SACRED HONOR

★★★★

SACRED HONOR

A BIOGRAPHY OF
COLIN POWELL

BY DAVID ROTH

ZondervanPublishingHouse
Grand Rapids, Michigan

HarperSanFrancisco
San Francisco, California

Divisions of HarperCollinsPublishers

Sacred Honor
Colin Powell: The Inside Account of His Life and Triumphs

Copyright © 1993 by David Roth

Requests for information should be addressed to:

🏛 ZondervanPublishingHouse
Grand Rapids, Michigan 49530

Library of Congress Cataloging-in-Publication Data

Roth, David, 1955– .
    Sacred Honor : Colin Powell, the inside account of his life and triumphs / by David Roth.
        p.   cm.
    Includes index.
    ISBN: 0-310-20656-1 (softcover)
    1. Powell, Colin L. 2. Generals—United States—Biography. 3. Afro-American generals—Biography. 4. United States. Army—Biography. I. Title.
E840.5.68R67 1993
355′.0092—dc20   93-4644
[B]   CIP

Edited by Lyn Cryderman and Dan Runyon
Interior design by Rick Devon
Cover photo by Linda L. Creighton

Printed in the United States of America

97 98 99 00 01 02/❖ DH/ 10 9 8 7 6 5 4

Contents

Acknowledgments

M Y F O R E M O S T appreciation goes to the Powell family. In addition to permitting me to ask them direct and sensitive questions, General Colin Powell and his gracious wife, Alma, allowed doors that have heretofore been either closed or merely cracked to those outside their immediate family to swing wide. Their son, Michael, and daughter-in-law, Jane (along with little Jeffrey, the pride of his grandparents) spared no kindness, assisting in many ways. Mike's friendship and candor was a source of encouragement and much practical help. The Powell daughters, Linda and Annemarie, were both gracious and offered special insights that seem to come only from daughters. General Powell's only sibling, Marilyn, along with her husband, Norm Berns, extended to me perfectly gracious hospitality while telling countless stories and fielding endless questions.

More than a little help came from my former colleagues in the office of the Chairman of the Joint Chiefs of Staff. Colonel F. W. "Bill" Smullen III made every effort to maintain some measure of professional propriety while giving me unprecedented access. He was successful, but I still owe him.

Although I had proposed the idea while still at the Pentagon, not until beginning work on this book did I find the time to create a computer database of what amounts to nearly all Powell's public words from nearly two hundred separate occasions while he was Chairman. It proved to be invaluable. Joan Asboth made sure that I got copies of speeches, videotapes, various transcripts and other documents, and she helped me keep up with Powell's activities after I left Washington. She spared no effort to provide whatever I needed, including ideas, to make this book as good as possible. Captain Robin Crumm, often a confidant and always a friend, was a big help in the early-ideas stage. Carolyn Piper, Betty Skinner, Sergeant Diane Gove, Commander W. D. "Dave" Barron, Major Antonino Fabiano, Senior Master Sergeant Scott Schlesinger, Sergeant First Class Cammie Brown, and Tech Sergeant D. J. Favaron were always there to help.

The person who best understands the mind and philosophy of Colin Powell is Army colonel and historian Larry Wilkerson. He has been Powell's principal speechwriter since his days as Commander-in-Chief of Forces command. His discussions with me, especially about Jefferson and Lincoln, have been of enormous value.

Marine Colonel Paul Kelly, who was the Chairman's key legislative advisor through four years in which relations between Congress and the military have been both exciting and challenging, offered insights into Powell's relations with Congress. Powell's senior aide, Major Rod von Lipsey, USMC, former speechwriter Captain Peter Swartz, USN (Ret.), and his successor, Lieutenant Commander Niel Golightly, as well as Air Force Colonel Dave Patterson, communicator Frank Angelo, and personal security officer Johnny Townsend, each helped in special ways. Nancy Hughes, Powell's confidential assistant and close co-worker for many years, was exceptionally helpful.

I would be remiss if I did not mention Sergeant First Class Otis Pearson. Otis has become something of a second son to the Powells, is a business partner with the general, and always a consummate gentleman. There are pieces of Colin Powell's life that only he knows, and I am fortunate to be privy to some of them.

General Powell's singularly intimate friend and professional colleague, Ambassador Richard Armitage, has guarded the privacy of their relationship jealously over the years. He stepped away from this principle of keeping silence by speaking with me entirely on-the-record for several hours on several occasions. His help was uniquely invaluable.

President Ronald Reagan has, since leaving office, declined all invitations to personally help authors. I appreciate, therefore, his taking a special interest in helping this project. He chose not to conduct a verbatim interview but decided instead to write longhand responses to my questions. And Cathy Goldberg made sure that they did not get lost in the shuffle.

President George Bush and Barbara Bush graciously answered my questions during their busy first days in Houston just after leaving the White House. Staffers Ann Brock, Paul Luthringer, Andy Maner, and Meg Offutt helped.

I owe a special debt to Mark Brender of ABC News, who gave me a home away from home on my many return trips to Washington and often kept me up to date on events as they were breaking. Many of my thoughts, some of them found on these pages, were tested on him first. Most important, his faithful friendship sustained a more-than-occasionally lonely and confused author. He and his wife, Sharon, have done their best to keep me warm and well-fed.

Fred Francis of NBC News, his assistant Tammy Kupperman, producer Naomi Spinrad, Wolf Blitzer who left the Pentagon beat and is now CNN's White House correspondent, and other friends and colleagues in the media were very helpful.

Many have photographed Colin Powell, but only a very few have an eye to see the man behind the uniform. David Hume Kennerly, a master craftsman, has singularly captured his subject on film. He generously made his pictures of Powell available for this book. The sequence of shots from which the cover photo by Linda Creighton of *U.S. News and*

World Report is taken, was brought to my attention by Kennerly. To them both, and photo editor David Friend at *LIFE* magazine, I am particularly grateful.

Military media colleagues pulled out all stops. John Primm, of Air Force Television, who helped me make Powell's "Kidvid" (and the unreleased Kidvid II), fellow reserve Captain Jack Pagano with whom John and I made Powell's Soviet Union video *Where West Meets East*, videographer Willie Cooper, Lou Wilkins, Douglas Welch, and Jerome Brown all lent a hand. So did Major Pete Keating of Army Public Affairs. I count them all as friends and comrades-in-arms.

I benefited from the astute military, historical, and sociological insights of Colonel Pete Herrly, who drafted Powell's "Joint Pub #1" and is now a professor at the National War College.

Colonel David Burpee of the Pentagon's Directorate for Defense Information offered assistance directly and indirectly. His staff members, especially the photo team, came through every time. Particular thanks to Ken Carter, Bettie Sprigg, Helene Stikkel, and Bob Ward; to Frank Falatko for press-briefing transcripts, and to Bob Whitmer and Laura Ricardo who provided audio- and videotapes of Powell.

Bob Pyle, who was with then-Major Powell in Vietnam when their helicopter crashed, was invaluable in reconstructing a confusing event. Every soldier knows that the troop next to you may save you; Bob was a hero, too. Let us not forget our corporate obligation to him and the likes of him, those whose names appear on the Wall and especially those who remain unaccounted for.

Julius Asboth; Al Blanchard; Bill and Kathleen Harding; Kitty Hernly; Renee Hohle; Air Force Captain Brian Holt; Major General John Hudachek USA (Ret.); Lieutenant Colonel Paul Lavendar, USA (Ret.); Walt McIntosh; Reverend Imagene Bigham Stewart; General John Wickham, USA (Ret.); Colonel Robert Williams, USA (Ret.); Marnie Wolfford; Bob Woodward; and the members of the staff of the

U.S. Army's Center for Military History each helped in their own ways.

In a very real sense, this is Lyn Cryderman's book. He asked me to write it, worked out the contract with Zondervan, and has been a helpful and dutiful editor involved in every step along the way. Thanks also to publisher, Scott Bolinder, and the whole team both at Zondervan and HarperCollins. Special mention must be made of David Whettstone, who first approached Lyn, and of Christine Anderson, Jonathan Petersen, Dave Anderson, Greg Stielstra, Paul J. Van Duinen, Beth Webber, Dan Runyon, and Mary McCormick.

Friends come and go in life. At the Little Portion Hermitage Community in Arkansas, where I have made my home most recently, faithfulness prevails. With my constant travels and repeated periods away from domestic and community responsibilities, John Michael Talbot and many others stood firm and prayed for many things—not least that this project would be completed on time.

Laura A. C. Roth sacrificed, kept home fires burning, and tended my children through both my time on Powell's/Pentagon team and again through the research and writing of *Sacred Honor/Colin Powell*. I shall forever be in her debt. From the earliest days of discussing the possibility of writing this book, Army Lieutenant Colonel Dave Gabbard, my historian brother, was a first-rate sounding board. Frank and Virginia Caponegro have always been my biggest moral supporters and lent help in more ways than I can count. Tanya Bartlett, my dear friend and able and devoted assistant, once again made the seemingly impossible happen. Someday I hope to repay her.

I am additionally grateful to others who chose to remain anonymous; and to any whose names may have slipped past me, I apologize.

It is not possible to acknowledge the full range of published materials that have been helpful. I will note a few books, however. For an understanding of Powell's philosophical roots a reading of Jefferson's principal documents is essential, especially the Declaration of Independence and his First and Second Inaugural Addresses. They are available in a number of editions. Probably the most accessible is *The Portable Thomas Jefferson* edited by Merrill D. Peterson. The number of Jefferson biographies, like those of Lincoln, is enormous. I owe a special debt to the analysis of Jefferson by Alf J. Mapp, Jr., whose nearly four decades of studying Jefferson led to a monumental two-volume history. The books are *Thomas Jefferson: A Strange Case of Mistaken Identity* and *Thomas Jefferson: Passionate Pilgrim*. Lincoln's words are also important to Powell. *Lincoln on Democracy*, edited by Mario Cuomo and Harold Holzer, is a handy resource. Powell's appreciation for Martin Luther King fits in the broader context of the Civil Rights Movement. While it is possible to get collections of King's words, both abridged and unabridged, possibly the handiest source for his and others' words is *The Eyes on the Prize Civil Rights Reader*, edited by Clayborne Carson, et al. For a general introduction to the movement, both the PBS video series and a book titled *Eyes on the Prize: America's Civil Rights Years 1954–1965* are a good place to start. I find it a good, ready reference. Vietnam books are too many to mention. The standard history, recently updated, is excellent. It is Stanley Karnow's *Vietnam: A History*.

Carl von Clausewitz is the central figure in the military education of Powell and his whole generation. His *On War* is the classic book on military strategy. It is available in a number of editions, but the standard one is edited by Michael Howard. He is also the author of a handy introduction in the Past Masters series titled simply *Clausewitz*.

There is a curious absence of detail about Powell in books written by his contemporaries. They all say a few nice things about him but hardly more. Both Ronald Reagan (*An American Life*) and Caspar Weinberger (*Fighting for Peace*) mention him very favorably, but the Powell mystique is only heightened by a lack of detail about him in these books. It is entirely in character for Powell to be outside the limelight when, in fact, his bosses relied upon him enormously.

The number of Gulf War books is now too many to mention. John Lancaster of the *Washington Post* is nearing completion of what will undoubtedly be an important book on the subject, on which Powell has cooperated with him extensively. Two others were good handbooks. They are Austin Bay and James Dunnigan's *From Shield to Storm*; and *Triumph Without Victory*, written by members of the *U.S. News & World Report* staff including Pentagon correspondent Bruce Auster. Of course, General H. Norman Schwarzkopf's opus, *It Doesn't Take A Hero*, includes a detailed account of the war as he saw it. And Bob Woodward's *The Commanders* is a book unto itself.

While on General Powell's staff, I was pleased to be able to offer some small help to Howard Means as he worked on his bio, *Colin Powell: Soldier/Statesman, Statesman/Soldier*. It is not an entirely satisfactory work and unfortunately is riddled with minor factual errors, but it is chock-full of quotes. I chose not to duplicate many of Means's interviews, especially with former Powell colleagues who have been repeatedly prodded to answer questions. I am happy to acknowledge Howard's hard work, and in some cases I have benefited from his published interview material.

Lastly, as anyone who has ever worked a day inside the Pentagon knows, the morning *Early Bird*, an official daily compilation of defense-related newspaper clippings, is the best day-to-day resource for following news about the military. Having it available throughout the research and writing of this book was an invaluable aid.

chapter one
A CLEAR SENSE OF FAMILY

IT IS FEBRUARY 20, 1991, and Colin Powell is irritated.

He thought the war plan was all worked out. The timetable had been okayed by President Bush.

Two weeks earlier, Schwarzkopf had said that his forces were "ready to go" and he wanted to get the ground war started by the twenty-first, give or take a couple of days in case of weather problems. Then it was agreed that the action would begin on the twenty-fourth.

Schwarzkopf slips down the hall from the Desert Storm command post and into his own private room to phone Powell. He breaks the news that the weather is not supposed to clear on the twenty-fourth, or the twenty-fifth.

Here it is the twentieth, and Norm wants a delay! *Powell thinks.* The offensive should have begun on the twenty-first as recommended.

But starting wars is never easy, even for tough guys like Stormin' Norman.

Their exchange is tense, terse. Schwarzkopf accuses Powell of giving in to the political pressure in Washington. Powell reminds him that Defense Secretary Dick Cheney and he were told point-blank by Schwarzkopf that he was "ready to go." Powell finally agrees to take the field commander's new recommendation to Cheney.

Half an hour later the forecast changes, and a week later the war is over—a mere hundred hours after the first tanks roll.

In the two months since the Gulf War ended, General Powell's life seemed busier than ever. At least, during the war, attention was focused in one place.

Not that things had turned out badly. America's men and women in uniform were heroes. So were the generals who led them. The number of invitations to public appearances and media events doubled, even tripled perhaps, and Colin Powell was both exhausted and exhilarated.

Not so long ago it seemed that it might not be possible to get everyone onto the battlefield on time. More than a half-million Americans and tens of thousands of coalition troops from around the world decisively answered the United Nations' mandate. By the time Desert Storm was over, the fourth-largest army in the world was roundly defeated, pounded from the air for forty-three days, and chased through the sands of the desert for just one hundred fateful hours. Sent running out of Kuwait, an uncountable number of Iraqis were killed. Still more thousands surrendered as Saddam Hussein's ruthless incursion was brought to an end.

But that was two months ago.

This week was supposed to have begun with a simple Monday afternoon visit to New York's Yankee Stadium to throw out the first pitch of the season. It turned into a jam-packed, nostalgic, quick visit home. There was the alum's proud return to his old school, Morris High. A visit to the Loral Corporation. A reception at the Bronx Borough Hall. Powell had a habit of calling his nearly-ninety-year-old Aunt Beryl each Sunday afternoon; he couldn't come to the Bronx without paying her a surprise visit.

In the Bronx, he met the family of Marine Captain Manuel Rivera whose Harrier jet, at the outset of the air war, crashed as it approached an aircraft carrier. The young flyer was killed instantly—the first casualty from the Bronx and from New York City. Powell shared hugs with his relatives. He knew their loss.

That evening there was a dinner. On Tuesday morning before returning to Washington he and Alma were honored guests at a Waldorf Astoria breakfast hosted by the Association for a Better New York.

At each event Powell made remarks or gave a prepared speech. There were hands to shake, new people to meet, old friends to greet, names and faces to remember, and many photos to be taken.

Powell returned to Washington Tuesday afternoon for a four o'clock White House meeting with James Baker, Brent Scowcroft, and Dick Cheney. The plight of the Kurds in the north of Iraq was a serious matter of concern, and the Warsaw Pact's military alliance was being disbanded. By 5:15 Powell was leaving 1600 Pennsylvania Avenue for the short drive back across the Potomac River. Ten minutes later he was in his office again for the daily wrap-up meeting with his staff. It lasted just minutes.

Otis was poised by the door with the engine running for the quick drive to the Chairman's quarters at Fort Myer. There Powell would change out of his workaday Army greens and into a general's blue, formal mess-dress uniform because he and Alma had another dinner to attend—a Congressional salute to the men and women of Operation Desert Storm at the Washington Hilton.

Wednesday, Thursday, and Friday proved almost as busy. But throughout the week he could not forget his return to New York. It was a proud time for Colin Powell, not so much for his own sake but for the young men and women he represented, the GIs he proudly called "my kids." As he boasted about the youngsters who went to the Gulf, he remembered his own experience of war. In the tumultuous 1960s and '70s, Vietnam was not a source of national pride. Those who came home were not treated as national heroes. In New York Powell had wanted to share his own joy and hope, so he told stories that made him proud. His kids had a purpose in life, worked hard, and WON!

Some people would think he was a sentimentalist, too mushy for a cool, nerves-of-steel general, but he meant every word when he said that ultimately, success in war belongs to those GIs in a cockpit, or a tank, or a foxhole, or on a ship at sea, who had put their lives on the line.

He told about troops like Private First Class Frank G. Bradish, a soft-spoken, quiet young teenager from Idaho. In the middle of a dark night in the desert, while wounded in both legs and having lost several fingers when his Bradley Fighting Vehicle was hit, Bradish pulled all of his buddies from that burning personnel carrier and saved their lives.

Because of his injuries, Bradish couldn't get the cap off a flare to signal the medics to come tend to his wounded buddies. So he bit off the cap with his teeth. Then he crawled back into the burning vehicle to get out all the ammunition. He was afraid that the ammunition would explode and kill everyone. Battalion commander, Lieutenant Colonel John Kalb, said that his men had to pull Private Bradish out of the vehicle. Only then did Bradish look down and realize that he was bleeding profusely. Powell was moved.

He retold another story in New York, one that was reported on ABC News. "I watched a special television show not too long ago—*Prime Time Live*, Sam Donaldson's show—and he was interviewing some of our troops in Saudi Arabia before the war began. He went to the heavy tank forces of the United States Army's VII Corps, which had just come in from Germany. He talked first to the Corps Commander, Lieutenant General Freddy Franks, who was missing his left leg just above the knee. It was blown off in Vietnam, but that didn't stop him. He got an artificial leg, moved up in the ranks, and now he's a corps commander, and Sam interviewed him while he was climbing off and on tanks and looking great.

"Then Sam followed General Franks to visit one of his

tank companies in the First Armored Division. As General Franks walked into the company area, he was greeted and escorted by a fine-looking, young, black Army captain who saluted him. You don't hear any words from the captain. He just escorts the general into the area.

"And some of the troops in this tank company are sitting around talking about the combat action they know will soon come. And Sam starts to talk to the individual soldiers.

"First you see an Asian-American soldier, then there's a white American sergeant who says a few words, and then a black soldier—an African-American, and then another white soldier, and then an old, grizzled black sergeant who says a few words and then, finally, another white soldier who says he's from Texas. He concludes the little piece by saying that he's honored to be an American and honored to be in the United States Army.

"But it's the first black soldier who said something that was so significant to me.

"He looked like he was about nineteen years old. His language wasn't perfect, but he was articulate.

"Here's what that young soldier said: 'All of us are family. All these guys right here are my family.' And then you hear the grunts and shouts of his buddies—*HUU-AHH! HUU-AHH!* You've heard it on a thousand interviews. All of those young teenagers, my kids, bonded together as a family, knowing they were going to face danger, said *HUU-AHH.*

"The bond in that family of soldiers, tankers awash in the middle of a sea of sand, was so strong that they would die for each other. That's what makes a hero. They'll die for each other, and they'll die for their duty. These young men and women come from all walks of American life. They're clean, smart, dedicated, trained, motivated, responsible, reliable, self-confident, selfless, patriotic, loyal, drug-free, respectful, tolerant, and caring.

"But wait a minute: Aren't these supposed to be the

clumsy, lazy, stupid, untrainable, drugged-up teenagers that aren't ready for the future?

"Only if you let them be."

These are my kids, Powell thought. His own father, Luther Powell, lived to see both his son, Colin, and his daughter, Marilyn, marry and have children. But Luther died before his son's rise to the highest military job in America. Luther never saw Colin with three million young men and women counting on his good paternal judgment.

Harlem was in its cultural Renaissance when an olive-skinned West Indian named Luther Powell arrived in New York. It was the 1920s. Though by race he would fit into America's most famous Negro community, neither city life nor the society into which he moved was familiar. Along with his fellow Jamaicans he brought a culture of his own to the United States, and only secondarily did he share race with those around him. Jamaicans' values and way of life were markedly different. Their experiences and values were colored by British colonialism and the institutions that shaped society under it. Black American traditions were as foreign to the new immigrants as life in the Caribbean was familiar. The heritage of slavery and segregation did not look so dark, nor was it so formative, to Luther and his sister as to those whose roots touched the soil of plantations in the American South, whose social identity was determined by the Emancipation Proclamation and a war that rent a nation along ideological and territorial lines.

Luther Theophilus Powell and Maud Ariel McKoy, whom he would marry, both came to the U.S. as young adults. The first two-and-a-half decades of the twentieth century brought to New York a large influx from the Islands. Harlem, in particular, received the largest portion of the nearly 150,000 West Indians, most of whom were black. They came to the United States when the Negro culture was blossoming. The 1920s was a decade of artistic efflorescence in Harlem. Duke Ellington, Bessie Smith, and Bill "Bojangles" Robinson entertained at The Cotton Club, Leroy's, and Barron's. Langston Hughes, Claude McKoy, and James Weldon Johnson were among the young writers whose names would become immortal in black literature. The local barbershop was a locus of social life for men. Although they were not shunned, West Indians generally, and Jamaicans in particular, were not simply absorbed into the fabric of black American life. Their distinctive identity remains in many ways to this day.

The route that brought Powell and McKoy to Harlem is not entirely clear. This much is known: Luther was the first member of his family to move to the States. There were seven other siblings. Eventually cousins would move to New York, and Luther brought his sister Beryl to New York as well. They were from the parish of St. Elizabeth in the westernmost county of Cornwall, a place called Top Hill. In the far north of Cornwall is the popular resort, Montego Bay. Top Hill is on the opposite, far southside of the island in a remote and rustically beautiful area with steep and rugged terrain. Situated near the base of the Santa Cruz Mountains, fewer than two miles from the Caribbean, the rocky, difficult-to-traverse land is anything but near the beach.

The Powells were peasant farmers there. Other family lived twenty miles away in Spur Tree and in the nearby city of Mandeville. Still others ended up in the Jamaican capital, Kingston, on the eastern side of the island. There seems to have been a time after leaving Top Hill before coming to New York when his parents lived deep in the island's interior in Christiana.

Maud's father was the overseer of a sugar plantation. He stayed behind as his wife, Alice Rebecca Coote McKoy, set out to make something for the family outside Jamaica. Left behind were Maud who was eldest, five other daughters, and three sons. Alice's trail is not entirely clear, however; she seems to have gone first to find work in the Cayman Islands, then Cuba. Finally arriving in New York, she first lived in Connecticut, then settled back in New York. Shortly thereafter the small, fair-skinned Maud joined her mother. Eventually the youngest child, Laurice Iola McKoy, twenty years Maud's junior, joined them.

Luther and Maud met while attending a picnic on an island in Pelham Bay Park. Known for its fishing, swimming, and beachfront walks on Long Island Sound, the park was a favorite summer getaway spot with shade trees and grassy expanses at the far eastern end of the Bronx. In the heart of Harlem at St. Philip's Church, on West 134th Street between Seventh and Eighth Avenues, they were married on December 28, 1929.

Luther Theophilus was a proud man who stood barely five-feet, four-inches tall, but those who knew him speak of his magnanimity, his ineffable spirit, his determination, and most of all—his kindness. Luther is always described as a person whose size was elevated by his bigness of heart. He was caring and compassionate.

Though outgoing, he said little—nor did he have to. His influence was in its own way, commanding. The children sensed and felt his love and devotion. Therefore, they respected his wishes. Luther was a man who liked order. He was almost never seen outside the house without a suit and tie. A charitable man of strong faith, Luther was always active in the Episcopal Church.

Maud, too, is remembered as religious. She was not sanguine like Luther but strong-willed and equally hardworking. In addition to holding down a job and performing the usual household duties, she took part in church activities, supervised the children's school work, and was the chief disciplinarian.

Both Luther and Maud worked in Manhattan's garment district. Maud was a seamstress, a finisher who sewed on buttons and trim. She did piecework, being paid for each garment she sewed. Every Thursday night she sat at the kitchen table and sorted her week's tickets—each one snipped from the garments she had worked on—and bundled them with rubber bands. The next morning she took them to work down to 34th Street, off 7th Avenue, to turn them in and get her pay. Luther worked for a company called Ginsburg that made women's coats and suits, at 500 Seventh Avenue. It later became Gaines Co. He was a warehouseman, a shipping clerk. In time he would become the head of the shipping department, a foreman, in a sort-of management position. He spent twenty-three years with the same firm until it closed. He then found a similar job with a textile company, Scheule and Company. Sometimes at the end of the season when garments were being discounted, Luther sold ladies' suits out of the apartment and around the neighborhood, often as a way to raise money for the church. His gentle, affable nature was the key to his small-scale entrepreneurial success.

Maud graduated from high school, but Luther never finished—one prideful fact that she, choleric by temperament, would use as an insult. From time to time she would mutter under her breath, "Him who never finished high school."

Upon being married, Luther joined his new bride and mother-in-law for a short while in their apartment on Bradhurst Avenue. The couple's own first home was in a brick-front apartment building on Morningside Avenue at 116th Street across from Harlem's Morningside Park. In this fashionable Negro neighborhood by Columbia University, their building had an elevator with an operator and an attractively appointed, formal, well-kept lobby. A ceramic-tiled fireplace graced the living room of their spacious flat, which had parquet floors throughout. It was a good location and made for a pleasant home. Still, in a sense, home would always be Jamaica. The word *home* was used that way. Family and friends came and went to and from "home." Despite separations from distant loved ones and the beginning of a new generation in a new land, Jamaica—as much a way of life as a place—was never far away.

In 1931 a daughter, Marilyn, was born in Presbyterian Hospital. Maud returned there on April 5, 1937, to give birth to a second child. Given the name of his father, Colin Luther Powell was born in the same hospital that his sister had been born in five-and-a-half years earlier.

By the late 1930s, the area was starting to change for the worse. Maud became concerned for the safety of her husband, who came home from work late each evening. The elevator no longer had an operator. The lobby might not be quite so safe. Like other immigrants who continued to seek a better life and whose means improved over time, Luther and Maud pondered moving across the Harlem River to another borough of New York, the Bronx. Friends who had recently moved there, the Witters, eventually moved to the Hunt's Point section of the South Bronx in 1940. This is where Marilyn and Colin grew up. It was just a bus or IRT subway ride from the city. The Powells took the trip often, especially Luther, who commuted early each morning and again in the evening for many years. And it would become Colin's route, too, in his early years at the City College of New York.

Hunt's Point was a neighborhood of three-, four-, and five-story rowhouses and apartments, of densely populated narrow streets and busy boulevards. Most of the residents had exchanged old tenements in Manhattan for newer ones farther out. When the Powells arrived, the solid working-class and lower-middle-class neighborhood was largely Jewish, with Italians and Irish, some Greeks, and the beginnings of a mix of other nationalities. Over the years it would become more black and Puerto Rican. The Powells and their extended family—it included Maud's sister, mother, and mother's brother, known to the children as Uncle Alfred—moved first into a four-bedroom apartment at 980 Fox Street. The extended family stayed there for three-and-a-half years.

Then, in 1943, the clan moved into a brown brick, four-story walk-up that was home to eight families. Just a few blocks from Fox Street, theirs was a roomy, third-floor, four-bedroom flat at 952 Kelly Street. Then, as today, you could hear the screech of train wheels from the elevated line down at the end of the block. It was just a short walk to the Intervale Avenue stop, on the elevated line, now closed. Shopping was easy, right in the neighborhood. Fat Mr.

Kaiserman had the bakery on the corner of Intervale and Kelly; he sold cheesecakes for less than a dollar. Sammy the Shoemaker was down the block. There was a storefront synagogue. The Powells, though, attended St. Margaret's Episcopal Church a couple of blocks away at 940 156th Street, between Dawson and Kelly. Luther became senior warden there, president of the parish board. In time, several relatives and so-called relatives from Jamaica moved into the neighborhood. Uncle Alfred Coote got married and moved down the street. Colin and Marilyn's grandmother stayed with them for eight or nine years, then she returned to Jamaica.

Luther had a reputation for helping people and opening wide the doors to his house. Stories about his hospitality abound. Most follow a similar line. One day the oil man came to the door. Luther called to Maud saying, "Put the coffee pot on, the oil man is here." He knew what to expect—this was to be a regular stop he looked forward to. After filling the oil tank downstairs, the two men would sit and talk and laugh and drink coffee. At Christmastime, Luther invited the garbagemen in for their annual holiday tip, a New York tradition in those days, but he did not merely give them their expected gift and exchange Christmas good wishes. He gathered them around the table to share a festive drink as the family's holiday preparations went on around them. This was classic Luther Powell. He often invited the mailman in and he made friends of total strangers. It did not matter who you were—you were a friend and guest and always welcome at Luther's. Family memories abound with tales of Luther Powell's standing out on the stoop, waiting for someone to pass by to talk with and possibly have into the apartment.

Colin Powell's wife, Alma, tells a story uncanny in its similarity. One day in the early 1970s when Colin and Alma were living in Burke, Virginia, outside Washington, D.C., she looked out the window. There was Colin leaning on the mailbox just waiting for a passerby to chat with. "And I thought, *Well, Luther, you're back,*" she recalls. Their son,

Michael, tells a story from Powell's days as post commander at Fort Leavenworth, Kansas. "We had this old house, built in the 1800s. It was a beautiful wood house. On Saturday morning everybody would be asleep, and Dad would come through with these people, giving a tour. He had just met them on the street. He'd seen them looking at the house and went out to explain things to them. Next thing, there would be these people walking by your room with strollers. And, of course, they were shocked. And he would say to them, 'Now look at this, look at this.' That's definitely Luther Powell."

On another occasion, the Powells hosted a small birthday party at the official residence of the Chairman of the Joint Chiefs of Staff, Quarters 6. A knock was heard at the front door. Jane Powell, Michael's wife, answered it. There stood two young men who identified themselves as Special Forces troops from the 82nd Airborne Division at Fort Bragg, North Carolina. They were just passing through Washington and wanted to meet their hero, General Powell. "I'm sorry, but we're having a family party right now," she told them, "perhaps you could come back a little later." They thanked her, turned on their heels, stepped down from the porch and strode down the walk toward the curb. "Who was that?" General Powell asked. When his daughter-in-law told him, Powell burst out the door and rushed out toward the car to prevent their driving away. Upon Powell's introducing himself, all three men went inside the house. Their host introduced them to family and friends. The two young sergeants joined the party for birthday cake, thanked their host for his graciousness, and politely dismissed themselves.

There was never a time more festive than holidays in the Powell's New York home. The whole family would come to Luther and Maud's place. Maud and her mother always prepared a special feast. Thanksgiving, Christmas, Easter— each brought its own culinary variations on a theme. Holidays meant extended celebration and festive multi-course meals. Both turkey and ham were always served.

There was some variety to the trimmings, but tradition always included peas and sweet potatoes. The cooking began days ahead of time. Guests came from out of town, cousins and so-called cousins, lots of them, and what were always referred to by the children as aunts and uncles. On the holiday itself people came and went all day long. At Christmas the visitors began their circuit of dropping in on the eve of the feast day. There were treats, of course, and a special eggnog served in true Jamaican style with overproof rum from home. But there was always a midnight service to attend at St. Margaret's. Then presents in the morning, followed soon thereafter by guests arriving. Many stayed for the meal. The table was set for more than capacity; there were always more than a dozen places for adults. A card table was set up in the vestibule for the children. The feast culminated with the cutting and devouring of the long-awaited Jamaican rum cakes in late afternoon. These special treats were baked well in advance, in those days between Thanksgiving and Christmas, according to their makers' personal recipes. When Maud baked hers, one was always put aside in a tin. It would be eaten on April 5 as Colin's birthday cake.

For a boy coming along in the 1940s and '50s the Kelly Street neighborhood was full of excitement. It was "a neat place to grow up," Colin Powell would say in 1989. Playing street games, making the walk, going to the movies—these were a few of the ways the young Colin filled his hours when not in school. There were always many books at home, and even at an early age Colin enjoyed reading. He liked to collect stamps and make maps, but while his sister might be practicing the piano inside the apartment, Colin was usually outside playing. He was one of the younger kids on the block, "always a kid" as he puts it, a year or two behind the other boys. His older friends watched out for him and didn't let him get into trouble even when they did. There was no shortage of games to play in the street, on the pavement, on the stoop. What they chose to do was partly decided by who was outside, and how many boys there were, partly by the time of day—when there was too much traffic there could be no punchball or stickball in the street using the manhole covers for home plate and second base. There was stoopball, which you could play alone or with another kid or two, and hide-and-go-seek, ring-a-levio, and hot beans and butter. There was shooting checkers made from bottle caps filled with wax. They tossed marbles against a cigar box trying to get them in through various-size holes, and they played Sluggo. Kites with razor tails tethered by glass cord were flown from the tenement roofs. And of course, especially in later years, they played games of football and baseball.

Colin's friends came in many colors. Among them were Gene Norman, Victor Ramirez, Tony Grant, Walter Schwartz, and Manny Garcia. "Growing up in New York, particularly on Kelly Street in the South Bronx, everybody was a 'minority'," Powell wrote in 1988. "I did not know what a 'majority' was. You were either black, Puerto Rican, Jewish, or of some strange European extraction."

Gene Norman, also black but not of Jamaican background, has remained a close friend throughout their adult lives. As teens, Gene and Colin rode their bikes everywhere. For them, having a two-wheeler was a sign of coming of age. It meant freedom. They could ride as far as Pelham Bay Park and back again. Speeding down Hunt's Point's steep "Bank Note Hill," named for the American Bank Note Company, was always a thrill. A nickel would take you anywhere on the trolley or subway, so the boys got around much of what was a safer city back then. The two of them sometimes took the trolley to the George Washington Bridge, then walked across it from New York into New Jersey. There they camped overnight in the woods of the Palisades. Powell's short-lived experience as a Boy Scout was in New Jersey. He recognized, in what was a non-integrated scout troop, that he was not too welcome there. It may not have been his first experience of being racially discriminated against, but it convinced him that the long trip from the South Bronx was not worth it.

A favorite pastime as a youngster was "making the walk," a counter-clockwise round of the neighborhood. Colin and his friends started at the corner of Kelly and 163rd Streets. They walked up 163rd, crossing Tiffany, Fox, and Simpson Streets. In each block they passed the Jewish bakery, a Puerto Rican grocery, a Jewish candy store, the Chinese laundry, and a variety of other stores. While the storefronts were all different, each block seemed much the same with the same kinds of shops up and down the street. At the wide Southern Boulevard they turned left off 163rd Street. Southern Boulevard was downtown, the center of commerce for their neighborhood. "It had three big movies and small and large stores containing almost every product you could want," according to Powell. The kids would gaze in the windows, pointing and stopping to look at the merchandise as they strode up the street. They turned left again at Westchester Avenue, known in the area for its variety of foods. There were butcher shops displaying their fresh cuts in the window with prosciutto and hard salami hanging from ceiling hooks, the strong, mixed smells of different cheeses emanating from open doors where wheels and wedges were poised inside glass cases, and other places where vendors sold fresh fruits and vegetables, stacked neatly with brown paper bags awaiting the hands of customers. There were candy stores and dry goods stores and places offering ethnic specialties to serve the area's many populations. The old Tiffany Theater was on the corner of Westchester and Tiffany, just a block before the turn back onto Kelly. This is where young Colin went nearly every Saturday clutching a quarter or two to cover admission. Most of that day was spent watching three or four B-westerns and serials. It was the beginning of his lifelong love for movies. At Kelly Street the last turn was made. They were back. The boys had "made the walk."

Young Colin went to kindergarten at PS 20. As American GIs fought World War II, the young Powell went to elementary school at PS 39 down at Kelly and Longwood. He was in the slow class as a fourth-grader and is remembered by friends and family as having been an ordinary child. He was quiet and easy-going. He hid in the shadow of his father and was overpowered by the strong academic prowess of his older sister.

For junior high he attended the then all-male J.H.S. 52 just up the street from home. He was class captain, took French, typed his reports, and earned mostly 80s and 90s. He graduated from intermediate school in June of 1950, just a couple of weeks after the U.S. pledged aid to the French, who had been heavily attacked by Soviet-backed, Communist North Viet Minh forces, and days before North Korea invaded South Korea.

Around the neighborhood, Colin learned a smattering of Yiddish. It was, after all, a sort of unofficial second tongue in the largely Jewish area. He has never lost the ability to sprinkle his speech with Yiddish words and idioms. In fact, Powell possesses a native's command of no language but English. However, the ability to adapt himself to the social and cultural and even to some extent linguistic demands of a situation—"code switching"—is something that seemed to come naturally to him. It is a skill that has served him well through the years.

Already as a young teenager, Powell had learned the habit of hard work. He held a variety of jobs, but one stands out. After school and on weekends he was a laborer and clerk at Sickser's, a couple of blocks from home at Westchester and Fox. It was a three-story store specializing in baby furnishings—cribs, strollers, carriages, and toys—run by a Jewish proprietor, Mr. Sickser, and his son-in-law Lou Kirschner. The two of them spoke Yiddish between themselves, and no doubt much of Powell's facility with the language was acquired there. One day, around age thirteen, Colin just happened to be walking past the store when the men needed some help. Mr. Sickser stopped the young boy and asked if he wanted to make a little money. Powell went into the store, did what was asked of him and, having worked well, was invited to stay on. Mostly he did general labor, assembling merchandise, unloading trucks, boxing things up for shipment, helping with setting up displays at Christmastime. He worked diligently, was polite, and always showed up on time. Most school weeks he put in twelve to fifteen hours for fifty- to seventy-five cents an hour. He stayed at Sickser's through his sophomore year in college.

Around this time Colin Powell's name underwent a transformation. Having British ties, the Christian name "Colin" was not uncommon. From birth his name was pronounced in the preferred way: KAH-lin. But one of the first acknowledged American heroes of World War II was a pilot whose plane was shot down after he bombed a Japanese battleship: Captain Colin P. Kelly, Jr. The pronunciation of what had become a household name was KOH-lin. "My friends in the streets of the South Bronx, who heard Captain Kelly's name pronounced on the radio and by their parents and other adults, began to refer to me by the same pronunciation," Powell wrote when the subject of his name arose in the *Times* of London in 1991. The story took a fortuitous turn when, in 1981, Brigadier General Colin Powell was assigned as Assistant Division Commander to the 4th Infantry Division at Fort Carson, Colorado. There he met his new Episcopal chaplain, Lieutenant Colonel Colin P. Kelly, III. His father, who received the Distinguished Flying Cross for heroism, had written to President Roosevelt in 1956 asking that his then eighteen-month-old son be afforded the opportunity to attend West Point if, when he completed high school, he wished to accept the appointment. Roosevelt agreed. The elder Kelly was killed. His son was appointed, commissioned, served as an armor officer in Vietnam, went to seminary, and returned to the Army. Upon their meeting, Powell immediately asked about the pronunciation of their mutual name. Both father and son were, indeed, called KOH-lin. General Powell was immediately relieved. "Thank God, you have been mispronouncing your name all your life also," he exclaimed. The different ways of saying the seemingly simple five-letter word was constantly evident when, as Chairman of the Joint Chiefs of

Staff, one of Powell's aides was a Marine corps officer, Major Colin F. Mayo. The boss was KOH-lin, his aide KAH-lin. But to this day Powell's sister calls her brother "KAH-lin."

In September 1950 Colin began high school. At Morris High he was very well-liked by both students and teachers, but those who remember him do not count him among the school's most popular members of his class. He ran track for a while but dropped out when he realized that running cross-country was not one of his strengths. Among the activities of which he is proudest is participation in the Service League. Like his sister and their many Jamaican cousins Powell took the college preparatory curriculum.

Kelly Street changed as rapidly as Colin grew up. For the most part, it changed for the worse—the family's once-suburban neighborhood started to become a place where danger lurked. One of the problems of his day was drugs. The teenagers were polarized into two groups—those who used drugs and those who did not. Marijuana and heroin were the major concerns. On the occasion of his first return to Morris High in 1991, thirty-seven years after graduating, the national Gulf War hero and native son addressed the school's students. He told them about his own experience. "We had lots of drugs in my neighborhood. It isn't something that's just been discovered in the last couple of years. On every street corner was some pothead or junkie trying to sell or deal or get others involved in it. I didn't do it. Never in my life, not even to experiment, not even to try, not to see what it would be like." He gives two reasons for staying clean. "One, my parents would have killed me, but the second reason is that . . . it was stupid. It was the most self-destructive thing you could do with the life that God and your parents had given to you." Powell knew about overdoses and saw the lives of kids he knew come to sad and abrupt ends. "Of all the kids that I grew up with on Kelly Street, Gene Norman and one or two others made it. Too many of the others did not make it. They went to jail, or they died, or they were never heard from again."

Colin stayed out of trouble in high school. He would not distinguish himself with high grades, but he was able to meet the requirements for graduation in just three-and-a-half years. He applied to two colleges, the City College of New York and New York University. Both accepted him. Upon finishing high school in February 1954, halfway through his senior year and two months away from his seventeenth birthday, he immediately enrolled in CCNY. His choice of school was simple: NYU cost $750 a year, and CCNY was only ten dollars.

Growing up, Colin Powell was surrounded by a close net of neighborhood family friends and actual and fictive kin—West Indian "aunts," "uncles," and "cousins" who saw his every move and made certain that he toed the line. This extended family and social network cared for its youth by both encouraging and challenging them. Social pressure to conform was only exceeded by an expectation that the immigrant second-generation was marked by achievement. And it was. Powell's sister, Marilyn, was graduated from Buffalo State College in 1952 and went on to become a bilingual school teacher active in multicultural education in Southern California. First cousin J. Bruce Llewellyn is an accomplished businessman and one of America's richest blacks.

He is founder of One Hundred Black Men, a charitable service organization, owns WKBW Channel 7, the ABC affiliate television station in Buffalo, New York, and is co-owner of a Coca-Cola bottling plant in Philadelphia. Not surprisingly, Colin Powell and Bruce Llewellyn have grown close over the years. Another cousin, Richard Lopez, was for some years the chief designer at Republic Aircraft. Jacqueline Lopez holds a Ph.D. in psychology and does counseling at New York University. Dolores Lopez Lowery is a biochemist in suburban Washington, D.C. Two cousins of Powell's generation became important judges. Dorothy Watson Cropper became a judge on the New York state

Supreme Court of Claims. James Lopez Watson followed in his immigrant father's footsteps by entering law. The senior James Watson started out as an elevator operator and distinguished himself by becoming the first black to graduate from New York Law School and the first black to be elected judge in both New York City and the state. The junior Watson became a senior judge on the U.S. Customs Court of International Trade. His sister Grace became a reading specialist for the Department of Education. Another Watson sibling, Barbara, was the first woman, and therefore also the first black woman, to become Assistant secretary of state and served as Ambassador to Malaysia from 1980–81. Another cousin, Arthur Lewis, now a private consultant in Washington, was a career foreign-service officer who became U.S. ambassador to the West African nation of Sierra Leone during the Bush administration. First cousin Victor Roque became a lawyer and is corporate counsel to a major New York utility. In Jamaica, other cousins with humble beginnings went to the finest universities abroad in England and Canada. They, too, have excelled and risen socially.

Powell's family members, while certainly unique in their particular accomplishments, are not uncommon representatives of Jamaican Americans as a group. Strong family ties and social cohesion, the immigrant spirit and belief in the American dream have combined to make blacks with West Indian family origins socio-economically elite. In the late 1960s the incomes of blacks of West Indian extraction in New York City were twenty-eight percent higher than that of other blacks there. They earned fifty-two percent more than African Americans nationally. Recent studies show that Powell's generation of sons and daughters of Jamaican immigrants earn a higher median income than their white contemporaries earn. As early as the middle of this century in New York, their clannish entrepreneurism and business acumen would cause American blacks to refer to them as "black Jews."

The cohesion of the family and the extended clan,

while nearly unheard of in most of American society and especially in the black community, was a given fact of life among Jamaican-Americans earlier in this century. Powell grew up with it, and so have his children. They still believe in the centrality of the family. Most Americans cannot comprehend the degree of importance that the Powells attach to home and family. High mobility and an emphasis on individualism in America since World War II have created a social state of disconnection, isolation, and strictly personal choices. These notions are foreign to Powell, his family, and their extended clan. David Maybury-Lewis of Harvard University, perhaps most widely known for his 1992 PBS television series, *Millennium*, says that three important "wisdoms" have been all but lost in our Western societies: First, a clear sense of family. Second, that the right and wrong of what you do is defined by the myths and rituals of family and society. Lastly, if you know these two, you learn the third—to balance the needs of the one with the needs of the many. When you have all three, you are whole, whoever you are. When you have all three you are home, wherever you are. Throughout his life, his career in the military and even today, Colin Powell seems to have understood and held onto these wisdoms.

chapter two
LEAD BY EXAMPLE

E N G I N E E R I N G seemed like a good field for the son of
Jamaican immigrants to pursue, and so Colin Powell did. He
was urged on by his mother, a frugal woman who pressed
her son to achievement and success. Colin himself was not
sure what he wanted to study when, at age sixteen, he
became a freshman at the City College of New York in the
second semester of the 1953–54 academic year. In fact, he
was not certain that college was for him. But, he acknowledges, "I went to college for a single reason: My parents
expected it. I don't recall having had any great urge to get a
higher education. I don't even remember consciously thinking the matter through." Maud Powell had urged her son,
"You got to go into engineering; that's where the money is,
man." The dutiful son complied by declaring it his major. So
back to Harlem he went, commuting along the same route
that his parents took daily to work.

Powell was not the only young man who chose CCNY
because it was virtually free, having been established as the
Free Academy in 1849, just more than a decade before the
outbreak of the Civil War. Its purpose was to make higher
education available to the working class. The list of distin-

guished alumni is impressive. They include Ira Gershwin, Bernard Malamud, A. M. Rosenthal, Abraham Beame, Edward Koch, Bernard and Marvin Kalb, Paddy Chayevsky, Jonas Salk, Edward G. Robinson, and Felix Frankfurter. Just as in his childhood neighborhood, most of Powell's classmates were Jewish. Like Kelly Street where he grew up, CCNY has since become mostly black and Hispanic.

There was a wintry chill in the air on his first day at college. "On that cold morning," he recalls, "I took the bus across the 155th Street bridge, rode up the hill, got off, met Raymond the Bagelman—a fixture on campus—and began my career as a CCNY student." He averaged a B in that first semester, not a bad showing in the demanding engineering program. He chose to enroll in summer school, taking a mechanical-drawing course, essential for an engineer. Sitting in class one hot afternoon, he concluded that no matter what his mother thought about engineering as a career there were certain things about the subject for which he simply had no aptitude. Powell remembers, "A professor said to me, 'Imagine a plane intersecting a cone in space.' I said, 'I cannot imagine a plane intersecting a cone in space. I'm out of here.'" It was the worst summer he ever spent and an important turning point.

During college, his summers were not all spent at school. Already accustomed to working part-time at Sickser's baby-furniture store during the week, Colin decided to return to a summer job he had first landed the year before. He worked in the near-by Coca-Cola bottling plant. He often talks about it when challenging and encouraging young people, especially minority youth. "Sometimes people get shocked when I tell them, when I was sixteen years old, I used to mop floors. Mop floors. Yeah, in the summer period as a college and high-school student, I would go to work in the soft-drink bottling industry of New York, and one of the jobs I got was to mop the floors at a very large plant that made a certain kind of cola. And black kids, well, of course you got to mop the floors, and white kids worked on the bottling machine. And so I mopped floors. The heck with it—ninety cents an hour, and I learned how to mop. When somebody comes and dumps about fifty cases of cola on the floor, I want to tell you, that is some serious mopping.

"I could mop floors as well as anybody right now. You know how you do it: left to right and not back and forth. There is a technique to mopping floors. And I mopped floors all summer long. I didn't complain. The man is paying me ninety cents to mop floors, and I mopped floors. At the end of the summer, the foreman came up to me and said: 'You mop floors pretty good.'

'You sure gave me enough opportunity to learn, sir.'

"He said, 'Why don't you come back next summer?'

"I said, 'To do what?'

"He said, 'We are going to put you on the machine.' All right. The next summer I went back, and I worked on the machine, just taking bottles out, and putting them on the conveyer belt. At the end of the summer, I was one of the top kids on the machine on the inspection part, and the next summer when I went back, I was deputy foreman on the machine."

Despite his disastrous showing in mechanical drawing, Powell continued in school. But CCNY's School of Technology, which included engineering and sciences in those days, was never easy for him. He switched majors to geology, also located in the "tech building," when school resumed in the fall of 1954. He discovered that he was not particularly gifted in physics, calculus, geology, history, languages, "or any of the other" subjects he enrolled in, but he did manage to make it through the required curriculum for a degree in geology. He says he did so by "mastering the rock formations under Manhattan."

Powell confesses that he may never have persevered had it not been that he found something he was good at. A short while into his first semester at City College he noticed a bunch of fellows wandering around Amsterdam and Convent Avenues wearing uniforms. "It was the local ROTC detachment," he would write for his college alumni magazine more than three decades later. "I had a certain interest in the military. My generation, after all, had essentially spent its elementary school years watching World War II and then, after a brief postwar hiatus, its teenage years watching and hearing about the Korean War. So if you were of that generation, the military made an indelible impression upon you."

Something about the uniform caught young freshman Powell's eye. He did not come from a military family, but he had seen newsreels each Saturday at the movies. An uncle had been a sergeant in World War II but got out as fast as he could once the war ended. Many members of the family of immigrants had been drafted, but they all hung up the Army green and khaki after their tours of duty were up. Nevertheless, the uniform had made a strong impression on him. (He confessed in 1991 to still feeling exhilaration every day that he put on the uniform.)

So Colin Powell looked into the Reserve Officer Training Corps. Unlike his academic course of studies where he never really felt at home. "ROTC was a natural. I enjoyed it. I did it well. I ran into some great young folks who remain lifelong friends," according to Powell.

ROTC was popular on college campuses in the 1950s. CCNY had the second-largest corps of cadets outside West Point and the other service academies and military schools like the Citadel and Virginia Military Institute. Some of his chums, such as Walter Schwartz who also went to City College, joined mostly because they expected to be drafted. Completing ROTC would guarantee them an officer's commission and the opportunity to finish their studies. In fact, some of his ROTC classmates never served a day on active duty.

Many college classmates thought of ROTC cadets as dull and out-of-date. The Beat Generation counterculture was flourishing in Greenwich Village. But while ROTC may have been square to some of his contemporaries, for Powell it provided a new order for his life. His sister, Marilyn Berns, believes that in a new way it gave him what he sought and was accustomed to—discipline. "I think he liked

the fact that it was structured. He came from a very
structured family with rules and order. . . . It gave him
security." At the same time it was new. In ROTC he was
able to emerge from behind the shadow of Luther Powell
and stand squarely in his own light. Colin Powell cut a good
figure in the uniform and was proud of it. He was tall and
lean with broad shoulders and a kind but serious face and a
toothy smile. Though he always appeared young, he had
the natural soldier-look.

There he learned drill and ceremonies, map reading,
basic infantry tactics, Army administrative procedures, and
rifle marksmanship. In the summers he went away to camp
where the classroom skills were tried out and field experience was gained. Army ROTC was not just a set of courses
required for a degree. It was a culture he was learning.
There was a clear sense of belonging.

There was social cohesion and even an elite class of
cadets—the Pershing Rifles. Powell recalls that upon joining
ROTC he immediately pledged Pershing Rifles and decided
to spend the next four years concentrating on ROTC. PR
members were distinguished by a whipped cord worn
through the shoulder epaulets of their uniforms. The cord
suggested that they were a little more serious than the
average ROTC cadet and possibly that they had made some
sort of tentative commitment to military service as a career.
"That appealed to me," Powell says. Their official purpose
was to be a precision drill team and honor guard. Many
hours were spent practicing or "drilling." They had an office
in the university's Finley Hall student center. It served as
the operational headquarters for what was as much a social
club as it was the campus brotherhood of gung-ho future
officers. Pershing Rifles became for Powell and his friends a
kind of fraternity whose four-year initiation ended in a
career, and the beginning of a surrogate family where a
home could be made wherever there were other troops. His
college friends, all fellow cadets, were the clean-cut, "good
kids" on campus. They stayed out of serious trouble but did
not miss an opportunity to throw and attend parties and

visit one another's families around the city. Luther and Maud liked Colin's college friends, who were always treated like extended family in their home.

Among them was a fellow two years his senior, Ronnie Brooks. Ronnie was a mentor and role model and at the same time, a friend. The son of a black Baptist preacher who ministered in the churches of Harlem, he seemed to understand West Indians in a way that some American blacks did not. Colin felt cared for and accepted by him in a special way. Brooks seemed driven to achieve and was a real motivator to the other cadets. Colin Powell looked up to him and emulated him. In turn, Powell seemed to follow Brooks into every position he held in the Pershing Rifles, including the top spot of company commander. His fellow cadets had Brooks pegged as a future career officer, what is often referred to as a "lifer." But after only six months on active duty he reverted to reserve status so that he could attend Brown University, where he earned master's and doctorate degrees in chemistry. He later married a West Indian from British Guyana.

Brooks demonstrated for Colin Powell a fundamental military officer's principle: Lead By Example. In time Cadet Powell, too, would practice his own version of one-step-ahead leadership. In his junior year, at the beginning of the ROTC "advanced program," Powell was put in charge of recruiting for the Pershing Rifles. Twenty-one new members were initiated. Among them was a young man just entering college and ROTC, Tony Mavroudis. Like Powell's following Brooks, the new cadet became both Colin Powell's protégé and his friend.

Through his college years Powell lived at home with his parents. They moved from the South Bronx to Queens in 1956. Though small, this was their first single-family house, and freshman Tony lived nearby. Their friendship was a powerful one. Powell, who grew up with only an older sister, admits that he loved Tony dearly, "like a brother." He describes Mavroudis as one of the craziest guys he ever met—smart, sharp, raw, coarse, and "a hell of a soldier."

They palled around, double-dated, and "learned about girls" together. "I lived in his house and called his parents Mom and Dad, and he lived in my house and called my parents Mom and Dad," Powell remembers. In their intense two years of day-to-day camaraderie together they managed to destroy both of their fathers' cars. Like his mentor, the Greek-American Mavroudis was expected to make a career out of the military.

Looking back, Powell confesses that he simply tolerated the academic demands of college, dashing from ROTC to visit the requisite classes held in the ivy-covered, metamorphosed black shale, Manhattan schist buildings that comprised the campus of CCNY. His heart, however, was with his comrades-in-arms as they conducted precision drills at the Ludwig Lewisohn Stadium. Most of Powell's attention was focused on Pershing Rifles activities.

Along with his fellow cadets, Powell was a regular patron at a few of the drinking establishments near school, among them a tavern on Convent Avenue, the Emerald Bar. He describes himself as having been "a loyal client of the place." On graduation day as the time for the ceremony approached, soon-to-be-college-graduate-and-second-lieutenant Powell was sitting on a stool sipping a rum and Coke. Maud Powell was across the street in the stadium where Colin spent so many hours marching in formation. As she glanced across the five hundred students who were assembled to graduate that day, she noticed, as only mothers can, that he was not among them. "And as my mother knew me well," he recalls, "she knew where I was and sent some friends over to ask me if I'd be kind enough to join the graduation ceremonies." Through her emissaries she let her son know that she had waited four-and-a-half years for the opportunity to see him graduate, so she expected him to show up. He did.

On June 1958, he was graduated. Despite what looks like a less-than-stellar academic performance—his overall average was barely above a C—his military accomplishments were impressive. He received straight A's in all military subjects, was Pershing Rifles company commander with the rank of cadet colonel, and was designated a Distinguished Military Graduate. He counted his B.S. degree in geology "an incidental dividend."

Notwithstanding his modest academic performance, Powell today believes that City College gave him a strong and valuable education. "It provided me with an appreciation of the liberal arts; it gave me an insight into the fundamentals of government; it gave me a deep respect for our democratic system." Looking back on his career, he adds, "Although I was forced to compete with West Pointers and Ivy Leaguers, lo and behold, my CCNY foundation was so solid that I never regretted going to City."

Perhaps more important to young Colin Powell than his college diploma was his commission as a second lieutenant. True, he could not become an officer in the Army of the United States without earning the degree. But a scroll bearing the signature of Secretary of the Army Wilber M. Bruckner, issued on behalf of the President, made him a *reserve* officer. He was one of two black second lieutenants in CCNY's commissioning group. Unlike cadets who attend West Point and receive Regular Army commissions, those who become officers through ROTC and enter active military service receive Reserve Army Commissions. Powell, however, as a Distinguished Military Graduate, would remain a reserve officer for less than a month. On June 30— *after* West Point's cadets were commissioned—Powell, too, became a Regular officer. It was a way of ensuring that Academy graduates were senior to College DMGs. "What was most important was—and this was expected of me by my parents—that I had a job, even if it was in the military. In those days you went to school to make yourself employable."

Just days later, in June 1958, a proud Second Lieutenant Colin Luther Powell, left the Bronx. He headed south in a Greyhound bus. His mother waved good-bye and was heard saying, "Do your three years, come home, we'll get a job, we'll be all right."

———————

The month that Powell began at City College, Senator Joe McCarthy turned his investigation of Communists to the Army. A week later the U.S. detonated a hydrogen bomb six hundred times more powerful than the one dropped on Hiroshima. In the last month of his first semester, the fifty-five-day-long French resistance of a Communist Viet Minh siege on Dien Bien Phu collapsed. Ten days later on May 17, in the *Brown v. Board of Education* case, the Supreme Court ordered an end to segregated "separate but equal" schools.

As Powell donned the uniform of a cadet for the first time in September 1954, a quarter of a million North Vietnamese fled to the South bringing the refugee total there to five hundred thousand. Less than a month later Ho Chi Minh returned to Hanoi after eight years underground. Within weeks of Cadet Powell's eighteenth birthday on April 5, a civil war raged in the streets of Saigon with the U.S. and France taking opposite sides. Ngo Dihn Diem and the United States emerged as victors in May. On May 14, the Warsaw Pact united the Soviet Union, Poland, Czechoslovakia, Hungary, Rumania, Bulgaria, Albania, and East Germany in a military alliance against the West.

In the spring of 1956, during Powell's sophomore year, Negroes boycotted buses in Montgomery, Alabama. Their leader, Martin Luther King, Jr., was jailed. Before the year was out, Soviet tanks rolled into Budapest. In September 1957, as his last year of college began and classes resumed for children around the nation, troops escorted nine black students into Little Rock's Central High School. By the end of the year, however, a federal judge approved delaying school integration there. This was the rapidly changing world in which Colin Powell learned to be a soldier who could lead by example.

chapter three

THE ARMY AND ALMA

AT FORT BENNING, Georgia, Colin Powell took
five months of full-time schooling in how to be a soldier.
Benning is the home of the infantry, backbone of the Army.
Traditionally the infantrymen become top-ranking generals,
the truest of the true warriors. Only in recent times, with the
advent of tank warfare, has the status of the infantryman
been challenged—by tankers, men in mighty fighting
machines. In fact, by the time Colin Powell entered the
Army the mechanized infantry was emerging as a compan-
ion force to fight side-by-side with tanks from the moving
platform of the armored personnel carrier.

Lieutenant Powell's first stop for training was the
Infantry Officer Basic Course. IOBC was held in those days
in a cluster of low cinder-block buildings at the heart of the
main post just across from the two-hundred-fifty-foot tow-
ers where he would later learn to land harnessed to a
parachute. IOBC is a review of many subjects learned in
ROTC, plus new subjects, and there is plenty of field
training. Mostly the new lieutenants learn to conduct
frontline fighting. There are no classes in the grand schemes
of strategy. No historic battle campaigns are discussed.

There are no civics lessons or readings in the art of warfare. Rather, small-unit tactics are learned, such as how to deploy the rifle squad in offense, establish a perimeter defense, follow staff administrative procedures, fill out government forms, order and allocate supplies, call artillery fire and use a radio, rate and counsel subordinates, maintain motor vehicles, and identify enemy equipment. IOBC also teaches procedures for handling prisoners of war, how to avoid becoming one yourself or to escape, survive and evade recapture, how to use small arms (especially the rifle), hand-to-hand combat, and land navigation both at night and during the day. An array of physically demanding obstacle courses and outdoor field-training exercises are also part of what new lieutenants must learn and relearn.

Doing so in Georgia in the hottest, muggiest months of the year can make Fort Benning the nastiest thing a GI ever hopes to experience. Despite efforts to keep canteens filled there are frequent "heat casualties." Its similitude to hell, more than one troop has noted, is enough to bring the most macho of men humbly to his knees. Powell fared well and kept a hopeful spirit despite the less-than-pleasant circumstances. When others were about to drop, Powell seemed able to squeeze out a smile, tell a joke, and drive on.

During the Basic Course, new lieutenants begin drawing real officer's pay. Powell earned $222.30 monthly plus bachelor officer's quarters, not much more than a dorm room. It is the beginning of an officer's social life. He joins the Officers' Club with its dining rooms and lounges and its officers-and-guests-only recreation facilities: tennis courts and a pool. In the late 1950s Fort Benning had its main O-Club and a couple of small, more colorful annexes at different parts of the installation—one at Custer Terrace and another near the Airborne School at Lawson Field.

A lieutenant is qualified to serve as an infantry-branch officer upon successfully completing the Basic Course. Few wash out; some go on to complete more specialized schools that qualify them to serve in the Army's more elite and specialized units. Powell asked for and received orders to attend both the Ranger and Airborne schools. Completing them would qualify him to serve in just about any capacity as a "grunt" or infantryman. The three-week airborne course involved lots of punishing, humiliating, and simply repetitive physical training: running from one place to the next all day long, dropping down for push-ups, repetitions of various exercises. There were daily inspections in formation with spit-shined boots—before sunrise. These were intended to be part harassment and initiation, part mental and physical toughening for future paratroopers. There were also practice parachute-landing falls, exits from the mock door, counting "one-thousand, two-thousand, three-thousand, four-thousand" then checking for an open canopy, jumping from the thirty-foot high practice tower, being dropped from the two-hundred-fifty-foot-high gondola and, in the end, real parachuting from a static line with classmates. The school taught him how to jump out of airplanes, land safely, and continue the work of an infantry officer. He earned his wings, became "jump qualified," and was no longer "just a 'dirty leg.'"

Ranger school is the ultimate foot-soldier's training ground, an extended, high-powered magnification of all that is muddiest, sweatiest, most tiring and taxing in the infantryman's life in the field. Long-range night patrols through swamps filled with snakes and snapping turtles are only offset by long road marches carrying fifty-pound field packs, with a rifle or machine-gun slung over the shoulder while wearing a steel pot on the head as the sun bakes it. Boots serve as furnaces for the feet sewn in them.

On one all-night patrol Powell's unit set out into the sleepless darkness of the swamp. They would keep moving all night long. Powell and his friend Bill McCaffrey were the tallest men in the unit and therefore assigned not regular M-1 rifles but heavy, bulky machine guns. A unit's success, soldiers are told early on, depends upon teamwork—buddies helping buddies. It was not uncommon, therefore, for someone to offer to relieve the machine gunner of his burden along the way. On this evening no one offered to lighten either man's load until two or three A.M., when someone took Powell's machine gun in exchange for a rifle. A short while later Powell turned to McCaffrey and exchanged his rifle for the machine gun.

At age twenty-one Powell was no longer just an "average kid" as he is often described by those who knew him on the block. While no one seems to have picked him out as a future four-star general, many of his contemporaries were impressed with his maturity. When things got tough, Powell didn't give up. He conveyed self-confidence and never lost his sense of humor. When other mouths were down-turned, he could still muster a smile. He conveyed the qualities of a natural leader mature beyond his years.

Powell finished his first round of Army schooling and set out for the "real Army" in January 1959. He was assigned to guard a section of the Fulda Gap in Germany at the focal point of what was expected to be the Soviets' avenue of attack into Central Europe. The East German border was less than fifty miles away. Assigned to Gelnhausen as a member of the tank-heavy Third Armored Division, Powell's team included infantrymen in armored personnel carriers. His first job was as a platoon leader with forty men, initially with Company B, Second Armored Rifle Battalion, 48th Infantry, known as "Bravo Company, Second of the Forty-Eighth." He later served with Company D in the same battalion where he was Company Executive Officer, the commander's right-hand man. He also served as the company commander for a few months. Through the bitter cold and biting wind of the winters of 1958–59 and 1959–60, Powell with a jeep and his troops, twelve to a vehicle, sat in M59 armored personnel carriers and looked eastward. They faced the men of the Eighth Guards Army, the vanguard of what was feared would be a massive sweep of Red Army forces. It was here that Powell first demonstrated an essential skill for all combat-arms officers who hope to climb the ranks: He was able to adapt, to do any job, and to do it gracefully. His superiors reported that Lieutenant Powell was a fine rifle platoon leader. For a while he was in charge of the company's heavy mortars, and he served for several months in an administrative job as an assistant adjutant. In each case his service was exemplary. He was promoted to first lieutenant two days before New Year's Day 1960.

On November 9, 1960, John F. Kennedy was elected President, and Powell was en route to a stateside assignment. He would spend nearly two years with the recently reactivated Fifth Infantry Division then based at Fort Devens, Massachusetts. The Fifth was mechanized infantry, more APCs than tanks. Serving there afforded Powell his first opportunity to command troops. A company command typically goes to a captain, but Powell would get his as a first lieutenant. He was in charge four months before moving on in February 1962 to serve on the battalion staff as the unit commander's personnel and administrative officer, a senior captain's job. He became a captain in June 1962.

Just before Thanksgiving 1961, Colin Powell met Alma Johnson on a blind date arranged by her graduate school roommate, a New Yorker named Jacqueline Fields. They were studying at Emerson College in Boston, and Alma was working as an audiologist with the Boston Guild for the Hard of Hearing. Jacqueline had met a lieutenant from nearby Fort Devens one weekend while Alma was away at a conference.

"When I got back," Alma Powell recalls, "she said 'I met this really nice guy, and he's coming in this weekend and bringing his friend.' I said, 'Oh, really? I don't go on blind dates,' and I let it pass." As the day approached, she decided that she really didn't want to go on the date. Alma told her roommate she would not be there when the GIs arrived. "I said, 'I don't go on blind dates, and I definitely don't go out with soldiers. How do I know what is walking in that door?'" She and her roommate had an argument, and Jackie prevailed. Alma decided, "All right, I'll stay here, but whoever this date is was going to be sorry! I dressed myself up as a femme fatale. I put on a beige, very form-fitting dress, not distasteful because I did wear it to work but a straight dress. It showed off my figure that was then ninety-eight pounds. There wasn't much of it there. And I made up my face so I looked very sophisticated.

"I still have a visual picture of them walking in the door. He looked like he was about twelve years old. He was cold, so his cheeks were rosy, and he had a very close haircut, and I thought, *All right, who is this baby?* So we sat and chatted for a few minutes and then I excused myself and went in the bedroom and changed my clothes and washed my face and came back. He still has not told me what he thought was going on."

Alma returned wearing a much less provocative dress that was more her style. "It must have been very conservative because sometime later he asked me why I dressed like a librarian. But modesty was a defense, because attractive girls get lots of unwanted attention. To avoid that, I looked 'professional.'"

There was nothing special about the date. They went to a night club and then got a bite to eat in some noisy place. But Alma thought the young lieutenant was nice. She saw him again the next weekend. In the weeks that followed he invited her for what was to become a weekly trip to Fort Devens. She took the bus there on Friday night, spent the weekend, and Colin drove her back to Boston on Sunday.

Fort Devens was her first introduction to Army life. She found it fun. Although he lived with other bachelor officers, Powell also had friends living on-post who were young married couples with children. "A lot of times we were with them, visiting their homes or having dinner with them. Much of it was in the white frame Officers' Club at Fort Devens. I liked those young couples and the way they lived." She was attracted by the social life of the officer's "family" and something much bigger and more inclusive about Army life. "It's a sense of community and belonging. Military people reach out to people very easily because of the very transient nature [of being in the service]. You make friends and you welcome new ones, and I liked that very much."

From the start, Alma Powell acknowledges, "I knew

[Colin] was a very nice person, probably the nicest person I had ever met. I was surprised the first night when I asked him how long he would be in the military. This was when the draft was still in effect. He said, 'I'm making it a career.' I thought, *What kind of nut is this?* Every young man I had ever known in the military had been drafted and counted down the days [to when he would be discharged]. I had never met a career military officer. I'm not sure I knew there was such a thing. There were no military installations near to where I grew up so I didn't know anything about the military."

The relationship became steady in January. Alma was heading for Tennessee for Christmas. She attended Fisk University in Nashville as an undergraduate, and her sister who lived there was nine months pregnant. Before she left, Colin told her about his parents' traditional New Year's Eve party. He asked if she would come to New York for it. "Maybe I will," she told him. Her sister's baby was born on the thirtieth of December, and the next day she caught a plane for New York to attend Luther and Maud Powell's party.

"It really was wonderful. It was marvelous. They enjoyed all holidays immensely. All of their friends and relatives and children of their friends were invited, and their little house was just full of people. Music was always playing on the dilapidated record player in the corner— West Indian music. There were all ages there, from little ones all the way up through the grandmothers and grandfathers, aunts and uncles. Lots of dancing, music, celebration, lots of good food. I was impressed. I thought, *These are nice people.* My parents were very conservative. We never had parties. I don't know why. Maybe they worked too hard, but his parents did, too. It was just not their makeup. So I liked this family gathering that included all the age groups."

The Powell family paid close attention to this young black woman whom Colin brought as his date. "I was being looked over very carefully. Every time I turned around,

Aunt Beryl was at my elbow. She was looking me over from top to bottom all night long. And I know now, knowing them as I do, that when I left that evening there was great discussion about whom he had brought home. And believe me, when they discuss somebody they do it thoroughly."

Alma thinks they were concerned about the fact that she was not Jamaican, especially once the relationship was serious and it seemed likely that they might be married. After the New Year's Eve party Colin and Alma spent more weekends in New York. He drove into Boston, picked her up, and they went to New York for the weekend. There they spent time with his family and met the friends with whom he had gone to college. By this time she dated him exclusively. In February Alma's mother, who founded Girl Scouts for black girls in Birmingham, came to New York for a scouting meeting. Alma made arrangements to meet her there. "Colin drove into Manhattan, picked us up, and took us out so that my mother could meet his parents. We had a very nice dinner, then chatted in the living room; Colin's mother was talking about her silver and linens. His father said, 'You know, maybe one day you'll have a daughter-in-law to give them to, you never know.' He was a sweet little man."

Alma's family seemed concerned that at age twenty-four she had not yet found a husband. By the time she finished college at Fisk, the "Harvard" of traditionally black colleges and universities, most of her friends were engaged. Meharry Medical School, which has graduated more than half of the seven thousand black physicians in America, was just across the street. It was assumed that Fisk girls would find young doctors to marry. Alma remembers one girl from Cleveland whose parents transferred her to Fisk from the University of Michigan precisely for the "social exposure." While she does not remember similar pressure on her, her family did not expect Alma to marry a GI. Her father did not meet Powell or his family until the weekend of the wedding. "If I were living at home and met a soldier, I think my father would not have let him in," Alma figures. Her mother met him in New York, however, and approved.

Perhaps of more concern for her father was the fact that the Powells were Jamaican. On the day of the wedding Mr. Johnson acknowledged, "I've spent my whole life trying to get away from West Indians, and now my daughter marries one." West Indians were perceived by American blacks a bit uppity. Alma suspects the difference is tied to the British colonial influence on West Indians and values that differed from those of blacks who grew up mostly as field laborers in the American South. Colin Powell thinks another difference is found in the emphasis upon education in the British colonies.

But Alma Johnson's parents were not exactly farmhands. They met in Birmingham though neither was born there. Her mother grew up in Kentucky. Her father was born in Ohio and went to Alabama as a young child. When Alma's parents were married, during the depression, they moved in with her father's parents. Three generations of Johnsons remained together under one roof.

Very much like Colin's kin, the Johnsons were people who worked hard and expected their children to do something with their lives. "All my life, everyone in my house worked," Alma asserts. "I remember when they began to talk about women's liberation, how women have to get out of the home and go into the work force! Our women always worked. Some were fortunate to have careers, but everybody had a job."

Alma's mother was the youngest child. By the time she finished school her sisters and brothers were already teachers. An older brother and sister had gone to Birmingham and, shortly after her grandfather died, sent for her grandmother and mother to join them. Her mother began to teach primary school. Her parents met at a church social and were married soon thereafter.

For most of his life Alma's father was an educator, but he would regale the children with stories of other jobs. He worked in a steel plant, as an undertaker, and sold insurance. Early in the 1930s he went to work in the Birmingham School System. By the time Alma was born in 1937, he was an elementary school principal in the segregated schools. At one point during World War II he held four jobs at once. It was approaching Christmas. He was principal of two schools on opposite sides of the city, working in the Post Office at night, and making embalming fluid on the back porch (due to the war it was hard to get). The hard work had its pay-off. Says Alma, "We were not well-to-do, but we owned the house we lived in, which was unusual, and we had a car, which was unusual." In 1944, her father became the third principal of Parker High School. With more than three thousand students it was the only black high school in Birmingham.

One day in late July 1962, Colin received a phone call from his dear friend and former Pershing Rifles mentor Ronnie Brooks. Brooks was attending graduate school at Brown University. A classmate from Birmingham had told him about Alma Johnson. Brooks called Powell and said, "I have to come up to Boston. I hear there is a girl who is really something, and I want to meet her." Colin responded, "Forget it, I already did." They decided that Ronnie should come anyway and look her over. They met in Boston for dinner at Alma's place. They talked. At one point Brooks got up, kissed Alma on the cheek, patted Colin on the shoulders, and said, "You found it."

Not until August 12 did Colin Powell propose marriage, if you can call it that. Lieutenant Powell had received orders to go to Vietnam and told Alma the next weekend in Boston.

"Oh, really?" she responded.

"Yeah, and I'll be gone a year."

"I don't want to tell you I'll be here when you get back, I'm too old for that," she told him, adding, "I may write, I may not. But I don't really want to go through all of that."

The next weekend he returned and said, "Okay, this is what we are going to do. We'll get married in two weeks.

You'll go home next week to get ready for the wedding, I'll come down the week after that, and we'll get married."

They called her parents, who immediately began painting the house. Friends started hand-writing invitations. Alma went out and in less than an hour bought a dress. Powell's parents were not surprised when he filled them in on their plans. But Luther and Maud were not too excited about the prospect of going to the South. "We're not going to Birmingham. You're crazy. Have a happy life," Luther told his son. But Powell's sister, Marilyn Berns, and her husband Norm, who is white, were eager to be there. In the end, the elder Powells decided that they would attend, too, reasoning that "if they lynch Norm we all ought to be there." On August 24 they were married. Ronnie Brooks was best man, and Alma's sister was matron of honor. Colin and Alma had four months before he went to Vietnam.

A month after the wedding they left Boston for Fort Bragg, North Carolina, home of the 82nd Airborne Division. Powell was sent there to attend a six-week course in training for Vietnam. Because it was a temporary assignment, Alma was not authorized to accompany him, and no quarters were available.

They spent several days looking for a place to live. There seemed to be no place for blacks in Fayetteville, the town outside Fort Bragg. One option was a house littered with old paint cans, sitting in the middle of a field. Next they visited an old black man who was a notary public, a real estate agent, and perhaps a preacher. Upon meeting Colin, the man called his wife and said, "You know those folks you got living in the back room? Kick them out. I got somebody else." But the Powells backed out when they saw the dingy room and were told that they needed their own sheets and could use the kitchen. Their possessions were still in the back of their VW Beetle when they hastily left to have dinner with a buddy of Colin's and his wife, Joe and Pat Schwar. Joe and Colin had been in the Infantry Officer Basic Course and served in Germany together. Now the

Schwars were assigned to Fort Bragg and lived in on-post housing.

When they arrived, Joe was not yet back from work. Pat was preparing supper and tending the three little children, ages three, two, and four months. As the Powells told her their tale of woe looking for a house, Pat proposed that they move in with them. When Joe walked in the door, she inquired, "Can't they, Joe?"

"What?" he asked.

"Can't Powells move in with us?"

"Sure, when do they want to come?"

Alma excused herself to go to the bathroom. When she returned, Colin discreetly asked her, "Do they really have room?" She delivered her scouting report—three bedrooms.

The Powells slept the next six weeks on bunk beds previously occupied by two Schwar boys who had moved in with the baby. "We were just one happy family," Alma Powell remembers fondly. And those three children had two mommies and daddies."

Pat, a white northerner from Philadelphia, got a lesson about life in the South one day when she and Alma went shopping. She proposed stopping for a Coke. Alma said, "You can go, I can't."

"What do you mean you can't?"

"I can't go to that lunch counter."

Pat got mad and said, "We're going anyway."

But Alma had to say, "Sorry."

Or they would be sitting around after dinner and Pat would say, "Come on, let's don't just sit here. Let's go bowling."

And Alma would have to say, "You can go; we can't."

chapter four

WAR IN BIRMINGHAM, WAR IN VIETNAM

T H A N K S G I V I N G 1962 the Powells spent together. Before Christmas they would be on opposite sides of the globe. Colin was promoted to captain in June, just two months before he and Alma married. Within months of the August wedding they conceived a child. Colin Powell left for Vietnam knowing that his wife would give birth while he served his one-year tour of duty.

Most United States citizens knew very little about Vietnam when Americans first went there as advisors. In May 1954, the colonialist French army suffered its final defeat by Viet Minh forces led by General Vo Nguyen Giap. This defeat marked the end of what had been called Indochina, which included Laos and Cambodia. In its place, the July 21 Geneva Accords established a divided Vietnam with a demilitarized zone at the seventeenth parallel. The north would become the Communist Democratic Republic of Vietnam and the south a non-communist coalition-governed nation called simply the Republic of Vietnam. They were referred to, of course, as North Vietnam and South Vietnam.

As part of the effort to stop the expansion of communism, the U.S. Military Assistance Advisory Group was formed to shore up the new South Vietnamese government headed by President Ngo Dinh Diem. It was thought that an American presence might also help create cohesion in the multifaction south by assembling a national army. A unified military, it was believed, would help prevent civil war. By the time Powell left for Southeast Asia and despite eight years of direct U.S. military involvement there, remarkably little was being reported in the American press.

While the Powells were staying with the Schwars in their Fort Bragg quarters, Joe Schwar's Special Forces unit was put on alert and then deployed in response to the Cuban missile crisis. The Powells were there to support Pat and the boys in what were very uncertain days. By the time Powell shipped out for Vietnam a little more than a month later, Joe was back. He and Pat helped Alma through one of the most difficult transitions she would make. She returned home to Birmingham, Alabama, to spend the year with her parents and have her child.

"To say that Birmingham was a powder keg in 1963 is an understatement," says Alma Powell. "Birmingham never was the nicest place in the world to live. Parents worried about their children with good reason. I was stopped by police just because I was black. You were in danger from the police as much as anybody else. And anybody who wanted to do anything against blacks was not likely to face any consequences for doing it."

Ten days after the French were defeated in Vietnam, the United States Supreme Court passed down the land-mark civil-rights decision requiring school integration in the *Brown v. Board of Education* case. A year-and-a-half later, on December 5, 1955, bus boycotts began in Montgomery, Alabama, launching the grass roots civil-rights movement. As events approached culmination seven-and-a-half-years later, just a few months after the hundredth anniversary of Lincoln's Emancipation Proclamation, national attention would turn to Birmingham.

Birmingham's role in the Negro rights movement came

to national attention on Mother's Day 1961 when thirteen Freedom Riders set out from Atlanta on two buses bound for Birmingham. The Greyhound bus was stoned as it stopped at Anniston en route. Two hundred angry whites met it there; its tires were slashed. When the bus stopped six miles out of town to fix the tires, it was surrounded and a firebomb tossed inside the back door. Passengers fled out an emergency exit as the bus burst into flames. Meanwhile a Trailways bus carrying the rest of the Freedom Riders pulled into the station at Birmingham, where a mob assaulted the passengers. One passenger was paralyzed for life. Apparently public-safety commissioner "Bull" Connor told the police to stay away, ostensibly because of the holiday. It was learned, however, that the police were kept away precisely so that there would be no interference with the mob.

The national black weekly newspaper, the *Pittsburgh Courier*, called Birmingham the "worst big city in the U.S.A." It was Alabama's most populous city. Forty percent of its 350,000 residents were black. The median income for whites was more than twice that of blacks. Whites were three times more likely to have graduated from high school than blacks. Three-quarters of all whites were skilled laborers; of those blacks employed, only one in six held a skilled job. In 1962, white city officials closed thirty-eight playgrounds, sixty-eight parks, six swimming pools, and four golf courses rather than allow them to be desegregated in accordance with a federal court order.

Between 1957 and 1963 there were eighteen unsolved bombings in black neighborhoods. Violence and threats of violence were commonplace. Some began referring to the city as "Bombingham." Alma Powell remembers, "It was ugly. The first bombings took place when I was a child. There were the church bombings, but initially it was homes that were bombed. These bombings didn't cause a ripple anywhere. We would all drive by to see it, and shake our heads, but then you didn't expect anything different."

Another incident involved a carload of drunken whites and a black man in Birmingham in September 1957. "It was

Labor Day when a friend called. I was in college and he was in law school. I said, 'What's going on?' and he said, 'They just castrated a guy last night who was standing by the side of the road talking to his neighbor. For no reason. *For no reason!*' "

This event reminded Alma of other racist encounters from her childhood. "My mother, when we were very small, worked for Girl Scouts. She was the first person to provide scouting for black girls and eventually became a professional on staff. She was conducting a camp-counselors' training session at the camp we planned to use for blacks. Several white friends from other places around the country came to help with the training. In her tent set off in the woods by herself, she woke up one night hearing voices. She got up and walked through the woods in the dark and came upon the Klan surrounding the white women's tent. They were saying, 'You'd better get out of here. By sunset tomorrow you'd better not be here.' We knew that sometime all of this racism was going to have to be resolved, and it was not going to be done peacefully."

Birmingham seemed quiet when her Colin left for Vietnam at the end of 1962, but it didn't last. The reputation of Reverend Doctor Martin Luther King, Jr., seemed to be waning after his participation in Albany, Georgia, protests that ended without the desegregation of city schools. Municipal parks were closed rather than be integrated. The public library was opened to blacks, but all chairs were removed. King himself was depressed. But the Reverend Fred Shuttlesworth, who was chain-whipped when he tried to enroll his daughter in a white school, whose wife was stabbed in the same 1957 incident, and whose house was leveled by a bomb in 1956, coaxed the Southern Christian Leadership Conference and Dr. King to make Birmingham their next step in the movement for civil rights.

In January 1963, King, Shuttlesworth, and others met for a three-day retreat to plan a strategy for Birmingham. A national tour followed to promote support for what was being called Project C. "C" stood for "confrontation." It was to begin in March. King implored President Kennedy to issue a second emancipation proclamation on the centennial of the first one. Kennedy declined but did send a civil rights bill to Congress, where it died in committee. By the time that protests began, city officials, especially Bull Connor, were ready for action. When violence struck, it became nothing short of a war on the city streets.

The home of Birmingham's civil rights movement was the Sixteenth Street Baptist Church. "Nobody was surprised as things began to explode," Alma says. Churches took the forefront because they could organize people. Reasoning that blacks contributed to the city's economy by purchasing from local merchants, the movement's leaders organized boycotts and picketed stores. Picketers were jailed. City government was in turmoil. In a referendum unrelated to the protests, one form of municipal government was replaced by another. In what was a contested election, the old commission was replaced by a city council. In the interim, however, Bull Connor remained in control of the police. When A. D. King, the brother of Martin Luther King, Jr., led an April 6 Palm Sunday prayer-march through the streets of downtown Birmingham, police loosed German shepherds and swung night sticks to put down the demonstrators. On April 12, Good Friday, after a half-mile of marching in the streets, Martin Luther King, Jr., was arrested, along with others. Demonstrations continued with King, Jr., in jail although the number of participants declined. Eight days after his arrest King was freed on bond.

A new strategy was proposed by a veteran of student sit-ins, James Bevel. It involved school children as protesters. Unlike adults, children would only miss school, and their arrest would not hurt the financial stability of black families. On May 2, Martin Luther King, Jr., addressed the first group of young demonstrators, ages six to eighteen, before sending them out. Bull Connor arrested 959 that day. Attorney General Robert Kennedy called King to urge calling off the protests, arguing that children might be hurt. The protests went on.

More than one thousand young people marched instead of going to school the next day. Before the demonstration could get off the ground, however, Bull Connor met the children with ferocious police dogs and the fire department's high-pressure hoses that put out a stream of water at one hundred pounds per square inch. Children were thrown into the air, leveled to the ground, rolled down the street, tossed against parked cars, and slammed into trees by the force. There was fury in the eyes of Birmingham's black people. There was shock across America at the sight on television.

Alma's uncle was principal at Birmingham's newly opened, second black high school. Her father remained principal of the original one. "It was difficult for my father and uncle because they felt responsible for the students," she explains. "Every day those who were demonstrating came to get children to leave school and march.

"The rationale was that the police wouldn't hurt children like they hurt adults. But, the children who marched were only the ones foolish enough to go. Many of us sat at home and said, 'This needs to be done, but we're not going to go do it.' My father and uncle thought that if parents sent children to school, then it was the school's responsibility to keep them there." Alma's father had a simple way of handling the situation. He met with the demonstrators every day at the door to say, "If their mothers want them to march, let them come and tell me. As long as they are in this building, I am responsible for them."

"Of course," Alma remembers, "the demonstrators didn't have any good things to say about my father and uncle. But I remember my uncle's sitting at the table saying, 'The children, the children, why do they have to use the children?' And I said, 'Because those are the ones who can do it. They are the ones who have to make the change.'"

Although they lived outside of central Birmingham, the Johnson home was not entirely insulated from violence. One late afternoon shortly after she gave birth to baby Michael, Alma was hanging diapers on the clothesline when she heard gunshots. A black neighbor was returning home from work. As he turned into his driveway, a car sped around the corner and took a couple of shots. Fortunately, they missed him. Mr. Robert Johnson did not just sit by in the midst of such dangers. He was always ready to take up arms in defense of his family. Once, Alma's father instructed her to put the newborn Michael in an underground recess below the floor as the two of them took guns and stood watch. His instructions: "Anything that comes up that driveway, you shoot first and ask questions later." She remembers, "My father liked guns. He had his own gun collection. Mother said that it was probably the tragedy of his life that he never got to shoot anybody. He was always prepared to do so."

The number of Birmingham demonstrators grew following the police and fire departments' horrifying response on Friday, May 3. By Monday, May 6, more than two thousand people were jailed. Governor George Wallace, whose inauguration speech included the words—"Segregation now! Segregation tomorrow! Segregation forever!"— supported Bull Connor's continuing strong-arm response. President Kennedy, however, wanted a settlement. A truce was negotiated with local businessmen, and Kennedy dispatched Army troops to make certain it would not be sabotaged. On June 11, Wallace personally blocked the entrance of a University of Alabama building to keep two black students out. Later in the day he stepped aside when confronted by Alabama National Guard General Henry Graham. Black students entered for the first time. That evening President Kennedy went on national television and announced that he would send a new civil-rights bill to Congress that would give the "elementary right" to be served in facilities that are open to the public to every American. It was delivered on June 19. But Birmingham would see still more violence.

On September 2, Wallace sent state troopers to Tuskegee High School to prevent its integration. On September 5, Birmingham shut its schools scheduled for integration. On

September 10, the schools were integrated as Kennedy
federalized the Alabama National Guard. Then on September 15, a bomb went off in the bathroom of the Sixteenth
Street Baptist Church during a Sunday service. Four little
girls were killed. Although she did not attend there, it was a
place Alma knew well. To this day she remembers the wet-concrete smell of the bathroom where the girls perished.
She, her mother, and her aunt were across town at church
when they received a call from her uncle telling them that
the bomb had gone off; they were to come home by a back
route. On the way they stopped for a stop sign. A black man
came up to the car and told her, "You better get out of here.
You're too fair to be here."

As young Captain Powell faced combat for the first
time, twelve time-zones away, he had no idea of the war
that was being waged on the home front. His wife and her
family, while not combatants, were on the front lines. His
first and only son was a potential casualty. Communications
were not good in Vietnam. When his plane landed in
Saigon, he entered a new world of little contact with home.

From Saigon Powell traveled north to Da Nang and on
to Hue, where the First Infantry Division of the Army of the
Republic of Vietnam (or ARVN) was based. It was South
Vietnam's cutting-edge unit in I Corps, with troops in the
two northernmost provinces nearest the DMZ. His job was
to serve as an advisor to the 2nd Battalion, 3rd Regiment, or
"2d of the 3d," one of the First Infantry Division's units, to
help build leadership and unit cohesion among the Viet-namese. His destination—a rugged, remote, mountainous,
and relatively uninhabited area, the A Shau Valley along the
Rao Loa River near Vietnam's border with Laos. Those who
lived there were not Vietnamese but so-called Montagnards,
literally "mountain people"—Mon-Khmer minorities whose
ancestors probably migrated to Indochina from islands
south of Southeast Asia. The U.S. Special Forces organized
the local people into a Civilian Irregular Defense Group

camp there in April 1963 to stop the North Vietnamese regular forces from infiltrating from Laos. This is where Powell spent most of his tour.

Assigned as an advisor to an ARVN unit, Powell often went for a couple weeks at a time without seeing other Americans. A Marine helicopter brought food and mail, but usually he was in the jungle looking for the enemy. Patrols lasted days or weeks. On his head Powell wore a steel helmet with a canvas camouflage cover held on by an elastic strap. Over his green fatigues he wore suspenders connected to a web belt. Attached were ammo pouches, grenades, and a couple of canteens. His pants were bloused into his boots; sewn up tight to keep critters out. A poncho attached to his "ruck" pack doubled as a semi-waterproof shelter. No longer riding around in an armored personnel carrier along the East-West border, Powell was now a foot soldier, "light" infantry, carrying a heavy, M-14 rifle. He was "a lean, mean, green fighting machine."

Powell spent most of his time on patrol—through swamps, over mountains, down valleys, in jungles. Despite the heat, sleeves were mostly worn down because the razor-edged elephant grass could cut flesh. Blood-sucking leeches fell from the trees. Monotonous, never-ending work. Walking. Starting. Stopping. Looking for signs of the enemy. Avoiding mines and booby-traps. Doing what "grunts" do. Humpin' and sweatin' day after day. Days were long; nights even longer. Some patrols led to fire fights. Most did not. But Powell remembers being ambushed nearly every morning just before sun-up. "They could find us more easily than we could find them."

The purpose of patrols in the A Shau Valley was to keep the North Vietnamese regulars and Viet Cong—black-pajama-wearing Communist troops from the south—from bringing weapons, ammunition, and supplies into South Vietnam. The complex set of roads, rails, paths, and trails known simply as the Ho Chi Minh Trail ran through this area, north-south through Laos. Another objective was to keep the Viet Cong from establishing stable bases of operations in the border region.

This was work for the Army's finest. Advisory teams made up of the best and brightest of America's young officers were first sent to Vietnam's Joint General Staff and Defense Ministry, and then to its Army, Navy, and Air Force military schools and training centers. Finally, they were sent to its divisions and to units in the field.

In the early 1960s America saw Vietnam as a regional skirmish, a small war, a "police action." But the opposition was an extension of the Soviet threat. American soldiers were selected to gain wartime experience in preparation for a possible European war with the U.S.S.R. Powell had punched his ticket right. He had the right training. He proved himself on the front lines as a platoon leader at the Fulda Gap. He met the criteria for service in the delicate position of advisor to the South Vietnamese Army.

Powell was an excellent officer. Physically fit, mentally tough, a proven leader competent in tactics, experienced with weapons, and knowledgeable in how to use them, he was also by nature diplomatic and culturally sensitive. Not stuck in his own little parochial world, he could work with people, and he authentically liked them, whoever they were. There are countless horror stories about the wrong GIs being assigned a job because of "the needs of the Army." This assignment, however, was an example of the Army personnel system at its best. Colin Powell was perfect for the assignment, despite the less-than-pleasant circumstances. Besides building good relations with the Vietnamese, Powell's efforts helped raise the battalion's combat readiness rating from satisfactory to excellent in the time he was with them.

The advisor's job is both to accompany ARVN troops on their operations and to provide training. In Army doctrine, operations and training are two parts of a whole; they go hand-in-hand. Advice was given on how to conduct military operations and how to maintain combat equipment "in the field." Advisors also assisted with rifle marksmanship training, small-unit tactics, land navigation, and other basic soldiering skills.

The Vietnamese offered local knowledge and experience. The Americans complemented this with extensive leadership and soldiering skills. While thousands of Vietnamese had served under the French, few were given leadership responsibilities, let alone training in how to lead. Even experienced South Vietnamese soldiers had little technical training. Fundamental command and staff experience was lacking. By the time Powell arrived in South Vietnam, the majority of ARVN troops were conscripts. It was a massive and growing force of 243,000 troops in need of formation. Unfortunately, Americans were trained to fight a different kind of war. Having recently faced the North Koreans across another "demilitarized" zone, the Americans were prepared for traditional tactics in which battle lines were clearly drawn. But the growing threat in South Vietnam was from within. War was being fought in little skirmishes and thousands of ambushes with countless snipers. The opposing forces were locals fighting in unconventional ways. For Americans out with ARVN units it was mostly a guerrilla war against the Viet Cong, the VC, "Victor Charlie," or simply Charlie.

Powell remembers the ARVN troops as being good soldiers. Their officers seemed well-trained. The one he remembers best was his first Vietnamese counterpart, Captain Vo Cong Hieu. They served side by side for several months. Powell and Hieu became close, living and working together day after day. But after Hieu was reassigned, Powell lost track of him. When South Vietnam fell to the communists in 1975, Powell suspected that his friend was either killed or imprisoned. In fact, Hieu was captured and interred in a Communist reeducation camp.

Shortly after becoming Chairman of the Joint Chiefs in October 1989, Powell received a letter at his Pentagon office. Enclosed was a photograph of six Montagnard children assembled with the two captains. The picture was taken in front of an A Shau Valley hootch in 1963. Powell recognized the photo. He had a copy of it among his own Vietnam memorabilia. The letter was from Hieu, telling of his thirteen-year detention and recent release. He included a plea for Powell's help in getting to the United States. One of his family members had escaped as a boat person, he explained. Her name was Mrs. Thuyet Do. After her arrival in the United States, eventually she settled in suburban Minneapolis, Minnesota.

Powell called his friend Rich Armitage and former Chairman of the Joint Chiefs of Staff General Jack Vessey who had been working with the Vietnamese government in search of American POWs and MIAs. In 1991 the former Colonel Hieu—he had been promoted since serving with Powell—along with his wife, children, and grandchildren joined Thuyet Do. They settled in New Hope, Minnesota.

On November 7, 1991, Powell was scheduled to speak that night to a group called the Minnesota Meeting in Bloomington, just outside Minneapolis, Minnesota. That same afternoon as Powell entered the lobby of the hotel where the event was to occur, Hieu was standing there in anticipation of their reunion. He had been in the U.S. only two weeks. Powell remembers his looking forlorn, in a poorly matched coat, tie, and trousers, and underdressed for the early winter chill. He looked as though he were "freezing to death," Powell says. When the two men's eyes met, they both grinned broadly. They walked toward one another and embraced. Powell asked and Hieu consented to be his honored guest at the black-tie occasion that evening.

When Powell left for Vietnam in 1962, he knew that Alma had to have a way to get word to him about their child's birth. Once in Vietnam they worked out a plan. She would write a letter with the details. On the outside she should write the words "Baby Letter." At headquarters back in Hue, Powell left word to keep watch for the Baby Letter so that when it arrived he could be called on the radio and immediately read the news.

The letter arrived but sat unnoticed in a pile with other mail waiting to be sent to the field. Meanwhile, Powell received another letter dropped with supplies from an airplane flying over the jungle. The letter was from his mother, who filled him in on all the usual Jamaican family goings-on. There was news of this aunt and that cousin. She and Dad were fine. After signing the letter, "Love, Mother," she added a postscript. "Oh, by the way, we are absolutely delighted about the baby." Was it a boy or a girl? When was it born?! She didn't say. Powell immediately got on the radio and exclaimed, "Look in the damned mailbox!" The letter was there, and he learned that his son, Michael, had been born on March 23.

On July 23, 1963, Powell was out on patrol as usual, moving to a vantage point to deploy one of the battalion's rifle companies when he stepped into a pit where a simple but effective Viet Cong booby trap was hidden. In the pit was a sharpened, poisoned bamboo stake with a point. Known as a "punji stick," it could pierce the newest of Army boots. It went through the instep of Powell's right foot and came out through the top. Despite the wound, he performed his duties, then made the two-hour trek back to a U.S. Special Forces camp, using a makeshift cane. By then his foot was an ugly purple, badly swollen, and he was in severe pain. A Medivac helicopter took him to the hospital at First Division Headquarters in Hue. In just a few weeks, the recipient of a Purple Heart, Powell was back again near the Laotian border.

In August, with fewer than four months of duty in Vietnam left to serve, Powell was assigned to ARVN's First Division Headquarters back in Hue as an advisor on the general staff, responsible for improving training throughout the division. He received a Bronze Star for this and other accomplishments throughout the tour.

On May 5, back home in the U.S., the Americans for Democratic Action issued a resolution demanding the withdrawal of all American troops from Vietnam. Three days later, twenty thousand Buddhists gathered in Hue for the traditional celebration of the Buddha's birthday. Seven children, one woman, and a man were killed, and twenty others were wounded at the orders of Deputy Province Chief, Major Dang Xi, a Diem regime official. Like Diem and his family, Xi was a member of the ten-percent Catholic minority, which Diem considered more "politically reliable." The Diem government blamed the Viet Cong for the incident. There were more Buddhist protests. A month later, on June 10, MACV Commander General Paul Harkins warned American military personnel to avoid duty with ARVN units that were suppressing Buddhists. The next day, Buddhist monk Quang Duc stepped out of a car on a busy Saigon street, sat down cross-legged, was doused with gasoline, and publicly immolated himself in a "respectful" plea for President Diem to show "compassion and charity" to all religions. Other such protests would follow.

President Diem's sister-in-law called the incidents "barbecues" and offered to supply matches. In July there were suspicions of a coup brewing. Diem's brother, Ngo Dinh Nhu, who headed the secret police and served as chief political officer, began attacking Buddhist pagodas. Shortly after midnight on August 21 his men raced through the streets of Saigon and surrounded Xa Loi, the city's principal temple. With semiautomatic rifles and tear gas they raided and ransacked it. Four hundred monks and nuns were arrested, including the eighty-year-old Buddhist patriarch. In Hue, Nhu's forces attacked the Dieude temple, and nearly two thousand people rioted in protest.

On August 24 the newly appointed U.S. Ambassador Henry Cabot Lodge received word from Washington that the U.S. could no longer stand Nhu's place in Diem's regime. Two days later Lodge met with Diem for the first time. The Vietnamese president refused to replace his brother or discuss other reforms. Lodge, joined by Saigon CIA chief John Richardson, urged the divided Kennedy administration to support a coup led by a group of South Vietnamese generals. On November 1, the dissident generals took over the presidential palace and toppled the Diem regime. Diem and Nhu escaped, but the next day were brutally killed. A few days later, Ambassador Lodge invited the insurgent generals to the embassy to congratulate them. He cabled Kennedy, "The prospects now are for a shorter war."

Powell was in Saigon in those early days of November 1963. As a young infantry officer his expertise was soldiering, not politics, or the art of war in any strategic sense. He had his orders and served proudly and dutifully to beat back the Communist bear. But he observed on returning home that the American effort in Southeast Asia was not enough to win. His assessment? "It'll take a half-million troops to succeed."

There were some 900 advisors in Indochina when Eisenhower left office in 1961. When Powell was assigned, there were 11,000. By the time he left in 1963, the figure was 16,000. At the height of the war five years later more than 536,000 Americans would be in Vietnam. Once again Colin L. Powell, serial number 083771, would be among them.

chapter five
VALOR WITHOUT VICTORY

J O H N F. K E N N E D Y was assassinated three weeks after Ngo Dinh Diem. Lyndon Baines Johnson was President when Colin Powell arrived home at the end of November 1963.

Colin and Alma Powell were reunited, and Powell was introduced to his six-month-old son, Michael. Their new home would once again be the home of the Infantry, Fort Benning, Georgia. After an "unaccompanied tour," the Army's term for being separated from your family for a year or more, Powell could count on this assignment's keeping them together for a couple of years. Since going to Fort Benning was what the Army calls a "PCS move"—short for permanent-change-of-station—the Powells were eligible for on-post officer's quarters. But there was a shortage of housing, and they could expect to be on a waiting list for months. Powell would have to find a place to live in the local area or remain separated from his family until government housing was available. Despite his being an Army officer and having served in Vietnam, being black limited his choices of places to live. Alma stayed in Birmingham with Michael. Powell remembers those days. "I was going back and forth to Birmingham every weekend while I looked in the local area for a place to live. But in 1963 it wasn't easy for me to find suitable rentals for my family, even though I could afford it—barely."

On one of his many trips between Fort Benning and Birmingham, Powell was driving his little German Volkswagen Beetle with New York plates on U.S. Highway 280 through Sylacauga, Alabama. Looking into his rearview mirror, Powell saw flashing lights and assumed that he was being pulled over for a traffic violation. But he had a bumper sticker on his car that read "All the Way with LBJ." When the patrolman came to the car, it turned out that he was handing out literature supporting Republican candidate Barry Goldwater. The patrolman looked into the foreign car where the young black man sat and said, "Boy, you ain't smart enough to be around here. You need to leave." "Yes, sir," Powell replied. Never again as an active-duty military officer would Powell express his political preferences.

Captain Powell searched throughout the area for a place to live. One place he scouted was in the nearby town of Phenix City, just over the Alabama border. "Alma and I heard about a place on 28th Avenue. It belonged to a preacher's family. It was a very nice brick house. It sort of looked like a preacher's house—comfortable, warm, touched by love. It was the first home for Colin, Alma, and Mike Powell. You can imagine the emotion we brought to it, the feelings, the sense of pride, the joy at being together as a family." Although they only lived there for a few months before moving on to Fort Benning, it was a cherished respite and sanctuary for the reunited family. In 1993, 28th Avenue was renamed: General Colin L. Powell Parkway.

One day in February 1964, Powell stopped at Buck's Barbecue, a hamburger joint just off-post in Columbus. He ordered a hamburger. The nice waitress asked him if he was an African student. "No," he replied. "Are you a Puerto Rican?" "No," he replied. "You're Negro?" she inquired. "That's right," Powell answered. "Well, I can't bring out a hamburger," she told him. The restaurant did serve blacks.

However, she said, "You'll have to go to the back door." Powell left without the hamburger. In July, President Johnson signed the most sweeping civil-rights legislation in American history, the Civil Rights Bill of 1964. It prohibited racial discrimination in employment, places of public accom- modation, publicly owned facilities, union membership, and federally funded programs. Shortly thereafter Powell returned to Buck's and ate his hamburger.

Powell's new job at the U.S. Army Infantry Board was not exactly the height of excitement in his career. He was a test officer. It was the sort of job somebody has to do. And it offered a very important fringe benefit: a regular schedule with weekends at home with the family. The Infantry Board was abolished in 1991 after seventy years as the Army's agency for user-testing new equipment. For example, once a new rifle such as the M-16, which was being tested there while Powell was working on other projects, had been developed and tested by industry, it would be sent to Fort Benning. There it was fired, dragged through the mud, cleaned by troops, beat against the ground, and given a realistic workout. Every newly developed item a soldier might use—each new rifle, field pack, helmet—was tested there for reliability, availability, and maintainability, known as RAM, according to specific standards established by the Infantry Board. Powell was a test officer from late November 1963 through June of 1964. He returned in May of 1965 and stayed until February 1966. His major responsibility in the Field Equipment and Special Projects division was testing a new radio.

One former colleague there remembers him as "very impressive as a soldier. It was in his manner, his demeanor. There was no foolishness but he was very friendly. He was an intense, hard worker. People liked him."

In August 1964, after his first nine months at the Infantry Board, Powell began the Infantry Officer's Advanced Course, the so-called career course. In those days it lasted nine months. This is where captains are prepared to become company commanders, the key first step in the list

of commands at battalion, brigade and, for the very few who
become generals, division and corps levels. It is also where a
"company-level" officer begins to get formal training in how
to work on the battalion commander's and higher staffs, as
an "S-1" (Personnel and Administration), "S-2" (Intelligence), "S-3" (Operations and Training), and "S-4" (Logistics). Of course, Powell's prior experience in Vietnam made
much of the classroom work a mere schoolhouse review.
Not only had he served side-by-side with Vietnamese
company commanders in real combat, but he had served in
the "3-shop." Of all the places a war-fighter should serve on
a staff, this is the most highly prestigious and where most of
the action is. At battalion and brigade levels there is an S-3
(short for "Staff" Three). At division and corps, because
they are commanded by generals, there is a G-3 (short for
"General" Staff Three). Eventually, at the highest level as
Chairman, Powell would have his own J-3 (J stands for
"Joint"). Powell had been at the right hand of the division
G-3 in his last days in Hue.

By the time he got to the career course he already knew
a great deal of the subject matter, and much of it was boring.
Classes were filled with laundry lists of things to be
remembered for tests. There were countless, catchy acro-
nyms for points of Army doctrine. Classes were taught in
large, dark lecture halls. Study groups met in smaller,
windowless rooms. Like all Army courses, however, it was a
ticket that needed to be punched for promotion. Without
being too eager to impress the instructors, Powell was
clearly gung ho, a determined, hard-working professional
who knew that much of what seemed like tedium or
harassment was just part of making a career out of the
Army. Powell's classmates remember him as a team player.
He may have been more serious than many of them, but he
was not a "glory hog." He did not make himself stand out.
Nor was he a complainer, the sort of guy who was just along
for the ride, dragging his feet. Classmates who knew him
well recall being impressed. More than one of them remembers thinking, *This guy is going to go far.* He surely cut the

right figure: tall, broad-shouldered, and slim but muscular, with a serious face and eyes that beamed as easily and sincerely as he smiled. He also was interested in more than his own success. Attentive and a good listener, Powell conveyed a genuine concern for his contemporaries. He inspired confidence and won it easily.

Never one to waste, Powell's experience at the Infantry Board is something he capitalized upon in the Advanced Course. In addition to skills specific to the military, young officers are expected to begin developing more general talents. Among them are leadership and management abilities. Officers are also expected to communicate well both verbally and in writing. Every Advanced Course officer was required to submit a research paper, more an exercise in organizational and writing abilities than anything else. Powell chose a topic he knew something about that, in its own way, was like late-breaking news to the few who might have read it at the Infantry School. It was a review of the "Distribution of the Lightweight Radio Transmitter AN/PRT 4 and Radio Receiver AN/PRR 9 (Squad Radio Sets) Within the Rifle Company, Infantry Battalion, Infantry Battalion (Mechanized) and Airborne Infantry Battalion." This was the new radio that he had tested at the Infantry Board. He concluded that these were better radios than the ones they would replace.

Two classes of two hundred young captains attended the Infantry Officer Advanced Course that began in August 1964. Almost all of them had either just returned from Vietnam or were about to be sent there. Powell is not the only one who would become a general. Among the several who would go on to receive stars was Howard Graves who, as a three-star, became Assistant to the Chairman of the Joint Chiefs of Staff under Powell and went on to become superintendent at West Point, the military academy's senior officer, equivalent to a college president.

Alma and Colin Powell conceived a second child at Fort Benning. Linda Powell was born at the hospital on-post on April 16, 1965. Following the career course and another nine months at the Infantry Board, in February 1966 Powell was called back to the Infantry School to be an instructor. There was no doubt that Powell was on the fast track. He was Airborne- and Ranger qualified. He had served at the Fulda Gap, the very focal point in the Cold War. He had been to Vietnam, was a combat infantryman, and had been awarded the Purple Heart and Bronze Star. Then Infantry called him home to Fort Benning—no small honor—and now it chose him to train others who would probably go to Vietnam, too. He was impressive on the lecture-hall platform and a good teacher, but once again schoolhouse life was anything but the exciting life of a warrior.

Powell remembers teaching officer candidates—mostly enlisted soldiers who had been selected for training leading to commissioning—who were being run through the Infantry School prior to being sent to Southeast Asia. Mostly, his Officer Candidate School classes were filled with tired, bored, impatient young men. He told Howard Means that "They'd come back in on a Friday morning after an all-night combat patrol. . . . They'd be allowed to shower, get a hot lunch, and then that Friday afternoon they had to get these dogged mandatory subjects that they had to have, and the doggedest of them all was how to fill out a unit-readiness report. And I got that every Friday afternoon. You haven't lived until you've had two hundred guys who are going to be second lieutenants tomorrow who have been up five straight days and nights, have just had a shower and a hot lunch, and they're in an air-conditioned room on a hot summer afternoon at Fort Benning—you have not lived. I never had to make presentations like the one I had to make at that time. I did anything [to keep their attention]. I threw rubber chickens at the class—I did it. I'm ashamed of it. But, they could fill out a unit-readiness report."

In May 1966, while teaching and writing infantry training manuals, Powell was promoted to the rank of major. It was a sign of his success. While he had never actually held a usually mandatory year of company command as a captain, he was a counterpart to ARVN commanders in Vietnam. But he commanded two companies briefly as a lieutenant, for three months in Germany and four months at Fort Devens with Alpha Company, 1-4 Infantry. With only eight years in the Army and fewer than four as a captain, he was selected "below the zone," meaning that his year-group of officers was not yet under consideration for promotion but he, along with a small number of others who were identified as exceptionally capable, was picked to be promoted early. Just over a year later, after fifteen months at the Infantry School and an uncommonly long period of more than three-and-a-half years at Fort Benning, Powell moved on to another key assignment.

For junior officers, military schooling is largely *pro forma*. Especially in the 1960s, every lieutenant and captain was assured that he would attend a Basic Course and an Advanced Course. These were taught by the different branches: infantry, armor, artillery, among others. But upon becoming a field-grade officer, beginning with major, the real competition among professionals begins. Attending the next level of military education is highly selective, but no one was very surprised when Major Powell was chosen to attend the Army's Command and General Staff College (CGSC), a nearly year-long course for experienced majors and lieutenant colonels, just a year after making major.

In a sense, CGSC is the real "career course." Those who attend it are virtually assured of staying in the Army for the twenty years required to retire. Unlike the advanced courses, which are offered at a number of places in different specializations, there is only one CGSC for officers of all branches to attend. It is offered only once a year at Fort Leavenworth, Kansas.

At Leavenworth, Powell made his mark. Out of a class of 1,244 officers, most of them his senior, Powell ranked second in the graduating class.

Much had transpired in the nation and the world during four and a half years of stateside duty since Powell returned from Vietnam. No longer were Americans there primarily as advisors. The United States was engaged in a bona fide war.

As Powell began the Advanced Course in August 1964, the House and Senate passed the Tonkin Gulf Resolution after American ships were attacked by North Vietnamese patrol boats. The bill, which was passed with only two opposing votes, was a virtual blank check for Johnson to escalate the war and would be overturned in 1970. In November, Johnson was elected to four more years as President. A month later, Martin Luther King, Jr., at age thirty-five became the youngest recipient of the Nobel Peace Prize.

On February 11, 1965, the U.S. began air strikes against targets in North Vietnam in retaliation for Hanoi-directed guerrilla attacks against American bases in the South Vietnamese Central Highlands. On March 31, Johnson committed two battalions of Marines with an offensive mission to Vietnam; a week later National Security Action Memorandum 328 officially authorized offensive operations. At the end of June, three thousand U.S. troops assaulted an area known as Viet Cong Zone D, twenty miles northeast of Saigon. The operation was called off after three days of making little contact with the enemy. For five days in August the Watts section of Los Angeles became a war zone. Set off by the arrest of a local black man on drunken driving charges and allegations of police brutality, the melee left thirty people dead, hundreds injured, 2,200 arrested, and millions of dollars in property damage from fires and looting. Antiwar protests were held across the country. On November 27, twenty to thirty thousand people surrounded the White House to oppose the war, among them Martin Luther King, Jr. Three days later a Quaker, the father of three children, immolated himself outside the Pentagon in protest. A week later a former Catholic seminarian did the same thing outside the United Nations in New York, as a protest against "war, all war." There was a truce for Christmas. Diplomatic efforts to stop the war seemed fruitless. By the end of the year units from the First Infantry, the 101 First Airborne, the First Marine, the First Cavalry, the 25th Infantry, and other American ground forces would be deployed to Vietnam.

In 1966, the Vietnam War dominated the world's attention. The number of Americans there increased from 180,000 to 280,000, plus 60,000 aboard ships in the area. Bombing of the Ho Chi Minh Trail in Laos, begun secretly in 1965, was stepped up but without much effect. The Viet Cong got what they needed to conduct operations in South Vietnam. In February, the Senate Foreign Relations Committee began televised hearings on the war. The Fourth Infantry and units that became the Americal Division, among others, deployed troops to fight. On the day after Christmas the Defense Department acknowledged that despite efforts to avoid civilian casualties, U.S. bombing in North Vietnam had hit such targets.

In February 1967 the U.S. began its largest assault to date with 25,000 troops in search of the Viet Cong headquarters near the Cambodian border. A month later Martin Luther King, Jr., at an anti-war march in Chicago, called the war "a blasphemy against all that America stands for." General William Westmoreland, commander of America's forces in Vietnam, asked for but did not get 200,000 more troops. He stirred controversy by saying that the enemy had "gained support in the United States that gives him hope that he can win politically that which he cannot win militarily." In September, military junta leader Lieutenant General Ngyuen Van Thieu, who had run South Vietnam for the last two years, was elected president. Protests continued. In November the air war accelerated, with Air Force and Navy planes striking targets near Hanoi and Haiphong. In a public-relations move, Johnson brought Westmoreland home to report that American operations around Dak To signaled "the beginning of a great defeat of the enemy." His remarks were constantly upbeat. Just before Christmas, Johnson visited American troops at Cam Ranh Bay to encourage them despite opposition at home and told them that the enemy "knows that he has met his master in the field." By year's end nearly a half million Americans were in Vietnam, 16,000 had been killed to date. One hundred thousand had been wounded in 1967. "Body counts" were a regular feature on the evening news.

On January 31, 1968—the lunar New Year known as Tet—Communist guerrillas shocked American and South Vietnamese forces by breaking a holiday truce and launching their most aggressive offensive of the war by attacking more than one hundred cities including Saigon and Hue. The American embassy was taken, and General Westmoreland's headquarters was attacked. Many cities were taken by Viet Cong forces, but by February 10 the offensive was largely put down. The former imperial capital of Hue would be devastated and take almost a month of house-to-house combat to reclaim. In military terms, Tet turned out to be an American victory. Twenty Viet Cong were killed for every U.S. and ARVN soldier lost. The overrun cities were reclaimed, but psychologically and politically Tet was a disaster. At the end of March, LBJ went on television to announce that bombing of North Vietnam would stop except near the DMZ, that 13,500 more troops would be sent, and more money would be needed for the war. And, he concluded, "I shall not seek, and I will not accept, the nomination of my party for another term as your President." Less than a week later, Martin Luther King, Jr., was shot and killed in Memphis; riots and looting followed in Chicago, Baltimore, Cincinnati, and Washington. After weeks of procedural haggling that included extensive discussions about the shape of the table to be used, the Vietnam Peace Talks began in May.

Duty, honor, country. Powell never lost sight of these time-honored principles. He carried them with him into a second tour in Vietnam. But the clarity of vision that prevailed in what he himself admits was a somewhat naïve way of going into his first tour five years earlier became clouded by the realities of an ugly war.

One of the most immediate, personal truths to be reckoned with was the 1967 combat death of his cherished friend and ROTC protégé, Tony Mavroudis. The two former Pershing Rifles both served as advisors in the early days of the war. Then, for a short while they were at Fort Benning together. But as Powell was being selected to go to school at Fort Leavenworth, his friend Major Mavroudis volunteered to go back to Vietnam. Unlike Powell, Mavroudis was single. Powell remembers Tony's telling him, "I got to go, I got to go. The only reason you're not going with me is Alma and the babies." But Powell replied, "I'm going to go in due course, Tony." Mavroudis was one of three CCNY Pershing Rifles from Powell's day to be killed in action.

Major Powell returned to Southeast Asia in June 1968. He was assigned the 3d Battalion, 1st Infantry, 11th Infantry Brigade of the 23d Infantry Division, known as the "Americal" Division. He was assigned to the 3/1st Infantry or "3d of the 1st" as the battalion's executive officer, or "XO."

The 3-1 Infantry had deployed south of Chu Lai in Quang Ngai province and was constantly searching for Viet Cong in the frustrating game of hide-and-seek that made up so much of the war. The Americans tried to root out and destroy command and communications posts, weapons, and supply caches. The Viet Cong would harass with snipers, mines, and booby traps. There would be occasional contact with North Vietnamese forces and actual engagements with the South Vietnamese Communists in firefights. Most of the time, though, it was cat-and-mouse, hit-and-run.

Powell came to the job of executive officer at the right time. The XO acts as the commander in his absence, but his day-to-day job is to keep things going in support of the fighting force's main effort. He handles administrative and logistical activities and oversees the commander's staff. His day is filled with making sure that mail from home and "beans and bullets" get to the troops, that vehicles are running and spare parts are ordered, that log books are filled out and records are kept. When Powell arrived, the battalion had been without an XO for two months. In many ways, especially in war, it is a thankless job but essential to keeping both morale and fighting capability high. Apparently Powell created order and efficiency out of what was just slightly better than chaos. Before he left, the unit was so highly rated in its Annual General Inspection that it was selected to represent the entire Americal Division in its annual inspection. His former commander, retired Colonel Henry Lowder, remembers that while Powell excelled at his job in the "rear"—not exactly a secure "behind-the-lines" place in a lineless guerrilla war—he was always looking for an opportunity to come forward. One time Lowder was reported to have been wounded—he reckons it merely a "scratch"—but without asserting himself too strongly Powell was on the next helicopter, prepared to take command.

Like so many of the assignments in his career, however, being a battalion executive officer would not last long, because someone higher up wanted to use him elsewhere. He was an XO for fewer than four months.

One day the Americal Division commander was reading his copy of the weekly newspaper *Army Times* when he saw a story about the most recent Command and General Staff College graduating class. There before him on the page was a picture of one of his officers, the number-two man in the class, Major Powell. The division commander, Major General Charles Gettys, is reported to have exclaimed, "I've got the number-two Leavenworth graduate in my division and he's stuck out in the boonies? I want him on my staff!"

Major Powell was given the G-3 post that is responsible for all of the division's operations and planning. He arrived one day, and his predecessor left the next. It is a senior lieutenant colonel's position, the top war-fighting post on the general's staff, and one of the most important jobs in the division after that of the commander himself. Later, when a colonel who was previously scheduled to fill the G-3 slot arrived, Powell would become his deputy. But General Gettys always appreciated Powell as a warrior. Gettys is reputed to have told Westmoreland's successor, General Creighton Abrams, who inquired about Powell upon meet-

ing him on a visit to the American headquarters, that he had
a major as his G-3 because he was "the best in Vietnam." In
the citation for the Legion of Merit that Powell received at
the end of his second tour in Vietnam, he is described as
having worked constantly, seven days a week, under
"intense mental pressure, and frequent hostile fire" while
visiting commanders and troops. He "always maintained
his calm and cheerful attitude, never reflecting the strain of
his great responsibilities." He was recognized even then for
what would become a hallmark skill in Washington: "The
briefings he conducted for commanders and visiting dignitaries were outstanding and earned him the respect and
compliments of those briefed." In addition to developing
complex plans for the division, "his ability, knowledge, and
helpful, cooperative attitude were so widely known that he
was frequently called upon by officers from other staff
sections for advice and recommendations far beyond the
scope of his assigned duties. He always gave so modestly[,]
and so freely of his time and knowledge that friction was
never created and, in fact, he earned the respect and
admiration of his superiors and subordinates alike."

In many ways Vietnam was a transient's war. Unlike
World War II where men and units stayed together over the
long haul, sometimes throughout the war, in Vietnam
troops were there for one-year tours. On the day they
arrived, many started "short-timers" calendars to count
down the days left in theater. In 1967, the Americal Division
was "reactivated," thrown together by combining a variety
of units specifically for service in Vietnam. Among them, the
name of the 11th Infantry Brigade in which Powell first
served is permanently etched in the annals of military
infamy.

On March 16, 1968, while Powell was still a student at
Fort Leavenworth, a platoon led by First Lieutenant William
Calley, Jr., entered the South Vietnamese village of My Lai.
He and his men herded more than three hundred unarmed
civilians—old men, women, children, and babies—into a
ditch and gunned them down. Before the slaughter, mem-

bers of Calley's platoon and other members of Charlie Company, 1-20th Infantry Battalion, battered, murdered, raped, and sodomized residents of the hamlet. As a result of a letter written by former combat infantryman Ron Rittenhour, the Army began investigating the incident. Six months after the brutal massacre occurred, Powell was serving in Chu Lai working for General Gettys. In a matter of months the entire chain-of-command—from the division commander down to the platoon leader—had changed. When representatives of the Army Inspector General's office showed up and asked Powell to look through the daily staff logs for "anything that looked like an unusual incident or a major contact with a large loss of life," he did not know what the investigators were hoping to find. As they looked over his shoulder, Powell discovered an entry about operations in the Batangan peninsula, probably the nastiest, most notorious of all places in the brigade's area of operations.

Typically, U.S. units would take enormous casualties there. The area was an undisputed Viet Cong stronghold. A journal entry showed that apparently there had been an extraordinarily high number of enemy killed in the village of My Lai on March 16, 1968. In a war that settled for the body count as a surrogate for clear, achievable objectives, it looked on paper as though some of the 11th Brigade's troops had accomplished something heroic and laudable. It was not until November 1969, when he himself was home and charges were brought against those involved, that Powell would learn what the inquiry was all about.

Unlike his first tour where Powell spent long days and nights on foot patrols through the jungles, much of his second tour was spent riding by helicopter from place to place, visiting units, often with the division commander. In November 1968, the 11th Infantry Brigade discovered twenty-nine North Vietnamese base camps. One of them, hidden in a deep, wooded draw west of the village of Quang Ngai, was captured on November 15 by one of the brigade's units, Charlie Company, 4-12th Infantry Battalion. It was a significant find because the camp served as the headquarters for provisional NVA units and was a training base for battalion and even regimental-size forces. Important documents, maps, and a supply of weapons were captured.

Because of the importance of the base, the battalion commander instructed the company commander, Captain James R. Smith, to clear a landing zone. Saws, chain saws, and other equipment were lowered into the area to make a clearing, but the steep, uneven terrain with a mountain on one side left the narrow opening in the trees just barely wide enough for a helicopter to set down. Before the day was out, however, the battalion commander's Huey flew in and landed three times to deliver supplies and bring out captured items. The pilot later reported that getting in and out required inch-by-inch precision maneuvering directed by the gunner and crew chief, who look out on either side.

Early the next afternoon, on Saturday November 16, Division Commander Gettys elected to visit the base camp with its classrooms and system of tunnels. With him were his chief-of-staff, Colonel Jack Treadwell, and Operations Officer Powell, with two aides and the helicopter's crew of four. What they did not know was that the brigade commander had tried unsuccessfully to land before them. As the colonel's chopper was dropping down, almost vertically, its rotor caught the tops of trees; the crew found it too tight to set down. His pilot flew to a larger, more permanent clearing nearby. The commanding general's crew was flying a new helicopter; it had ninety hours logged. At 2:00 P.M., General Gettys and those with him arrived in the area of the freshly cut landing zone. Those on the ground launched a red smoke flare to clearly mark the spot. There was virtually no wind. They made several passes as the pilot tried to figure out how best to make his approach. Warrant Officer James D. Hannan was at the controls and made one attempt to fly into the clearing but circled off because he believed he was approaching with too much speed. Flying in from the north, he tried a second time, much more slowly. The gunner told the pilot that he was clear on the right. The crew chief told the pilot that he was clear on the right but to lift the tail up. Then, as he lowered the craft down, Major Powell, who was looking out the left window, began to notice the tops of trees being chopped off. Leaves were flying. Small branches were being cut. The co-pilot was just about to key the mike to say to the pilot "I don't think we can make it" when, in an instant, the rotor caught a tree trunk nearly six inches around. The chopper tilted left—Powell reported that he bent over and grabbed his knees—then dropped straight down the twenty-five or thirty feet flat on its skids.

Powell and the gunner released their seat belts. Powell burst out the side door as the engine whined at a high pitch and began to smoke. PFC Bob Pyle, the gunner, was right on his heels. Powell yelled, "Get away, get away, it's gonna explode," but Colonel Treadwell and General Gettys could be seen still inside. Pyle recognized that the pilots, whose doors cannot be opened from inside, were also inside. He ran back. The pilot's door was crushed. Pyle slid back the protective armor plate and jimmied the door open. He tried to get out the pilot who was crushed, held in by an armrest. Meanwhile, Powell also turned back, went around the chopper, and got out the general, who was barely conscious and had a fractured shoulder. Powell moved him away from the chopper, and others carried him away. Powell returned again and reached for the colonel, who was not wearing a helmet. Others helped as he was carried away, unconscious, with lacerations on his head. Once again Powell returned to get the general's aide, who was seated in the middle, right under the engine and transmission, which had come down through the ceiling and onto his head. His face had been smashed against the radio, and he moaned as Powell, the co-pilot, and the crew chief pried him out of the chopper, which continued to smoke and looked as though it might explode at any moment. Finally, as Pyle turned the pilot around with the help of the co-pilot and he fell out the door, Powell helped others to pull the aviator, whose back was fractured, away from the wreckage. Everyone aboard lived.

Powell does not tell the story without being prodded,

and he downplays his role in the rescue. "I wasn't alone," he says. "It wasn't anything heroic," he told Ken Adelman in 1990. What Powell fails to mention is that he himself had sustained a broken ankle from the impact. It may have been all in a day's work for the hard-driving major, but General Gettys must have thought it was certain proof of his uncompromising devotion to duty. He saw to it that Powell was awarded the Soldier's Medal, the Army's award for bravery in non-combat heroism and the voluntary risk of life not involving actual conflict with an enemy.

Vietnam was not World War II. Colin Powell is not unlike many of his fellow war buddies who returned to a less than warm homecoming. He does not sit around and tell war stories. Colonel Bill Smullen, Powell's special assistant as Chairman of the Joint Chiefs of Staff, remembers his own return to Fort Benning after serving in Vietnam. Smullen was attending the career course at the time. "Just about everyone had just come home from a tour in Vietnam. Those who hadn't were on their way there. There we were at the Infantry Center, Building 4, home of the Infantry. Between classes we would stand outside and drink coffee or have a Coke. We talked about everything under the sun. We talked about sports, but we never mentioned Vietnam. We just didn't discuss it. Most Vietnam vets don't just sit around and tell war stories." Colin Powell has never seen a feature film about the Vietnam War although he loves to watch movies. Once his son, Michael, suggested that he see the film *Platoon*. "I don't need to see movies about Vietnam," his father replied, "I was there."

Is Colin Powell ashamed of his service in Southeast Asia? Not at all. It was an unwinnable war without clear objectives. It was a politicians' war, not a soldier's. Powell, like so many other young men and women who served faithfully, did so with the best of intentions, with a clear conscience, by following lawful orders, for the American and eternal ideals, for democracy's sake. In the celebratory wake of the Gulf War, Powell spoke at the Vietnam Veterans Memorial: *The Wall*, in Washington. The occasion was

Memorial Day. It was a deeply moving time for him personally. He elected to tell the story of his fallen friend Tony Mavroudis. And he addressed his fellow Vietnam vets. He said, "You need no redemption. You redeemed yourself in the A Shau Valley. You redeemed yourself at Hue. You redeemed yourself at Dau Tieng, at Khe Sanh, in the South China Sea, in the air over Hanoi, or launching off Yankee Station, and in a thousand other places.

"The parades and celebrations are not needed to restore our honor as Vietnam veterans, because we never lost our honor. They're not to clear up the matter of our valor, because our valor was never in question. Two hundred and thirty-six Medals of Honor say our valor was never in question. Fifty-eight thousand, one hundred and seventy-five names on this wall say that our valor and the value of our service were never in question."

Although the Vietnam War was not won, the valor of its warriors must not be forgotten. Powell chose to put Vietnam in the honorable context of serving one's country, when he told those gathered, "My friends, Americans have placed their lives, their fortunes, and their sacred honor in harm's way from Concord Bridge to Gettysburg, from Normandy to Pork Chop Hill, from the A Shau Valley to the Valley of the Euphrates."

chapter six
OPPORTUNITIES

W A S H I N G T O N was not a proud sight when Colin Powell arrived in September 1969. The anti-war movement was in full swing, and the nation's capital was its focal point. In mid-November a quarter of a million protesters marched from the Capitol up Pennsylvania Avenue to the Washington Monument. A month earlier, seventy-nine college presidents had appealed to President Richard Nixon for a speedier withdrawal of U.S. forces from Southeast Asia. The Vietnam Moratorium, a nationally coordinated demonstration, moved young and old, rich and poor, black and white, students and workers, to a variety of peaceful expressions of opposition to the war in Vietnam.

Powell was in Washington to go to school. Before leaving for his second tour in Vietnam, the Army had selected him for a fully funded, active-duty master's degree program. He was accepted at George Washington University, right in the heart of the District of Columbia. Powell remembers that "GWU was not exactly a hotbed of left-wing conspiracies, but there were demonstrations, and there was certainly an anti-war fever on the campus. I hung out with a bunch of other Army officers and a Navy officer or two who were my graduate school classmates.

"There was very little interaction with the rest of the students. I was in graduate school, not undergraduate school, so I didn't have to deal with the more volatile folks. Graduate students, for the most part, were government employees working somewhere and taking afternoon and evening courses, so the protesting was not anything to get swept up in. One demonstration got out of hand with tear gas busting all over the place, but it was essentially something to stay away from.

"I was glad to be back home and to be reintroduced to my family. We bought a house out in the suburbs, and except for living at Fort Benning for three years, it was our first home. The kids were growing up. Alma became pregnant shortly after I got back. And I was in graduate school for two years, so I never wore a uniform."

The demonstrations were disturbing, but Powell was attending business school. He was there to learn. While school meant a two-year hiatus from the military life, Powell asserts, "I didn't shrink from it. There was no hiding who you were. We weren't subjected to any stick-it-in-your-face sorts of comments from classmates. We were all in graduate business school, so it wasn't exactly a flower-child arrangement."

Most up-and-coming officers go to graduate school. In fact, promotion to the top ranks requires a graduate degree. Most of those who become generals, however, do not set out to earn master-of-business-administration degrees. The preferred field is usually international relations. "I think the Army wanted me to get the M.B.A.," Powell notes. "I was more interested in business than in just getting a soft policy degree. I think it was an agreement with the Army that an M.B.A. was where they needed the expertise, and that's what they inclined me toward. I've never had any formal education in national affairs, strategy, and policy, except for the National War College."

Some officers accept the Army's offer to attend school,

take the required tour of duty that follows it, and then start a new civilian career, or start working on their retirement plans. Powell had no such strategy. "I probably made myself better qualified to go into business in due course, but I wasn't focusing on getting out or retiring. It was something the Army wanted, and it was going to help me in due course."

After having excelled at the Army's Command and General Staff College, graduate school was an opportunity to make good outside the military arena, where he had excelled. He never forgot that he had not been at the top of his college class at CCNY and was determined not to repeat his previous ho-hum performance. "I really saw it as a way to improve my education, to sort of compensate for my fairly modest achievement as an undergraduate," Powell says, "and also make myself more employable to the Army, as well as after the Army was over."

By the eleven-year point in Powell's career he seems to have made his mind up that he would at least stay with the Army long enough to qualify for retirement at half-pay for the rest of his life. Besides, he had no other plans. "At that point a twenty-year career seemed right for everybody. We didn't know where we were going," Powell confesses.

While his studies at GWU were supposed to be largely quantitative and analytical, Powell's true interests were more people-centered. He found behavioral science and management classes most interesting. Powell admits: "I'm not a number cruncher, and I wouldn't consider myself computer literate. Management courses were fascinating to me, and math was something to be tolerated. There weren't that many computer courses then. I got straight A's except for a B in one programming course where one had to write a COBOL program. I didn't do that well. I busted one test, and I got a B."

On the modest income of a major, the Powells could not afford the fashionable neighborhoods of Northwest Washington, but the Virginia suburbs offered appealing accommodations within their price range. They bought a five-bedroom, single-family house in Dale City, just south of Washington. In nearby Woodbridge they also became active in a new Episcopal church bearing the same name as the one in the South Bronx that Powell grew up in—St. Margaret's. Like his father, young Michael Powell would become an acolyte there. Alma got involved in the Altar Guild and, in time, Colin became the senior warden, the top layperson responsible for temporal affairs at a time when money needed to be raised to build a growing church.

Powell developed a network of friendships with men in the parish. Those who knew him recall that he was one of the key figures in a nickel-and-dime biweekly poker game that the male leadership of the parish started as a social and fellowship time. Those who participated were either government employees or worked in defense-related business. Powell fit right in. He was the only black, however.

Once when Powell was hosting the game, one of the men left to go home to get a roll of toilet paper to wipe his runny nose. When he returned to the Powell house, Colin met him and said, "Get in here, quick! What do you want the neighbors to think? A white man comes to the black guy's house and has to bring his own toilet paper!" They both had a laugh.

One weekend, Powell and friends were painting the outside of the rector's house. Powell, who always drove old cars that he worked on himself, parked his beat-up white station wagon on the street in front of the parish house. While Powell worked in back, one of the men from the poker club applied a coat of red house paint to the driver's door of Powell's car, which had only a coat of primer. When Powell later went out to get in his car, he was not amused, but it was all in good fun. Some of the Poker Club men from more than twenty years ago still meet today, and Powell has always invited a few of them to his promotions over the years. The member of the club who was known for walking in the door and saying, "Shut up and deal!"—Powell played his cards conservatively. Despite the almost incessant chatter about life "inside the Beltway" with its political intrigues and partisan controversies, Powell and friends seldom discussed politics. "We were there to relax and play a little cards," says Walt McIntosh.

In the summer between his first and second years at GWU, Powell was promoted to lieutenant colonel almost without notice, except by the increase of $35.10 in his monthly paycheck. In the spring, the Powell's third child, Annemarie, was born at the Army hospital at nearby Fort Belvoir.

Powell knew when he returned from Vietnam that he could count on two years of schooling in Washington and an assignment as well. He was a highly sought-after commodity. "I knew I would go to the Army Staff somewhere."

Army Staff meant the Pentagon, the nearly mythical seat of power for the armed forces. The building has been called many things, including the Puzzle Palace. Five-sided, with five floors and five "rings" of office space with the A-Ring on the inside and the E-Ring on the outside, divided by ten corridors, the uninitiated might find simply navigating the layout confounding. With six-and-a-half-million square feet of floor space, its own indoor shopping mall and subway stop, an inadequate sixty-seven acres of parking space and office space for more than 24,000 people, the Pentagon is much more than a big War Room. It is easy for a lieutenant colonel to get lost and forgotten in such a building where generals are as commonplace as junior officers are elsewhere in the military. A successful assignment at the Pentagon depends largely on *where* you are assigned.

"There became a great flap over where I would go," says Powell. "I was going to the Assistant Vice-Chief-of-Staff's Office." Powell was originally slotted to work in the computer directorate—a logical assignment, given his degree. But, Powell recalls, "It wasn't really a happy shop down there." Fortunately, somebody in the programming directorate expressed an interest in him. Even though I had just received a degree in data processing, I really don't want to work there. So they put me into the programming part."

The assignment was a fortuitous, major shift-point in his career. As a thirty-one–year-old lieutenant colonel, Powell was working for the Army's number-three officer at the Pentagon, General William E. Dupuy. He worked with some of the fastest rising stars that Dupuy had assembled around him, men who would go on to become top generals, among them Max Thurman, Louis Menetrey, Joe Palastra. "It was a hell of a stable," Powell recalls. Powell was excited to work on a few projects specifically for Dupuy and to write some speeches for him. "He really fired me up. But I was only there for a short time before I went on to the fellowship."

One day in early 1972 an assignments officer in the Army's infantry branch office called Powell. They wanted him to apply for the prestigious White House Fellowship, open to young professionals in a broad range of fields. Powell was given one weekend to answer eight pages of questions, many requiring two-page responses. He was given only five hundred words, about two-typewritten pages, to write a memorandum for the President, making a specific policy proposal. He sent the forms off and gave the application not another thought.

Well over a thousand applications were received. Powell was among the one hundred thirty invited for interviews and became one of the thirty-three national finalists. What began as a soldier's simply following orders became something to invest himself in. His family was excited. Powell felt the pressure to do well, but the odds were still only about fifty-fifty. He decided just to get the final process over with and then go back about his business at the Pentagon. As a result, Powell says, he "had a lot of fun." For three-and-a-half days Powell and the other finalists were scrutinized at Airlie House, a conference center in Virginia, in interviews as well as social situations. At the end of the weekend, the fellowship winners were announced.

Powell was one of two African Americans selected among the seventeen to become Fellows. The other black,

James Bostic, a chemical engineer who had recently completed his Ph.D., at age twenty-three was the youngest member of the fellowship class. Powell, at thirty-six, was among the oldest Fellows. He would emerge as one of the group's leaders as well. Bostic, who has remained good friends with Powell over the years, told Howard Means, "He had more experience than most of us. He helped people with the perspective of what was important and what was not. He was a nice guy, a consensus builder. All the things people write about him now, they were there then."

White House Fellows do not all go to work in the West Wing at 1600 Pennsylvania; however, they are assured of a job at senior levels in the executive branch. Powell was invited for interviews with George Romney, then Secretary of Health, Education, and Welfare, as well as by FBI Director L. Patrick Gray. But in what was probably the most fortuitous appointment he could have received, and possibly because of his getting an M.B.A., he ended up at the Office of Management and Budget (OMB), where the annual federal budget is generated and numbers are made to do mysterious things. It was fortuitous less because he would learn the rest of what he had set out to master in graduate school than the fact that OMB was where he would meet an elite group of rising policy makers whose ranks he would eventually join.

Heading OMB was Caspar Weinberger. His deputy was Frank Carlucci. Each of these men would go on to become Secretary of Defense. Powell recalls that Carlucci hired him into OMB, but that he never had anything else to do with him because both Carlucci and Weinberger left shortly thereafter to go to the Department of Health, Education, and Welfare.

"The first four months I was there I just fiddled around," Powell remembers. He was working in the Old Executive Office Building for the Director of the Management office, the M-side of OMB. No one seemed to know what happened to presidential orders once they were issued, and President Nixon was upset that he would tell people to do things but nothing would happen. "I ended up doing some fairly modest research on what happens to presidential orders once they're given, and I described a system for tracking presidential orders," Powell recalls. This work on the "Weekly Compilation of Presidential Directives" got Powell into every cabinet department, and as a result he saw how the government worked. "It was fun, and I learned a lot. But it was make-work, because the Fellows program is really traveling and other things," says Powell. While he was "having fun with it," the really serious work at OMB did not begin until a new director arrived, following Nixon's election to a second term.

"Fred Malek became the director of OMB," Powell remembers. "He was on the board that selected me to be a Fellow. He monitored the program for the White House. So I wrote a note, congratulating him. The next thing I knew, he called me over and made me his special assistant. He had some really exciting young turks working for him at the time. Over the next eight months I had a chance, sitting at his right hand, to hone my skills on working between disparate organizations with different bureaucratic interests, watching how a budget is put together, seeing how the numbers are reconciled, how the issues are resolved, and looking at some of the management issues in handling large organizations."

It was at OMB that Powell first began to understand the importance of public relations and handling the media. By the end of his White House Fellowship year, Powell had a taste of the political side of Washington at the edge of its highest levels, just as he had of the Army the year before. And he had made more good impressions. People liked and would remember him. Fred Malek asked him to stay on, but Powell had an important ticket to punch. It was time for a battalion command.

The number of commands is limited. Even the most highly qualified officers stand in line, but Powell went to check with his assignment officer at Infantry branch to see if a command was available. Because they were "unaccompanied tours," one year with wife and family left behind, assignments to Korea were less sought after than those in the U.S. and Europe. The 1/32d Infantry, part of the Second Infantry Division in Korea, was coming open. Powell took it.

In Korea, Powell found the Army morale at an all-time low. Drug abuse and racial incidents were epidemic. The U.S. had pulled out of Vietnam while Powell was a White House Fellow in March 1973. Many who had been to Vietnam were demoralized by the combined effects of war itself and the anti-war movement at home. An assignment to Korea—where there was little to do but train and get in trouble in the towns that fed off the lonely GIs—often meant nothing but trouble. Powell's battalion was a hotbed of dissent and racial fighting between white and black troops.

In Korea, units of the Second Infantry Division were assigned to small posts covering a five-hundred-square-mile area. The 1/32d was based on Camp Casey, directly north of Seoul and just south of the demilitarized zone that separates North and South Korea. Its proximity to the DMZ placed Powell's forces, like his first platoon at the Fulda Gap, at the critical point of potential conflict. Had the North Koreans launched a war, Powell and his men would have been right there to meet the enemy.

The division commander, Major General Hank "Gunfighter" Emerson, decided that because Powell was black, he might be able to bring the battalion—one of the worst in the division—under control. The 1/32d had been nearly overtaken by its own version of black street-gangs. Before long the leaders were brought before the commander for nonjudicial punishment under the Uniform Code of Military Justice. Others were court-martialed. At the same time, Powell drew close to his junior officers, especially the young company commanders. He inspired their confidence. In retrospect, he is described as having been notably charismatic. Between Emerson's aggressive program to build discipline and self-confidence, and Powell's leadership of his battalion, it didn't take long to make the 1/32d a crack unit.

Powell held Emerson in high esteem. "He did things that you couldn't get away with in the United States with newspapers watching. You know, 'There will be no drugs.' and 'We're going to have race relations, and it begins tomorrow morning at eight o'clock. Any questions?'" Powell recalls one of Emerson's techniques for handling racial conflict off-post in Tongduchon. "There used to be a section of town where the white soldiers went, and there was another section of town called 'the Crack'—where all the black soldiers went. The black soldiers essentially said, 'Don't nobody come in here, or else.' One night Emerson got all the battalion commanders and said, 'We're all going to the Crack tonight—every damn one of us—and if anything happens, we're going to take the whole division in there and clean it out.' Further progress was made by tightening up on training. We started running them every morning for four miles and working their butts off, and they were too tired to get in trouble, too exhausted to think about drugs. When nightfall came, they collapsed. It was one of the best years of my life."

Powell's executive officer, then-Major Ben Willis, remembers that personal discipline was a strong inspiration to the other officers in Powell's battalion. "He let his company commanders command their companies, and he set a great example. He's a fine Christian person. There were no wives over there to speak of, but he cast a very jaundiced eye when any of his officers would stray downtown to visit the whorehouses. It's certainly something that he'd never do."

But Powell was no stick-in-the-mud either. He would often go to the Camp Casey Officers' Club with the officers under him. One night the division staff brought a group of teachers, women from Seoul, up to Camp Casey. To hear Powell tell the story, they were brought to the officers' club to see that the men were not animals. Then Powell and his men walked in. First, some of the young captains took the foosball machine and as a demonstration of their strength lifted it to the ceiling. When they dropped it, it smashed into pieces. Next, a young officer from the 1/32d poured a Coke down the slot of the jukebox. A fight broke out. Powell's executive officer beat up the division's senior administration and personnel officer. In the morning Powell was the Clint-Eastwood-style hero, but he also had to find money to pay the bill for two thousand dollars in damages to the club.

In another place at another time such a melee could have signaled the premature end to an officer's career, but in this instance, the whole occasion built up his image: Not just a bright young black officer who had been to the White House, he was a tough guy, too. So their fun had gotten just a little out of hand, and the teachers got a show of how tension on the "Z" could be vented.

Powell was the sort of guy that Gunfighter Emerson fancied himself and liked—rough-and-tumble, combat sea-soned, a no-nonsense kind of commander, as well as a nice guy—so the incident elevated Powell's status to new heights. Indeed Emerson had developed a romantic notion of him. But it was more than style and image that led Emerson to rate him as one of the top two of his battalion commanders and to be promoted to brigadier general "as quick as the law allows." It was not just his human-relations victories that won Powell such respect. He had taken a rag-bag bunch of men in fatigues and turned them into a fighting force ready for whatever they might face in combat. Powell proved himself to be a bona fide first-rate field commander, and more.

The events surrounding the break-in of the Watergate hotel and its cover-up by Nixon aides became news before Powell left Washington for Korea. In March, Nixon was named a co-conspirator by a federal grand jury. By July the Supreme Court, in an 8-to-0 decision, ordered Nixon to turn over additional tapes sought by Special Watergate Prosecu-tor Archibald Cox; the House Judiciary Committee recom-mended impeachment on grounds of obstructing justice. On

August 8, faced with probable impeachment, Nixon became the first President to resign.

On September 16, Vice-President-become-President Gerald Ford granted Nixon a full and unconditional pardon. On the same day he granted immunity to Vietnam-era draft evaders. Lieutenant Colonel Powell's year of command was over, and he began a new assignment at the Pentagon.

The return to Washington, home, and family also meant putting away the starched fatigues, the jeep, and the men. It was back to a desk, this time for just over nine months in the Defense Department's directorate for manpower requirements under the Assistant Secretary of Defense for Manpower and Reserve Affairs. He was a systems analyst just biding his time until attending the all-important War College.

The military has several senior service schools, to which only a select few officers are sent. Attending one of them is the fourth and last step that officers must take if they hope to become "general officers" (as opposed to branch-specific ones, such as infantry, or armor officers). Being chosen to attend a war college is no guarantee that an officer will become a general, but in Powell's case it seemed a certainty. Punching this ticket was all he needed to get a brigade command and get his first star. The Army's own senior service school, attended mostly by Army officers, is at Carlisle Barracks, Pennsylvania. But Powell was selected to attend the Harvard of war colleges, the National War College, a part of the National Defense University, located at Fort McNair in Washington, D.C. The National War College is the most prestigious such institution and provides an environment where all services are represented almost equally. The warfare taught is strategic. The philosophy is joint.

At war college, Powell became a disciple of Clausewitz, whose philosophy of war has most recently formed a generation of warriors. The eighteenth-century military strategist's book *On War* has become nothing short of Holy Writ in the era following Vietnam. Powell subscribes to it in earnest. Often disputed in the particulars, certain key doctrines stand out. For Clausewitz, war consists of three things: the directing policy of the government, the professional qualities of the military, and the attitude of the population. All three are important. There is no confusion between battles and the war as a whole. Strategy is the linking together of separate battles into a single war. The war has a final object, an ultimate goal. Military maneuvers are designed to lead to battles that have particular goals that support the ultimate goal of the war itself. Wars are not fought piecemeal with ambiguous or vague purposes. Quite the contrary. In what is probably his most famous assertion, Clausewitz held that *war is nothing but the continuation of policy by other means*. Therefore, the policy goal must be clear before the generals and admirals can go about the business of working out how to achieve militarily what will bring about the political end that is sought. The most magnificent of battles is a hollow show of force if it does not support the attainment of the political end. War is not fought for its own sake but for the sake of bringing peace.

To his way of thinking, the last word on conducting a war must rest in the hands of the political leadership, but it is generals who have the expertise in war, and political leaders are obliged to rely on them.

Clausewitz raised further questions about conducting wars that Powell would bring to other contexts later in his career. Among these are the inevitability of uncertainty, operating on information that is never complete, and making good judgments according to probabilities. Clausewitz's chapter "On Military Genius" defines qualities needed in a commander. Among them are high intelligence and both physical and moral courage. Two additional characteristics, however, are identified as particularly important: an *intuitive ability*—or commander's "perspective"—that sees and discerns the right military course to take without having to work it out step-by-step; and simple *determination*, the willpower that blends reason with moral courage. Clausewitz also outlines the good habits, or virtues, of those who make up an army. Ultimately, he concluded, moral factors are the key determinants in war.

Powell was promoted to colonel just two months before completing the course at the National War College and moving on to Fort Campbell, Kentucky. Fort Campbell is home to the 101st Airborne Division, the "Screaming Eagles," the Army's only division designated as "Air Assault." In World War II, the 101st distinguished itself as an elite division of paratroopers, second in prominence to the 82d Airborne. But with the development of helicopters as versatile battlefield aircraft the Army transformed the 101st into its single division that relied upon helicopters to get to the battlefield and "fight light" as foot soldiers. The 101st grew in prestige as its mission changed. The 82d Airborne remained the Army's air-droppable force, while the 101st became its air-mobile one. The Army even added a course fashioned after the Airborne School, where a different set of wings is awarded, the Air Assault School.

Powell was assigned to command the 101st's 2d Brigade. His boss, the division commander, was Major General Jack Wickham. His boss's boss, commander of the XVIII Airborne Corps, was Lieutenant General Hank Emerson, who had earned his third star since he and Powell were in Korea together.

Once again the job Powell did impressed his boss. "Colin was the best brigade commander we had," Wickham remembers. "He was best in his tactical knowledge, in his feel for soldiers, and his ability to communicate. He had a natural leadership style about him. He was very reassuring to those above him also. He didn't seem to have an agenda, and he got results."

When it was time to take most of the 101st to Germany for an extended training exercise called REFORGER, Wickham left Powell at home to watch the fort. "Colin stayed back with part of his brigade, and we took part of his brigade over there. He, therefore, was the most senior officer on the post and performed very well there." Even at that point, Wickham, who went on to become Chief of Staff of the Army, picked Powell, "as one of the brightest of our younger officers."

While at Fort Campbell, Powell's name was submitted as one of the Army's top candidates to become military assistant to Jimmy Carter's Secretary of Defense, Harold Brown, shortly after the new administration took over. This position, like all other military slots at the Pentagon, is filled without regard for the officer's political affiliation. A tradition that is observed, however, rotates the position among officers of the different services, and this was not Army's turn. Powell was not selected.

John Kester was special assistant to both Brown and his deputy, Charles Duncan at the time. His broad-ranging responsibilities included serving as political liaison to the White House. With enormous responsibilities and an all-too-small staff, Kester needed someone to serve as his own chief of staff. He looked through the nominations for military assistant in hope of finding someone who could be his gatekeeper and make sure that things got done. When he saw Powell's bio, he took notice: White House Fellow; proven soldier with the right commands; Vietnam War decorations; already experienced in the hallways of the Pentagon; and black. Race was a definite plus in the new administration. Powell was with his brigade out in the woods on a field training exercise when he received a call on a field phone. The call summoned him back to Washington. Out of six candidates interviewed, Powell was chosen.

He was confident, comfortable, straightforward. He did not seem overly awed by the corridors of power. Powell seemed capable of getting to the inside track on the service staffs, able to figure out what was going on, and how to get things done. In the interview Powell asked Kester, "How did you happen to bring me in here?" Kester replied, "I checked you out, and I heard a lot of good things about you." Powell replied, "Well, I checked you out, too, and it wasn't all good." Powell's candor impressed Kester.

chapter seven

PERSONAL AND
PROFESSIONAL JUDGMENT

AFTER FIFTEEN months of successful command time back in the "real Army," Powell was not displeased to return to Washington. The Powell family had spent more time there than anywhere else. With the exception of just over a year at Fort Campbell, the family had been in the capital city continuously since 1969. Their return would last another four years.

The Powell's son, Michael, was sixteen when the family returned to Washington. The move marked a turning point in his relationships with his parents. Mike Powell recalls: "In our house, when you were young, your mother was your primary parent. You were always very admiring of your father, but he worked a lot. He was on the job night and day; there was the Korea tour and Vietnam when he went away. But as I got older, there was an unspoken time when my parents handed me off. It's not that my mother backed out of the picture—she remained a friend and someone you loved—but at some point the serious life advice started coming from [my dad].

"I remember turning sixteen. Dad always had a difficult time with serious conversations about things. I remember getting this long letter that he must have written late at night. It was deep, heartfelt, and handwritten. It must have been twelve or fifteen pages. It was sort of Rudyard-Kipling-like: 'Now you're a man and what does it mean?' The tone was that over the coming years you are going to be exposed to evils from drinking to drugs, from sexual relations to this-and-that, and in the end you're going to be an adult. Just remember that the next four years are the most important four years you are ever going to experience. Just remember that our philosophy is that we show you right from wrong, and the rest is up to you. You don't do things according to our wishes. *You* make the decision of whether it's right or wrong in accord with the ways that we taught you. And he concluded by saying, 'Never forget, there is nothing too bad that you can't come and get our help.'"

"The funny thing, is that he would follow the letter up in action, but he would never ask you about them. You would get the letter sort of anonymously, and he would rarely even ask whether you read it. I always sensed that there was an uncomfortableness on his part to even talk about it."

Something similar happened with the great sex talk that boys are supposed to have with their fathers. "I might have been seventeen," Mike remembers. "One Saturday everyone was gone from our house in Burke, Virginia. It seemed odd to me that all the women were gone. I don't know where they were, but I was just on the couch in the den. Right next to the couch was a door that led to the garage, where Dad had this hobby of working on cars. He comes walking into the den with this brown paper bag in his hand. With one hand on the door, ready to go into the garage, he opens it and says, 'I got something for you. I'd really like you to read it. If you have any questions, just ask me,' and he tosses this brown paper bag, and it lands beside me. I said, 'Okay.' He walks out, gets in the car and leaves. I pull the contents out of the bag, and it's a book called *Boys and Sex*. That was his way of talking with me about sex. I read it, and after a while people finally got back to the house."

Rather than believe his father's discomfort to be a source of weakness, Mike has a different interpretation. "What was funny about this stuff is that he didn't have to say anything. Just watching him struggle to get the message across made you admire him so much and made you care about him so much and want not to hurt him so much that you just wouldn't.

"The kids in our family, even in our wildest periods, never presented our parents with the problems that other parents had. In high school I almost never had a drink, never wanted to, never thought about it. I wanted to be at home. I didn't feel driven from my house. Friday nights I was more likely to be at home watching TV with my parents rather than out in some field, like most of my friends, drinking all night. I was popular. I had a blast in high school, but I didn't seem to need the drinking to enjoy myself."

The Powell family's guiding philosophy for its maturing teens was based on three R's, according to Mike, "We're going to teach you right, we're going to teach you wrong, and we're going to teach you responsibility. If you have a problem and you mess up, you can always come and see us. But when you come and see us, you better tell us what you did about it. There was no such thing as being able to say, 'Oh, I screwed up. Fix it.' The first question was going to be 'What did you do about it?' You would get in more trouble for not taking responsibility for your mistakes than for the mistakes themselves." One time Mike ran out of gas, left the car in the middle of the street, and walked home. It was not running out of gas that earned his father's dissatisfaction but the fact that the car was not moved out of traffic.

Mike says that his mother and father never demanded submission to heavy-handed parental authority. His parents never demanded respect. "It had to do with being respected in our house and *you* didn't want to lose your parents' respect." In their house where there was no corporal punishment, Mike Powell asserts, "to be told that they were disappointed almost hurt more than a spanking."

What guided the Powell children's lives was the strong sense of family. "The family was more important than anything on earth, and don't go screw it up. Don't go do something that's gonna drive a wedge in the family," Mike Powell says. "It's a simple philosophy that worked across the board. You don't want to do anything that will make you ashamed of each other. That was something my dad learned from his parents."

According to Mike, such a philosophy both holds the family together and has positive personal aspects to it. "To this day nothing is more gratifying to any of us than to have our father say, 'I'm proud of you.' Or more likely, because that's not really his style, to hear him brag about you to somebody else."

When Colin Powell became John Kester's gatekeeper, he turned a newly created job into an important one. In the corridor that is home to the offices of the Secretary of Defense, on the third floor, E-Ring, named for General Eisenhower, an Army colonel does not command immediate respect simply based on rank. Powell knew that. One condition he had for accepting the job as Executive to the Special Assistant to the Secretary and Deputy Secretary of Defense was to create an office for Powell directly outside Kester's. No one went in or out without Powell's making a judgment. In a role that demands mutual trust and mature sensibilities about the workings of the Pentagon as well as a degree of political sophistication, Powell's job gave him significant influence over who and what got in, or did not get in, to Kester. This intensely political job could have turned out badly had Powell allowed himself to emerge as a partisan from behind his uniform. He never did. It was another of Powell's great successes. After nearly a year and a half Powell was asked by the Deputy Secretary of Defense, Charles Duncan, to become his senior military assistant.

Duncan identifies three qualities in Powell that others have echoed throughout his career. He works extremely well with people, he is a fast learner, and he has enormous energy and stamina. Working in the front office for the Deputy Secretary and daily contact with the Secretary of Defense, the White House, and Capitol Hill, also gave Powell opportunity to hone his political skills and learn how to make defense policy.

One evening, while Maud Powell was visiting her son and his family, Colin asked everyone to gather around for a family meeting, something they never did. "I didn't even know what a family meeting was," Mike Powell recalls. When everyone was seated, Powell looked around at everyone. Their attention was fixed on him. He said, "I just want to tell you this. Today the President said that I actually get to be a general."

"He said it in the way a little child would," says his son. His simple message took a moment to sink in. Then his mother jumped up with excitement. After twenty-one years in uniform, Maud Powell concluded that her son was probably going to be a career officer and everything was going to be all right. A proud Maud Powell was present when Colin's first stars were pinned on and would live to see him make major general. His father, unfortunately, died just before his son's promotion into the general officer ranks.

In the latter part of the last year of his presidency, President Carter asked Charles Duncan to move over to the Department of Energy. Once again Powell was where the action was. The year 1979 was an uncommonly turbulent year in the usually less than conspicuous government department. In May, Carter ordered an end to oil-price controls. By the end of June, OPEC had raised oil prices a total of fifty percent over the previous year. On July 15, Carter went on television, proposing a six-point package of energy measures including oil import limits designed to cut consumption by 4.5 billion gallons a day and reduce U.S. dependence on foreign petroleum. The summer's oil shortages led to long lines at the gas pump and higher prices.

Though still an active-duty officer, Powell became Duncan's administrative assistant at Energy.

Carter was defeated by Ronald Reagan on November 4, 1980. Before the transition between administrations began, Brigadier General Powell had returned to the Pentagon. Reagan's choices in the two top Defense Department posts were men Powell already knew. They had met eight-and-a-half years earlier at OMB. Reagan named Caspar Weinberger as defense secretary and Frank Carlucci as the new deputy. Following twelve years of Reagan and Bush administrations, some would grow to think of Powell as a de facto Republican. His prior association with Carter officials underlines his decided political ambiguity, however. When Powell was rejoined with those who first welcomed him to Washington, it may have been Providence or fate but it was not maneuvering. Weinberger and Carlucci walked into an office Powell already inhabited. He was the most experienced man in the office. The transition period, and Powell's five months at the beginning of the new administration, forged a future both professionally and personally.

Five months of working with Weinberger and Carlucci was enough for Powell to make a strong and lasting impression. More important, it sealed relationships for which Powell uses terms of quasi-kinship. Carlucci had chosen him for the OMB, became his boss as Deputy Secretary of Defense, and later in 1987 brought him along to the White House. Powell has described Carlucci as his "godfather of godfathers."

Carlucci was the key member in what turned out to be a sort of clan into which Powell was adopted. Carlucci's own career began with State Department civil service. He served under both Lyndon Johnson and Richard Nixon before working for Weinberger at OMB in the Reagan years. While at college in Princeton, Carlucci was on the wrestling team with Donald Rumsfeld. When Rumsfeld became director of the Office of Economic Opportunity, he brought classmate Carlucci into OEO as assistant director. When President Gerald Ford asked Rumsfeld to become White House Chief of Staff, he brought along an assistant from OEO, Dick Cheney. Rumsfeld went on to become Secretary of Defense in 1975 (just before Harold Brown) under Ford. Powell met him briefly when then-Colonel Powell was commanding his brigade at Fort Campbell. Although Rumsfeld was mentioned for the post again under George Bush, it was Cheney who succeeded Weinberger as defense secretary under whom Powell served, between 1983 and 1986, as military assistant.

Among those Powell worked with through the transition were two people who would become his lasting friends. Powell first met Rich Armitage, who spent his career in Washington as Assistant Secretary of Defense under Weinberger, when Powell was still a colonel-promotable working for Duncan. Over the years they have become best friends and mutual confidants. In 1992, Powell told Morton Kondracke, "I would trust him with my life, my children, my reputation, everything I have. There's no finer public servant I know, no finer American, no more honorable man." Shortly after they met—and especially when Powell was at the White House and serving as Chairman—Armitage and Powell started calling one another on the phone each day to share information they had heard and to bounce ideas off one another. They kept it up over the years and have become sounding boards for just about anything the other guy might want to discuss. Both men are "news junkies." Often they will talk, if only briefly, two or three times a day.

Weinberger brought a woman in her mid-twenties named Marybel Batjer with him into the Pentagon. She served as the defense secretary's personnel manager. Over time Powell, Armitage, and Batjer would become an inseparable trio with the pet nicknames Big Guy, Buddha, and Bimbo. Armitage says that Batjer "was younger than both of us and we took a protective attitude toward her. She was an attractive woman, and very bright, and needed some brotherly if not fatherly care. It began as a protectorate and developed into a real friendship among the three of us." Six years later Powell took her along with him to the National Security Council.

The three-way friendship had benefits for everyone including Powell. "With me and Marybel, Colin feels that we can put aside our own personal ambitions," Armitage says. "He asks, 'What do you think about such-and-such?' and he tries things out." The three would go out to eat regularly, especially to the Thai Room.

Powell saw the Reagan administration officials through the early days of getting settled into power. After five months, however, Powell had the opportunity to return to the Army and become the number-two soldier in a division. He jumped at the opportunity.

Frank Carlucci is proud of his role in Powell's career. According to Carlucci, "We put Colin out in Fort Carson to get him another star." In June 1981 Brigadier General Powell reported in at Fort Carson, Colorado, to serve as the 4th Mechanized Infantry Division's assistant division commander (ADC) for operations and training. There were two ADCs, right-hand men to Major General John Hudachek, the two-star general who commanded the division. One ADC was in charge of logistics and support, a "beans and bullets" man. The other was responsible for warfighting and training. It was an operational job. Given Powell's experience, it seemed tailor-made for him.

But in a turn of events that no one could have anticipated, Colin Powell was faced with his first and only resistance to promotion. Hudachek did not think that Powell should be promoted. As Powell's commander and the "rater" on Powell's efficiency report, he let the Army know.

Those who know Powell, know Hudachek, and know the story of what could have been an abrupt end to a flawless, fast-track career, speculate about what might have driven Hudachek to try to derail Powell. Some think it was a personality clash.

Powell's reputation was simply untarnished, and his friends were not about to let his career come to a stop because of one rating by one general who was himself about to retire. Powell moved from Fort Carson to another one-star position as deputy commanding general at Fort Leavenworth, where he had been second in his command and General Staff College class in 1967–68, fifteen years earlier.

Even at Fort Leavenworth there was no escaping Washington for Brigadier General Colin Powell. That same year, 1982, General Jack Wickham became Vice Chief of Staff of the Army and was nominated to become Chief. He formed a band of fourteen hand-picked officers, all bright lieutenant colonels and colonels, to prepare the way for his term as the Army's top soldier. Wickham asked Powell to head up the group that was known as Project 14. They were asked to do three things. First, Wickham wanted to know what policies he needed to sign up for in order to maintain continuity with his predecessor's work. Second, they were to identify policies he should revoke because they were either ignored, or at odds with the best interests of the Army. And third, they were to pin down the new initiatives that Wickham should adopt early so that he would have four years to get them into place. One of those new enterprises dealt with something Powell knew well—the light infantry. As warfare moved more and more toward tanks and mechanized infantry, the old light infantry, except for the elite airborne units, had slipped from prestige and prominence. Project 14 was instrumental in getting the present light-infantry structure into the Army.

Powell's eleven months at Fort Leavenworth were a refreshing interlude before he would pick up his second star and return to Washington at the behest of Secretary of Defense Caspar Weinberger.

chapter eight
CONDUCT AND CRISIS
IN WASHINGTON

C A R L U C C I and Weinberger already had a plan, when Powell went back to the Army as a one-star, to usher him back to the Pentagon as senior military assistant to the Secretary of Defense. He had not sought the job.

In July 1983, two years after his departure, Powell was back in Room 3E880, the Office of the Secretary of Defense, and less than a month later he made major general.

At the highest level of the Department of Defense a two-star general is not exactly a middle manager, but neither is he among the most senior. In a position where assertive action on behalf of the Secretary of Defense is a necessity, Powell proved himself able to wear the rank of his boss while maintaining the demeanor of a mere major general.

By all accounts he brought to the job wide experience both in the military and among the civilian, political leadership in Washington. He knew whom he was working for and had the absolute confidence of his boss. Powell had been beside the seat of power before and once again found himself in a position where his responsibilities and de facto authority were greater than his rank. Here he proved that it was possible to be a political general. He kept a public profile so low that it qualified, to use infantry language, as a low crawl. At the same time he was about as formidable as he could possibly have been. Best of all, he was fair, not self-absorbed with personal agendas that so often become the crux of conflict in Washington.

The term used in Washington for such a person is "honest broker." The military synonym is service. Powell looked out for Cap Weinberger with utmost devotion. Doing so meant being clear and accurate in winnowing and then conveying messages. A most discriminating gatekeeper, he stayed focused on the real issues. Often this meant sifting through complex issues to get to the heart of the matter. It was a job that required enormous powers of concentration and attention to detail on a wide range of issues but also the ability to cut through the minutia and get to the substance.

Powell was a master at conducting meetings. He understood that simply getting people into a room to talk about a subject is not sufficient. A meeting must have a purpose. If the purpose is clear, each person is able to bring something to the table. Positions can then be articulated in such a fashion that a decision can be reached. Powell ran a no-nonsense, stay-on-the-right-subject, get-business-done-and-over-with-it meeting. He did so fairly. And he was almost always the person best prepared upon entering the room.

The issues that occupied and sometimes preoccupied the Defense Department during Powell's tenure with Weinberger were diverse. We were building a military arsenal with an unsurpassed technological edge and revitalizing the human force that wore the nation's uniforms a decade after Vietnam. The Soviet Union was branded an evil empire and so-called freedom fighters in Central America were receiving covert aid from the CIA. Iran and Iraq were engaged in a war along their shared border. The Soviets downed a Korean jetliner, saying that it was on a spy mission, and blamed the tragedy that took 269 lives on the United States. In October 1983, two hundred and sixteen Marines were killed when a suicide terrorist drove a truck carrying more than a ton of explosives into the U.S. Marine peacekeepers' headquarters in Beirut. Four months later, Americans withdrew from Lebanon. In November nearly two thousand Marines came ashore on a tiny Caribbean island, shaking Grenada from the grip of those President Reagan called "Cuban thugs," in an effort to restore democratic government. A black American Navy aviator, Lieutenant Goodman, was shot down, captured, and subsequently released by Syria following an appeal from Jesse Jackson. In the ongoing war of Middle East terrorist acts, TWA flight 847 was hijacked by the radical Shiite group known as Hezbollah. Just before landing, passenger and Navy diver Robert Stethem was murdered. An American naval task force conducted exercises in the Mediterranean north of Libya as a show of force against Muammar Qaddafi, a supporter of international terrorism. Qaddafi's tangle with the U.S. by bombing a GI-frequented bar in West Berlin led to retaliation on April 21, 1986, by American air strikes of targets in Libya.

The most notable change to take place in the world, however, was the transformation begun in the Soviet Union. From February 1984 to March 1985, leadership changed hands from the old guard of Yuri Andropov and Konstantin Chernenko to Mikhail Gorbachev. Gorbachev called for immediate changes to the Soviet system. Upon meeting him, Vice-President George Bush was impressed. "If there ever was a time we can move forward with progress, I would say this is a good time for that," Bush said.

Watching events unfold and participating in making policy was the best possible on-the-job training for Colin Powell's future work at the White House and as Chairman. One tragic series of events played an essential role in his eventual service as deputy and then national security advisor to the President. Those events came to be known simply as Iran-Contra. The whole affair might have simply escaped him, for better or worse, had the Army's conventional wisdom prevailed. As he approached the end of his second year with Weinberger, Army Chief of Staff General

Jack Wickham eyed Powell for an assignment as command-ing general of an Army division. Wickham told Weinberger that it was time to pull Powell for what is considered an essential stepping-stone into the highest ranks. But equally important to a soldier with Powell's background, command-ing a division is often the moment of greatest personal satisfaction. While not the highest level of command, it is the assignment that puts a general both in touch with troops and also in charge of a major military unit.

Weinberger knew that taking a division was something Powell had worked hard for and possibly always dreamed of. But, says Wickham, Weinberger told him that he relied so heavily on Powell that he simply could not let him go. The men struck a deal. Wickham recalls saying, "Cap, I'll leave him there but when the year's up I want to put him in Europe and give him three stars to command a corps. That will do the same thing for him [as leading a division]." In 1986 that's exactly what they did.

Meanwhile, however, a memo on "U.S. Policy Toward Iran" dated 17 June 1985 came across General Powell's desk. It signaled the beginning of the Iran part of the Iran-Contra affair. The memo was a directive from National Security Advisor Robert C. "Bud" McFarlane addressed to the Secretary of State and the Secretary of Defense. Its purpose was to explore possibilities for improving relations with Iran. Nine policy options were laid out amounting to a grand scheme for romancing the government of Ayatollah Khomeini that had taken and was still holding American hostages. First on the list of options, in an attempt to "reduce the attractiveness of Soviet assistance and trade offers" was selling "selected military equipment as deter-mined on a case-by-case basis."

Powell wrote a cover note to Weinberger saying that the document had arrived "Eyes Only" for the Secretary and that he recommended passing it along to Rich Armitage for analysis. Weinberger wrote his own note: "This is almost too absurd to comment on. By all means pass it to Rich, but the assumption here is: (1) that Iran is about to fall, and

(2) we can deal with that on a rational basis." Weinberger equated the plan to "asking Qaddafi to Washington for a cozy chat."

Rich Armitage was indeed consulted. His assessment was that the whole scheme was both absurd and fundamentally wrong. On more than one occasion Colin Powell made a point of strongly expressing to Weinberger his own displeasure with the initiatives that seemed to be gaining momentum. With Powell's help, Weinberger tried to kill the idea of selling arms to Iran, but the initiative would not die. Weinberger, the faithful friend and servant of Ronald Reagan, would wonder if he should resign over the whole mess. Despite his devotion to Reagan, Weinberger repeatedly told Rich Armitage that his own mistake in the affair was not stepping down over it. But the idea of making arms available to Iran, despite an embargo, picked up steam without the support of the Defense Department. Weinberger argued that a direct transfer of arms from the military to Iran would violate the Arms Export Control Act. Besides, if it was a covert action, the CIA, headed by William Casey, another old friend of Reagan and one of the minds behind the Iran-Contra scheme, should take the lead. In January 1986, in what might look like a way of washing their hands by using a technicality in the law, Powell, under the direction of the Secretary of Defense, visited his old friend and then-acting Vice Chief of Staff of the Army General Max Thurman to arrange the transfer of 4,508 TOW missiles from the Army to the CIA. Powell gave Thurman no indication of the destination of the missiles.

The technicality is known as the Economy Act. It provides for one government agency to provide goods or services to another agency so long as they are fully reimbursed. Rich Armitage asserts that "Weinberger used it as a vehicle to slow things down. He saw it as a way to stop the problem." It didn't and the TOW transfer turned out to be just the beginning. The scheme would involve some of the most colorful, often tragic, and sometimes shady characters in the history of American foreign policy. The scheme kept employed a special prosecutor who, over six years and an expense of thirty-five million dollars, seemed determined to indict everyone who had ever heard about Iran-Contra.

Powell gave depositions to congressional staffs and the special prosecutor. In June 1992, Weinberger was indicted on charges of perjury and obstruction of justice when it was found that he had not told special prosecutor Lawrence Walsh of notes he wrote in his daily log about events as they happened. Powell testified that he gave Weinberger a report related to a November 1985 shipment of Hawk missiles from Israel to Iran. Weinberger said that he did not remember receiving the report. Powell went on record stressing Weinberger's opposition to the initiatives and made a point to attend a show-of-support tribute and fundraiser to help defray legal costs for Weinberger in September 1992. In a pre-Christmas move designed to bring an end to Iran-Contra, Weinberger, along with others, was granted a pardon by outgoing President George Bush. His trial had been scheduled to begin January 5, 1993.

When Powell left the Office of the Secretary of Defense for Germany in June 1986 he could not have anticipated that what started as a memo from Bud McFarlane would still play a part in public life six years later. For his part, Powell was pleased to be given command of V Corps. It was both a three-star command and a sentimental return to Germany where he began his career. It was a return to the site of the anticipated great battle between East and West at a time when a notable shift in the wind of U.S.-Soviet relations was not far off. And yet, instead of having forty men under his command, Powell had seventy-two thousand American soldiers. Instead of anticipating another platoon, it was the 8th Guards Army, about equal in size to his corps, that faced him. From the V Corps headquarters in Frankfurt, Lieutenant General Colin Powell could get onto his commander's helicopter and in a matter of minutes land at any of the installations where his troops were located. Once again he could wear to work the forest camouflage-patterned Battle

Dress Uniform, which replaced the fatigues he wore in the early days. He was soldiering again and working with warriors.

It seemed, however, that no sooner had Powell arrived in Europe when he got a call from Frank Carlucci. In November, five months after Powell's move to Germany, the Iran-Contra affair became news. Ronald Reagan fired Admiral John Poindexter, his National Security advisor, along with Oliver North. The President asked Frank Carlucci—who had nothing to do with government at the time and had no contact with the shenanigans within the McFarlane-Poindexter-Casey-North fellowship—to become the new National Security Advisor, to clean house, and to restore confidence in the National Security Council. Carlucci accepted but was in desperate need of help. He needed a deputy who was beyond reproach. He needed Colin Powell. When he called to ask Powell to join with him, the happy soldier replied, "Frank, you're going to ruin my career."

Carlucci appealed to one of Powell's closest friends, Grant Green, whom Carlucci had already recruited to be executive secretary of the NSC, to lean on Powell. But when Green called Germany, Powell urged him to talk Carlucci out of bringing him back. "I don't want to come back to Washington," Powell insisted. It was Jack Wickham, who called Germany and told his former protégé that it was in the best interest of the nation for Powell to accept. But Wickham discovered that "Powell was happy as a clam over there." Powell was not being coy when he let Carlucci know that it would take a call from the Commander-in-Chief to get him back to Washington.

Ken Adelman, a good friend and associate of both Carlucci and Powell, who headed up the Arms Control and Disarmament Agency at the time, was with Carlucci when he phoned Powell. Adelman told Howard Means how the call from Ronald Reagan to Colin Powell was made. "Three days after Carlucci's call, Colin calls me and says, 'What's the buzz?' Three days later, it's the same thing—'What's the buzz? Where's the President's call?' He's calling me all the time asking, What's the story? So I go to these little round-faced guys who work for [White House Chief of Staff] Don Regan, and I say, 'What's the buzz on this call to Colin Powell from the President?' They say, 'Well, we never got a form requesting a presidential call.' So I used the typewriter right there. I give the secretary two bucks to go get coffee, and I use her typewriter and fill it out right there. Regan apparently had his own candidate for the deputy's job. When Reagan got the slip, he made the call to Colin. Colin has been seen [by some] as the reluctant warrior, but he wasn't so reluctant. He was delighted to do this job."

Delighted, perhaps. Honored, surely. But Powell enjoyed his command and had done very well without actually seeking positions. Perhaps he remembered Thomas Jefferson: "Whenever a man has cast a longing eye on offices, a rottenness begins in his conduct."

By the time Powell arrived at the West Wing of the White House in January, Carlucci was already cleaning up the National Security Council mess. Within three months the NSC's politico-military office, which included its covert operations, was abolished, and half of the staff members were replaced. Except in times of crisis, everyone went from eighteen-hour workdays, six days a week, to a Monday through Friday, out by 6:00 P.M., schedule. Carlucci focused on working directly with key cabinet members and the President. Powell ran the day-to-day operations, chaired meetings, and cleared speeches. Having mastered the role of unofficial spokesman from his days as Weinberger's military assistant, he also frequently spoke to the media. Carlucci and Powell stuck together, worked as a team, and things started getting done.

There was no handbook for running the NSC when they arrived. The legislation that established it in 1947 defines its purpose: "to advise the President with respect to the integration of domestic, foreign, and military policies relating to the national security so as to enable the military service and the other departments and agencies . . . to cooperate more effectively in matters involving the national security." Nowhere does it say how.

Powell wrote in 1989, "When Frank Carlucci and I took over, we found no law which spelled out the duties of the position. There was no job description, there was no directive, and there was no specific guidance from the President. . . ." Tossed into a difficult situation at a difficult time, Carlucci and Powell chose a middle ground. "The model we adopted, which seems to have worked rather well, was a combination of two extremes. The national security advisor, first and foremost, had to be the manager of the process. It was his job to make sure that the bureaucracy functioned well and the trains ran on time. At the same time he had to be a powerful figure in his own right not only to make that happen, but to use the same power to provide advice to the President on foreign policy issues even when that advice was contrary to that of the Secretary of State or other cabinet officials."

The bottom line was, "to serve the President, to serve the President, to serve the President."

In very little time Carlucci and Powell had the NSC up and running, serving the President. Their offices were right next to one set aside in the West Wing for the Vice-President. George Bush liked Powell and was impressed with how he ran meetings. "He'd run them and get them over with in a hurry. He was thorough, and he presented people's positions very, very fairly and objectively as national security types have to do. He was crisp and strong in the way he put on the meetings, even with the President."

On March 4, following the Tower Commission investigation's report, Ronald Reagan went on television to address the American people about Iran-Contra. In his speech, the President admitted that things had gone awry and he took "full responsibility" for the affair. The speech had been worked and reworked by veteran speechwriter Landon Parvin in consultation with the President's wife, the new Chief of Staff Howard Baker, and others. The day before Reagan's address, Powell proposed an addition to the speech that did not make the final cut. Had it been included, the American people would have heard the President say: "As a matter of simple fairness, however, I must say that I believe the commission's comments about George Schultz and Cap Weinberger are incorrect. Both of them vigorously opposed the arms sales to Iran, and they so advised me several times. The commission's statements that the two secretaries did not support the President are also wrong. They did support me despite their known opposition to the program. I now find that both secretaries were excluded from meetings on the subject by the same people and process used to deny me vital information about this whole matter."

Powell had greater success when he proposed strong language for a Reagan speech given three months later at the Brandenberg Gate in West Berlin. Despite State Department objections the President delivered the words, "Mr. Gorbachev, open this gate . . . tear down this wall."

By the time congressional hearings into Iran-Contra dominated the summer's television viewing, the NSC was busy with new issues. The May 22 attack of the USS Stark by Iraqi jets firing Exocet missiles left thirty-seven American sailors dead. In early June the streets of Seoul, South Korea, were filled with violence occasioned by uncertainty over presidential elections. The Soviet Union and Eastern bloc nations were gradually being transformed and Ronald Reagan seemed to have an uncanny appreciation of their significance.

Powell's influence on policy was felt more than seen. Since he was not a principal policy maker but rather an advisor, the public remained unaware of the role he played in events. In the first act of an epic drama, Powell worked to send U.S. Navy ship escorts into the Persian Gulf with reflagged Kuwaiti tankers beginning in July 1987. He held a strict line on the subject of negotiating with terrorists. To stop feeding a no-win cycle of violence Powell opposed taking retaliatory, hit-and-run military action against those who held American hostages in Lebanon, even when videotape of the brutally beaten and killed Lieutenant Colonel Rich Higgins outraged human sensibilities.

Colin Powell was immersed in the President's business when, on June 27, the Powells received a sobering phone call from Germany. Mike Powell had followed in his father's footsteps. Although he was accepted into West Point, he chose to attend a private college. He was the first of all three Powell children who would go to Jefferson's alma mater, the College of William and Mary. He enrolled in ROTC there. On May 12, 1985 he was graduated and commissioned a second lieutenant. His father presided at the commissioning ceremony. Two years later, First Lieutenant Powell was serving in Germany as executive officer of a cavalry troop. Returning one afternoon after a day-long reconnaissance, Powell, with a junior lieutenant and the jeep driver, were in the fourth and last Army vehicle in their convoy driving down a two-lane autobahn. At about 1800 hours, 6 P.M., Powell's M151 jeep began to drift to the right toward the guard rail. For just a moment the driver, with the wind blowing in his face, was beginning to doze. As he realized what was happening he turned the wheel sharply to the left, so sharp that he was headed into the oncoming lane of traffic. A truck was fast approaching. In a split-second he jerked the wheel to the right. The Army jeep was out of control at sixty miles an hour with no roll-bar, no doors and no way to gain control. It missed the truck but began to flip side-over-side. The driver's side went down and Powell's came over it. Mike was thrown into the air and landed on the road. The jeep landed on him before it continued spinning right side over left. Within minutes a German ambulance arrived. The other lieutenant, miraculously, was up and walking around suffering only minor injuries. The driver was hurt, but Powell was in very bad condition.

When the medical team got him to the hospital the doctors wanted to give him up for dead. His pelvis had been crushed by the jeep. Parts of his lower back were broken. Internal injuries were massive. When the other lieutenant heard talk of giving up, he insisted that everything possible be done until Mike could be taken to a U.S. Army hospital by helicopter.

Colin and Alma Powell flew to Germany immediately upon learning that their son was near death. Ronald Reagan authorized the Powells' use of an Air Force aircraft to take them. When they arrived, Mike was rigged with several bottles dripping blood, medicine, and water into his veins. He was retaining fluid because of the broken pelvis, and swollen beyond recognition. Troops from his unit made a special trip to give blood. In just over a day he received twice the blood that normally courses through the body. He was in critical condition and in intensive care. Mike's father insisted that his son receive the very best possible care. They would not give up his life so easily. It was decided that the only place to treat him was at Walter Reed Army Medical Center in Washington, D.C.

Michael was put in the intensive care unit at Walter Reed. Alma Powell stayed with her son around the clock. Michael's father made a point to see his son for as long as he could manage away from the White House each day. They prayed and prayed and prayed. Surgery fused discs in his lower spine. In July doctors used an ingenious steel frame that pierced the flesh to hold his pelvis together. There were constant infections. There were more tubes and bottles and needles. A less critical but nonetheless serious problem was the disposal of waste. In the accident Michael's urethra, through which urine passes, was torn. An irritating tube from the stomach was used to shortcut the usual plumbing until doctors could begin to repair the damage. His condition remained touch-and-go.

Just four days after Mike Powell returned from Germany, the ICU was overwhelmed with trauma patients. A round had gone off in training, immediately killing a number of soldiers and leaving several others without limbs. Besides tending to her son, Alma Powell helped care for the other patients in the unit.

Mike Powell did not die. The steel frame held his pelvis

together until it was safe to remove it in October. In all, he was hospitalized from June 27, 1987, until March of the next year with only occasional releases for a few days to go home to his parents' quarters at Fort Myer. His short military career was brought to an abrupt and premature end. He was medically retired from the Army with 100 percent disability. While he gets around well, today Mike walks with a bit of a stoop due to the fused lower vertebrae. As of this writing he had a total of fourteen surgeries and has averaged one a year to deal with residual problems since his release from the hospital.

The accident rallied the Powell family. Colin and Alma's prayers were answered. Mike lived. Out of the tragedy came a special joy for all the Powells. At college, Mike Powell had dated Jane Knott. When they both graduated, Second Lieutenant Powell went off to the Army and remained good friends with Jane. After the accident, Jane, who was working in Washington, came to be with Michael every day. As the months passed and other friends came less and less frequently, Jane continued to visit every day. When Mike was released and moved home to continue recuperating at his parents', the romance had already been rekindled. In October 1988 they were married.

When Mike was just six years old and his father was in Vietnam, he wrote a letter in pencil on the wide-lined paper used to teach penmanship. It read something like: "Dear Dad, I hope everything is fine. I'm fine. Mom's fine. We miss you. Right now I don't know what I want to be when I grow up, either a lieutenant colonel in the Army or a lawyer. Come home soon. We miss you, Michael."

In May 1993 Mike Powell finished law school at Georgetown University.

In November 1987, Caspar Weinberger resigned after seven years as defense secretary. Ronald Reagan recalls, "When Cap resigned, Frank Carlucci was the obvious choice to move over to the Pentagon." Weinberger, Carlucci, and

White House Chief of Staff Howard Baker all recommended Powell for the National Security Advisor's job. "With the NSC spot open, I knew immediately that there could be no better man for the job than Colin Powell," said Reagan. "I had previously brought him back from Germany to serve as my Deputy National Security Advisor, and from the moment he arrived he was seen by everyone on the NSC and White House staff as one of the most knowledgeable and intelligent men in the field. Sometimes you just know that someone's right for the job. That's how I felt about Colin Powell," says Reagan. Reagan's feeling made Powell the first and only black to become Assistant to the President for National Security Affairs.

Weinberger as Secretary of Defense and George Schultz as Secretary of State had been at loggerheads long enough. The two men were both longtime Reagan associates from California. When they came to the administration, it was expected that they would be like two hands working together. In fact, they seemed to be policy adversaries and at times downright nasty toward one another. Whether Weinberger's reason for stepping down was (as he reported) his wife's health or the constant friction with Schultz, Carlucci, as Weinberger's successor, could and did break the cycle of constant mutual frustration between the two departments, and Powell was well prepared to advise the President on national security matters.

Powell learned early that competence and character go a long way toward building credibility. He made it a personal hallmark to deal with his bosses directly. Ronald Reagan appreciated the Powell approach. "I have always been appreciative of Colin's candid assessment of situations," he said. "Finding someone who will talk straight to you in Washington is a rare and valuable asset. But to find someone who is straightforward and loyal is invaluable," says Reagan. In the last months of Reagan's presidency, Powell's service would prove comforting to the President.

The President's fatigue was visible in the final year of his second term. In seven years Reagan had been served by

a half-dozen men who bore the title of National Security
Advisor. Not all of them served his best interests. A couple
were definitely loose cannons. What Reagan needed, he
found in Powell. "I had tremendous confidence in his
ability," says Reagan. "He had substituted for Frank Carlucci from time to time in security briefings when Frank was
away on official business. Colin and I hit it off right away
and I always respected his judgment—everybody did."

Much would happen in the brief time between Reagan's November 5 announcement that Powell would be the
new National Security Advisor and his officially assuming
the post in December. A report issued seven months after
House and Senate panels began reviewing Iran-Contra
assigned "ultimate responsibility" for the affair to the
President. More significantly in the long run, Reagan and
Gorbachev met in Washington and the two superpowers
agreed to eliminate all intermediate range nuclear weapons.

Powell coordinated the planning of that summit. He
left no detail unattended, and the meeting went flawlessly,
unlike the earlier October 1986 summit in Iceland that
collapsed over the issue of the space-based Strategic Defense
Initiative known as "Star Wars." When Powell briefed the
international press on the eve before the end of the
Washington summit, he diplomatically glossed over the
continuing SDI disagreement in such a fashion as to keep
attention focused on the historic common ground claimed
by Mr. Gorbachev and Mr. Reagan.

This was Powell's first of three U.S.-U.S.S.R. summits.
He coordinated two others in 1988, one held in Moscow in
May and another on Governor's Island in New York in
December. In all, he oversaw seven summits that included
Canada, Mexico, NATO, and an economic summit. He
worked on a free-trade agreement with Canada.

The scope of issues that Powell dealt with as National
Security Advisor included some that were ordinarily verbo-
ten for military officers. Since America's national security

Powell inspires sailors aboard the USS Wisconsin in the Persian Gulf at the beginning of Operation Desert Shield, September 14, 1990.

Young Colin in his Sunday best, age 7. "On the block" on Kelly Street, South Bronx, **(right)** with friends (left to right) Victor Ramirez, Tony Grant, Colin Powell, Manny Garcia. The Powell family **(below)** at the time of sister Marilyn's college graduation from Buffalo State College, 1952.

(left) Cadet Sergeant First Class Powell sporting the distinctive Pershing Rifles cord on his shoulder. ROTC cadet Colin Powell at summer camp **(top),** somewhat out-of-uniform sporting a Coca Cola T-shirt under his fatigues. Lt. and Mrs. Powell on their wedding day, **(above)** August 25, 1962. Maud and Luther Powell are on the newlyweds' left. To the right are Alma's parents, Mr. and Mrs. Robert Johnson.

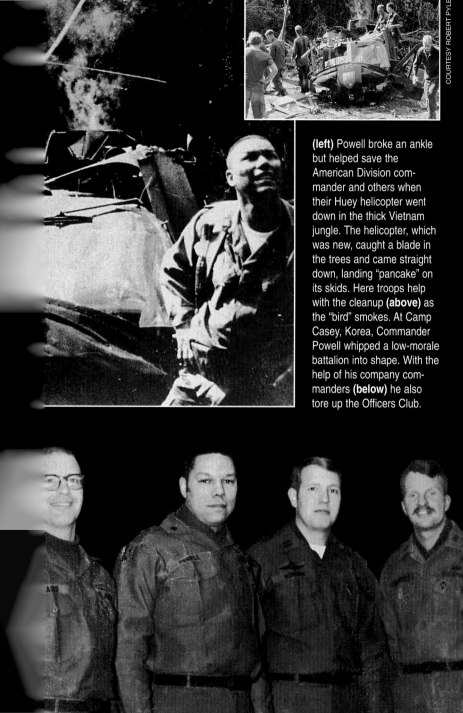

(left) Powell broke an ankle but helped save the American Division commander and others when their Huey helicopter went down in the thick Vietnam jungle. The helicopter, which was new, caught a blade in the trees and came straight down, landing "pancake" on its skids. Here troops help with the cleanup **(above)** as the "bird" smokes. At Camp Casey, Korea, Commander Powell whipped a low-morale battalion into shape. With the help of his company commanders **(below)** he also tore up the Officers Club.

(above) In the relaxed atmosphere of the president's California ranch, National Security Advisor Powell advises President Ronald Reagan as White House Chief of Staff Howard Baker looks on, November 25, 1987. They were preparing for the historic December Reagan-Gorbachev summit that cut U.S.-Soviet nuclear arsenals.
(left) Secretary of Defense Dick Cheney conducts the swearing in of Powell as Chairman of the Joint Chiefs of Staff, October 3, 1989.

Powell is a serious Volvo restorer and auto mechanic, shown here in his one-car garage behind the Chairman's official residence, "Quarters 6" at Fort Meyer, Virginia. Lieutenant Mike Powell and his dad, then V Corps commander, were both assigned to Germany at the same time. Here the whole family gathers **(right)** not long before the accident that ended the junior Powell's career. In the driveway of Quarters 6 **(bottom right)** the Chairman's official residence, Powell next to this cherished 1953 Volvo.

Airborne, **(above)** the Powells relaxing en route to the Soviet Union, 1992. A woman of grace and charm, Alma Powell as America's first lady of the military, 1992.

DEPARTMENT OF DEFENSE PHOTO

(above) Powell mugs with Soviet officers visiting the U.S., October 1990. **(right)** On December 7, 1991, Powell remembered Pearl Harbor. In Hawaii, a half-century later, he meets survivors of the fateful day that brought the U.S. into World War II. Disciplined young cadets salute **(bottom right)** as the Chairman proudly passes by. Powell worked hard to bring new Junior ROTC programs into schools such as the Charles C. Rogers Academy near Detroit. The school, attended mostly by black youth, is named for the deceased African-American Army general.

COURTESY JOHNNY TOWNSEND

©DAVID HUME KENNERLY/LIFE MAGAZINE

WHITE HOUSE PHOTO BY DAVID VALDEZ

OCJCS PHOTO BY MIKE OLSON

President George Bush honored Powell with the Presidential Medal of Freedom. The special affection between Powell and the Bushes is visible on the faces of Barbara Bush, Colin Powell, and the President. **(left)** Norman Vincent Peale published the Colin Powell success story in *Guideposts* magazine and visited the general to present his annual Positive Thinking Award. **(below)** Flanked by the service Chiefs and the Vice Chairman.

DEPARTMENT OF DEFENSE PHOTO BY HELENE STIKKEL

A visit to Tactical Air Command forces in the Saudi Desert. The Air Force with its precision-guided munitions was preparing for the largest and most accurate show of force in the history of warfare.

Powell getting ready to take a snapshot of some of the GIs he affectionately calls "my kids," December 21, 1990, Saudi Arabia. Ever concerned for the troops, **(right)** Powell visits an injured airman at the field hospital in Saudi Arabia.

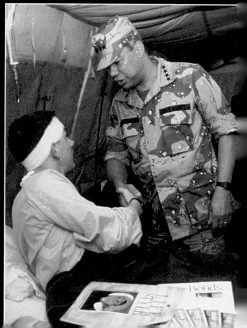

At the end of the first week of Desert Storm, Powell points out Iraqi anti-aircraft forces as he briefs the media. In the Pentagon briefing, **(right)** Powell and Cheney assess bomb damage and coalition air losses before the press, January 23, 1991.

Concern and relief were on the faces of the Powells and the Cheneys as they welcomed home downed American flyers who were held as POWs by the Iraqis. **(left)** The commander-in-chief, the field commander "Stormin'" Norman Schwarzkopf, and the Chairman in the Oval Office before the Gulf War Homecoming Celebration, June 8, 1991.

"Poppy" runs with grandson Jeffrey across the lawn in front of the Chairman's official residence, "Quarters 6." Powell, Defense Secretary Les Aspin, and President Clinton following a weekend meeting in the Oval Office. Noting that "for once I am better dressed than you," Clinton inscribed this photo **(right)** as a birthday present to Powell.

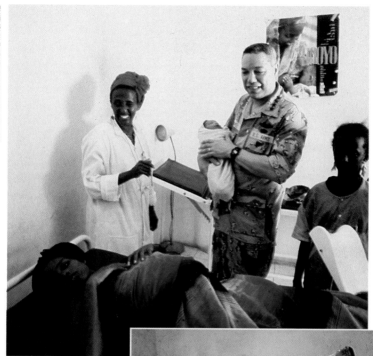

On his 56th birthday, April 5, 1993, Colin Powell holds a baby born less than an hour before his arrival at a clinic outside Mogadishu, Somalia. Accompanied by a member of the joint task force responsible for bringing aid to Somalia, Powell visits a feeding center **(right)** where corn meal was distributed to the hungry.

The Chairman, in a rare quiet moment, returning from Somalia.

interests include economic and geopolitical issues, therefore during his two years at the NSC Powell was called upon to operate outside his usual portfolio.

In a unique speech delivered to the Economic Club of Detroit less than a month after Bush was elected and barely a month before Reagan would retire, Powell spoke with such conviction about economics and national security that it is hard to believe he was merely holding a party line on behalf of the boss. In it Powell touted post-World War II "economic liberalism" that was copied around the world so successfully that the world economy was invigorated beyond our wildest hopes. The present state of international competition is a result of the free world's success.

Powell said that the "energy shocks" along with growing trade with the East has demonstrated that economic considerations, as much as defense and foreign policy, is a national-security issue. Access to markets is a persistent problem. An example of success is the bilateral U.S. Canadian Free Trade Agreement. "It is precisely our partnership with our allies that helps resolve those problems. It is our common political values and security interests that give both sides a powerful, overriding incentive to resolve the disputes fairly," said Powell. Global security cannot be achieved without a strong international economy extending to the lesser developed nations. Creative solutions can and must be found for dealing with Third-World debt, but "internal structural distortions must also be addressed." This means putting together sound macro-economic plans because resources from developed nations will not help if the internal system itself does not foster incentives, productivity, and investment.

The United States has a responsibility to back up its words with resources, Powell stressed. One- and one-half percent of the Federal budget spent on international programs is not enough and, when adjusted for inflation, has actually declined in recent years. This must be corrected.

Protecting the global environment, too, is a national security issue. Deforestation, the depletion of the ozone layer, and acid rain are topics that must be addressed multinationally.

There are "economic issues at home that can have a large impact on our national security if we don't keep our house in order," Powell said. While not gutting America's national defense, getting control of the budget and trade deficits is a challenge that must be faced. Turning around the trade deficit is neither easy nor quickly possible. "But one thing is certain," Powell told his audience, "the solution is rarely found in protectionist guidance or in national guidance from Washington."

Calls for import restrictions in the name of national security are often attempts to freeze time, to insulate the U.S. economy from the need to adapt to international competition. Powell called foreign investment "a vote of confidence in the U.S. economy." It promotes growth and creates jobs, he said.

"We believe the marketplace allocates resources more efficiently than the government. Thus we have never favored an industrial policy. However," Powell suggested, "there may be an argument for reviewing what the government can do to encourage the private sector to invest more to foster technological excellence in critical industries."

Closing on a theme he stressed even after leaving the NSC, Powell called an educated workforce "the backbone of the economy." Having the world's best educational system is a national security concern, he said, and all children must learn from the earliest age that drugs lead to disaster.

When George Bush roundly defeated Democratic candidate Michael Dukakis in the November 1988 presidential contest, Colin Powell fashioned the December summit with Gorbachev so that President-elect Bush would play a significant and visible role beside Reagan. The day after the election, Bush had asked Powell to stay on into the new administration. Or, if he wanted he could become CIA director. If he preferred the idea of going over to the State

Department, he could have the number-two spot there. Powell told Bush that he had chosen the military as his career and was a soldier first. Rich Armitage confirmed that CIA was not Powell's style. The deputy's position at the State Department was one step too far down the ladder.

Powell chose to return to the Army, where he walked into a four-star promotion and the largest command in the military. The Powells prepared for a move that would take them ever so briefly to Forces Command near Atlanta. In February, just as Colin Powell was leaving Washington and Rich Armitage was involved in the transition from one administration to another, Marybel Batjer's parents were both diagnosed with cancer. Big Guy and Buddha kept up their daily calls and took turns to make sure Bimbo had whatever moral support she needed. One or the other called her each day.

By October General Colin L. Powell would be brought back to Washington to become the principal military advisor to President Bush.

chapter nine
GOD AND COUNTRY

C O L I N P O W E L L' S faith is quiet but runs deep. His
father, Luther Theophilus Powell, was a devout Anglican.
With Maud he attended church each Sunday. They wanted
their two children to know the Lord whose three persons
and ineffable attributes are recounted in the Creed. Marilyn
and Colin were baptized and confirmed and received the
sacraments at the appointed times. They attended Sunday
school and received religious instruction at home. Profess-
ing a personal faith in Jesus Christ and following his father's
example, Colin became an acolyte in St. Margaret's Episcopal Church in the South Bronx, where his father was senior
warden, president of the lay board. Twenty-five years later
Colin, too, would become senior warden in St. Margaret's,
but this was a church in Woodbridge, Virginia, a suburb of
Washington, D.C. He served on the vestry there for three
years in the mid-1970s. His son, Michael, became an acolyte
like his father. Powell publicly acknowledges that his
mother's hope for him was not that he might become a
soldier but rather a member of the clergy.

"I'm a dyed-in-the wool, unreformed Episcopalian of
the 1928 *Prayer Book*," Powell told an interviewer recently.

For Powell this statement packs a lot of meaning. His point is not that he likes his religion dusty and old, without feeling, and steeped in hollow ritual. Rather it is a nostalgic comment. Powell finds recent reforms in the ancient, deeply rooted church of his childhood troubling. Yes, he loves the cadence of the King James translation. He finds the seemingly timeless and transcendent worship and traditional hymns spiritually stirring. But he has trouble with recent turns in the government of the Anglican Communion. As a military leader who knows that certain unchanging, fundamental principles undergird the conduct of war, preaching and teaching that Christianity is not rooted in certain unchanging truths such as the Resurrection is more than unsettling; it is simply unacceptable. Much of the supposed reform of liturgical worship that followed the Catholic Church's Second Vatican Council has touched the Episcopal Church as well. The modern-language edition of the *Book of Common Prayer* introduced in 1976 and so-called folk liturgies fail to stir Powell's heart in the same way that the traditional Anglican service did. Like many other evangelical adherents to the Church of England, he sees that faith and institution are at odds. While he now attends Sunday Eucharist only occasionally, it is not because of a lack of belief in God. He simply finds it difficult going to church as a celebrity where too much attention is paid to him.

His favorite passage of the Bible is the thirteenth chapter of Paul's first letter to the Corinthians. This classic text on love moves him deeply. But there is so much to be found in Scripture, he adds. In true Powell style, those things dearest to him do not evoke many words. He does not say more. When asked by young people about what books he would recommend, he suggests the ones written by fellow Anglican C. S. Lewis—notably the allegorical *Chronicles of Narnia* series, especially its first volume, *The Lion, The Witch, and the Wardrobe*. He read them to his own children. He does not elaborate.

As a brigade commander concerned for the spiritual welfare of his soldiers, Powell made it his practice to attend

the Episcopal service each Sunday. After attending church
with his family, he would return to the unit chapel at Fort
Campbell, Kentucky, to take in the worship services that his
troops might be attending. These ranged from a black
Baptist to a classical Pentecostal congregation, from a
Catholic Mass to a non-denominational "General Protes-
tant" service.

Powell may not wear his faith on his sleeve, but during
his term as Chairman of the Joint Chiefs he made a point
more than once to be publicly identified as a man of God.
He wrote in the November 1991 issue of *Guideposts* magazine, "I'll never forget when I was confirmed, the bishop
laying his hands on my head and intoning, 'Defend, O
Lord, this Thy child with Thy heavenly grace; that he may
continue Thine forever; and daily increase in Thy Holy Spirit
more and more, until he comes unto Thy everlasting
kingdom. Amen.' These words gave me a deep assurance,
and every year thereafter when I heard this supplication,
that feeling of God's watching over me was reaffirmed.
Along with it was a sense of needing to live up to His
expectations."

On the occasion of the annual Congressional Prayer
Breakfast in 1992, hosting senator and longtime friend Ted
Stevens of Alaska asked Powell to offer the opening prayer.
Powell accepted this uncommon invitation. This particular
role—leading the nation's members of Congress and other
leaders in prayer—was not traditionally fulfilled by a
military officer. General John Vessey, one of Powell's
predecessors as Chairman and a soldier whose Christian
faith is well-known, was asked to lead this prayer several
years before, perhaps setting a precedent but without
establishing a tradition. Powell wrote his words of invoca-
tion himself. Many were inspired as he led the national
leadership in prayer.

Powell praised the work of the International Bible
Society, which provided low-cost Bibles to troops who
served in Operation Desert Shield. "The Bibles you distributed to our men and women in uniform were a testament to

the spiritual need that must be met on the battlefield," the general wrote. "If they helped only one soldier survive the searing sands of Saudi Arabia, then I am thankful that need was fulfilled."

In times of great need, Powell has not hesitated to plead with God, praying with great fervor for the young men and women he affectionately called "my kids," America's GIs. This was true particularly during the Gulf War.

When his only son, Michael, was so badly hurt that the doctors had given him up for dead, there was nothing Powell could do but pray. Powell prayed. He remembers it as perhaps the greatest single moment of testing of his faith.

When Colin Powell was invited by former Watergate conspirator and converted Christian Chuck Colson to be interviewed for *Inside Journal*, the bi-monthly newspaper read by more than a quarter million men and women in prison, he accepted without hesitation. Colson's Prison Fellowship was a ministry that Powell could relate to. Powell is no evangelist but is able to inspire and motivate others. The front-page headline read, "He's Cool, He's Tough, & He Works Like a Dog"—a tough-love teaser to an article that spells out his hopes for prisoners in less-than-evangelist talk. His exhortation is tailored to prisoners, but at core is classic Powell: Despite your situation you can make something of your life; refuse to accept the view others have of you; attach yourself to something positive—family, church, or school; take it slow but just stick to it; be your own person and make your own decisions; if you work hard and invest what is required to be successful, you can make something of your life. But when asked what he believes Powell spelled out a simple, straightforward personal credo: "I believe in the country we live in; I believe in the system we have in this country; I believe in the fundamental goodness of people; I believe in my family; I believe in myself; I believe that God gave us life to use for a purpose."

If Powell's few words about religion hide his faith, his deep convictions about fundamental human and societal values and a guiding political philosophy are not quite so easy to obscure. Powell has read widely, especially from history. He does not claim to have heroes from among history's great figures. His personal inspiration comes from more ordinary types—his parents and family, and friends he knew growing up. Yet three figures do loom large in the mind of Colin Powell. Preeminent among them is Thomas Jefferson, followed by Abraham Lincoln and Martin Luther King, Jr.

Powell affectionately calls him "T.J." From the shelf behind his desk in the Pentagon, a bronze bust of Jefferson looked down over Powell's shoulder. Jefferson's *words* are the basis for many of Powell's strongest convictions. His favorite documents include the Declaration of Independence that Jefferson drafted and which, though edited by one-fourth on the part of Congress, launched the American enterprise. For Powell, the document is more than symbolic and not merely a prosaic statement of lofty ideals. Both in its historic setting as a manifesto severing ties with King George and the British throne as well as its broader, perennial meaning, Colin Luther Powell treasures these epoch-making words. They are the source for his own meditation. All men are created equal. They are endowed by their Creator with certain (Jefferson wrote "inherent and") inalienable rights. To secure these rights, governments are instituted. Governments derive their just powers from the consent of those who are governed. When a form of government becomes destructive to these ends, it is the people's right to alter or abolish it and institute a new government built on such principles and organized in such a way that will most likely bring about their safety and happiness. Jefferson and his brethren enumerated the infringements of these principles under which the colonies were suffering. It was their right and even their duty to throw off the yoke of oppression. Trusting in God's providence, those who gathered together by taking this bold stand pledged their lives, their fortunes, and their sacred

honor for the cause. Colin Powell chooses to join them in
the cause of democracy.

Army colonel Larry Wilkerson, a historian, fellow
infantryman, and Powell's principal speechwriter from his
days at Forces Command through his chairmanship, probably knows Powell's political philosophy best. According to
Wilkerson, "All the decisions he makes, all the policies that
wind up a part and parcel of Colin Powell are imbedded in
that fundamental [Jeffersonian] understanding of our political system and our culture." Much attention has been paid
to the forty-second President William Jefferson Clinton's
particular interest in the third President, whose name he
bears. Clinton's populist rhetoric and eager desire to hear
from the American people as he conducted the 1992
campaign marked his personal style as eminently Jeffersonian. That fact notwithstanding, Wilkerson asserts that
Colin Powell's comprehension of the true Thomas Jefferson
is singular in American public life today. "While Colin
Powell is a brilliant tactician—he can maneuver within the
labyrinth of Washington politics as well as any, perhaps
better than most—he nonetheless keeps in mind, and every
action is motivated by not just the tactical situation but also
this greater understanding of how our system works, why it
works, and for what it works. Preeminent is the American
people. They are what should drive the system. Powell truly
understands that."

He also preaches it. Speaking to members of an
American Legion post in San Diego about their efforts to
educate area youth about the democratic system he said, "I
talk about democracy all the time. Reporters come to my
office and ask questions and talk about things, and they are
surprised to suddenly see me reach down from my bookcase
a copy of presidential speeches, and I always go to Thomas
Jefferson's First and Second inaugural addresses because in
those two main speeches of the Jefferson era he captures the
essence of democracy. People don't think a man in uniform
studies those sorts of things, but I do because my life is on

the line for democracy, and I lead three million men and women who live and are willing to die for democracy."

He continued, in these remarks made shortly after the collapse of the U.S.S.R., "Recently, I have been teaching a lot of democracy to my Soviet friends. A year and a half ago in Vienna, Austria, I sat down with thirty-five chiefs of defense, my counterparts from all over Europe, to include Soviet counterparts as part of this new cooperation with the Soviets. It was a military doctrine seminar where we are supposed to talk about war. I didn't talk about war. We talked about democracy and then talked about peace.

"I told them what it was like to be a soldier in a democratic nation, how we are accountable to the people and how they in the Soviet Union have to become accountable to the people and respond to the wishes of the people. The people of the Soviet Union told their leaders what their wishes were just one month ago today."

Early in 1992, Brian Lamb of C-SPAN conducted an interview with Powell in a Pentagon television studio. When they arrived on the set, the general's bust of Jefferson had been placed on the table between him and his questioner. Lamb asked him about his special appreciation for the statesman from Virginia. "Well, T.J. is an inspiration to all Americans, and I gain great strength from reading about him and reading about his life," said Powell. "I find his words so prophetic and his definition of what the American experience is and what democracy is all about very inspiring. From time to time I pull out his First Inaugural Address, which is one of the most perfect statements ever made of what America is all about. You also have to read his Second Inaugural Address after he had been President for four years and been kicked around a lot. It's not like his First Inaugural Address. He's more argumentative and bitter in his Second Inaugural Address. But you see a man who believed in the country and yet knew there were problems in the country. He struggled with those problems, and you can see that he had ups and downs but never lost faith in the basic goodness of the people of America, in the basic truth that human rights and individual liberties are the bedrock principles of our nation and will overcome all obstacles placed in our way. So I continue to find Mr. Jefferson an inspiration."

Nearly twenty-five years after writing the Declaration of Independence, Jefferson delivered his First Inaugural Address. He spoke once again of "sacred principles." "Though the will of the majority is in all cases to prevail, that will, to be rightful, must be reasonable; that the minority possess their equal rights, which equal laws must protect, and to violate which would be oppression." Jefferson called for a common unity. "Let us, then, fellow citizens, unite with one heart and one mind. Let us restore to social intercourse that harmony and affection without which liberty and even life itself are but dreary things."

Tolerance is essential to democracy. Jefferson's concern was no longer the religious intolerance of a quarter-century before but a growing political one and the possibility of one party and its views dominating the rest. Jefferson would not have his own party persecuting the Federalists. In America, in Jefferson's view, all are republicans, or federalists, or democrats.

Powell agrees that, in Jefferson's words, "every difference of opinion is not a difference of principle." At least it need not be. "We have called by different names brethren of the same principle" that guides the "strongest government on earth." Jefferson's description of the American system and its status in the world is repeated habitually both in formal speeches and in conversation by Colin Powell. There is but one superpower more than two hundred years after its founding. Its singular global position despite its imperfections is based upon those principles enumerated in the Declaration, Constitution and Bill of Rights. Most of all, its strength is found in their incarnation in the American people.

"Preeminent is the American people. They are what should drive the system. Colin Powell understands that," asserts Wilkerson. "How many of our Nation's leaders, if you would have a private conversation with them, would have that come to them as one of their first thoughts? The American people are what this entire business is all about. Too few government officials consider that they are indeed the servants of the Constitution and the American people. That is always foremost in Powell's mind."

Jefferson's idea, and America's principle, of the "supremacy of the civil over the military authority" is based upon a fundamental trust in the will of the people as exercised through elective government. Belief in the rightness of this doctrine allows a politically capable, Washington-savvy man like Powell to serve under a Commander-in-Chief whether or not he agrees with his various policies or party politics. He is a soldier. While wearing Army green, his commission is to salute smartly and execute the orders of the one chosen by the people to preside over the executive branch of government. This is why he could disagree with Ronald Reagan and George Bush in more than one area of policy and still serve the nation. As Chairman of the Joint Chiefs his particular area of responsibility is to advise the President and national security team on matters pertaining to the military. In the end, however, the President is the top commander; the Chairman is a staff member at his service.

But Powell is not merely a soldier. As he does with his faith, he hid his politics quite successfully behind the uniform during the 1992 presidential campaign. When asked about possible political ambitions, he responded, "I am a soldier." As early as May 1991 he boasted, "Nobody knows my politics." In partisan terms this is true. But his Jeffersonian philosophy spans the full extent of the man from Virginia's teaching. In religion as well as in matters of "domestic" policy there is kinship between them. During the presidential campaign of 1800, Jefferson was too proud to respond to charges that he was an atheist. But in his First Inaugural Address he at once professed his faith and took an ecumenical stance. "Enlightened by a benign religion, professed, indeed, and practiced in various forms, yet all of them inculcating honesty, truth, temperance, gratitude, and the love of man; acknowledging and adoring an overruling Providence, which by all its dispensations proves that it delights in the happiness of man here and his greater happiness hereafter." By juxtaposing the words "enlightened" and "religion" Jefferson brought together reason and faith, hoping to reconcile them. While his affection for Enlightenment thinkers Bacon, Newton, and Locke was widely known even during his lifetime, few in Jefferson's day had an inkling that he read from his Greek/Latin/English New Testament each day.

Like Powell, whose Christianity raises concrete, practical questions, Jefferson asks, "With all these blessings, what more is necessary to make us a happy and prosperous people? Still one thing more, fellow citizens—a wise and frugal government, which shall restrain men from injuring one another, shall leave them otherwise free to regulate their own pursuits of industry and improvement, and shall not take from the mouth of labor the bread it has earned. This is the sum of good government, and this is necessary to close the circle of our felicities." Wise government. Frugal government. Good order. The opportunity to work, learn, and earn more. In very concrete ways, Powell's personal life reflects these traits of character. He likes proverbial wisdom—pithy, insightful, and useful maxims, which he writes down as a form of self-government. He is personally frugal. Perhaps occasioned by so many years of living on a GI's pay, he very rarely buys himself anything of value. His greatest expense of recent years has been sending three children through college at Jefferson's own distinguished alma mater, William and Mary, now a modestly priced state-supported school. He demonstrates his belief in hard work and the good stewardship of resources. What he believes he personally lives, and what he lives he believes to be the course of true democracy.

Jefferson is often hailed as the great liberal, yet conservatives, too, identify him as a patron saint. A close reading of him reveals no simple political category. He offers

a "creed of our political faith" as he himself called it, and
Powell subscribes to these "essential principles of our
government" devoutly. He has not given public speeches on
the particulars of specific articles of this creed. Senior
military officers are traditionally apolitical, at least in their
public personae. Powell plays all his cards close to his vest,
especially those politically sensitive ones that might cause
controversy outside the bounds of his own responsibilities.
However, he has addressed certain subjects. Freedom of the
press is one example.

"As a government official I have always felt keenly my
responsibility to account to the American people—through
their media—for my actions," he told the National Newspaper Association in 1991.

"Recently, some of you may recall, I gained a little bit of
notoriety at a Desert Storm press conference when I leaned
forward at that press conference and asked the press and
the American people to 'Trust me, trust me.' I'm very, very
grateful for the trust that many journalists, editors, reporters, and other Americans showed in me and in my
military colleagues over the past seven months. But because
I believe in a free press, I also believe that when we talk
about relations between the military and the media, trust is
not the issue.

"Thomas Jefferson said that if he were forced to choose
between government and newspapers, he'd pick the newspapers. There was a very sound reason behind his choice—
and it had nothing to do with trust. He knew, and I know
that the most effective means of ensuring the government's
accountability to the people is an aggressive, free, challenging, untrusting press—one that goes about its business
afflicting the comfortable and championing the oppressed,
and taking it out on the government. The media can't afflict
the comfortable and champion the oppressed by trusting
government officials. In fact, when both are doing their jobs
properly, there should be tension, skepticism, and friction
between government and the media. As I tell my staff, we

should always be just on the verge of having a food fight with each other.''

Powell's audience laughed, as did he. But ever since his days in the Office of the Secretary of Defense he has made friends among the press. Weinberger was once a journalist. When Weinberger became Secretary of Defense, relations between the military and the media had been bad for many years. All trust had eroded. His hope was to stop the Pentagon's routine evasion of the press. He instituted a new policy summed up in new "Principles of Information" that were hung framed on the walls of every media relations office in the building. They signaled a new open, responsive, and timely way of working with the press. Powell let it be known to numerous journalists that he was there to help the Secretary communicate. Veteran NBC correspondent Fred Francis recalls, "Powell said to me one day, 'Fred, if you ever need to know what's going on, just call. Call me anytime.'" Even as Chairman, Powell regularly would take calls from old friends in the press. He often dashes off a note to praise a particularly good story, or picks up the phone to voice his objection to an inaccurate one. He also responds to the Fourth Estate. When CBS ran a story about GIs who had lost limbs in the Gulf War and could not get state-of-the-art prostheses, Powell got on the air the next day to say that something would be done about it. It was—that day.

Powell often glosses other Jeffersonian principles— besides freedom of the press—by a simple reference to his mentor, T.J. They include exact and equal justice for all, the support of states' rights; "economy in public expense, that labor may be lightly burdened," the payment of government debt and "sacred preservation of the public faith," the encouragement of commerce and agriculture. Powell has touched from time to time on the troubling matters of America's economy, U.S. competitiveness in the world marketplace and the federal budget deficit. He says in private what he could not publicly utter while in uniform. The swollen budgets of the Reagan era were a scandal. We must take seriously what there is to learn from the successes in other economies, especially Japan's. There must be ways to provide individual incentives to greater productivity. The federal budget must be cut drastically. Free enterprise and competition need to be more encouraged.

In public he has argued for a prudent but severe reduction in both the number of troops and the armaments in the military. Yes, the end of the Cold War makes it possible, but more important, responsible government makes it compelling. We must not rob the military of its might—history has shown the disastrous effects of doing that—but Congress must not be allowed to keep National Guard units without a mission in their home states for personal political benefit at a high cost to the taxpayer. Pork barrel has no place in the budget. Politics is surely the art of the practical brought about by compromise. Powell is as astute a politico as can be found in Washington, but Jeffersonian democratic principles must always take priority over political self-interest. Therefore, Powell is in many ways a fiscal conservative.

Like Jefferson, he believes in the importance of free enterprise and personal property to spur individual incentive. And he is more than suspicious of big government. While he would not eliminate entitlement programs—many of them were paid for by the hard-earned dollars and taxes of those who need them most, elderly Social Security recipients, for example—Powell has solutions other than handouts. How they would take shape is not quite clear. They would be based, however, on old-fashioned hard work, personal initiative, personal discipline, and living with financial obligations within our financial means. Powell favors social, moral programs over governmental social programs.

One specific government plan he has put forward capitalizes upon the successes of the military and the lessons learned there. In a time of deep defense-budget cuts, additional funds are being appropriated to expand high school Junior Reserve Officer Training Corps (JROTC) programs. Speaking to the Council on Foreign Relations in

Chicago in November 1992, Powell explained his plan: "As we enter this new and uncertain period in our nation's history, a time when a lot of people are asking worried questions about what happened to our spirit, our morals, our morale, our pride, our vigor . . . can we offer some of the spirit that we're giving to our young people in the military to the rest of society? I think we can." Retired officers and NCOs currently teach military subjects in fifteen hundred secondary schools. Powell has gotten approval to double that number and hopes it might eventually be expanded even more. "We are not trying to militarize our youngsters; we are just trying to make them a little more proud of themselves, of their country, a little more able to take advantage of the opportunities in this country. . . . It's a wonderful way to get role models back into our schools, to show youngsters, fourteen, fifteen, sixteen, and seventeen years old what it means to be good Americans, what it means to work hard and to achieve. . . . Overcoming our nation's domestic challenges will require exactly those kinds of high standards, that kind of discipline, that sense of purpose."

In his Second Inaugural Address, Jefferson addressed the question of a balanced federal budget and excessive government expense. The subject was war. In peaceful times taxes on foreign imports were sufficient to support the national government and to return funds to the states for their particular projects, including rivers, canals, roads, arts, manufacturing, and education, among others. But in times of war, Jefferson suggested, these funds might have to be cut so as to make it possible to "meet within the year all the expenses of the year, without encroaching on the rights of future generations, by burdening them with the debts of the past." Economic accountability was for Jefferson a matter of ethics and morals. While he was speaking specifically about conducting war and foreign affairs, the principle applies also to fiscal policy: "We are firmly convinced, and we act on the conviction, that with nations, as with individuals, our interests soundly calculated, will ever be found inseparable from our moral duties." In both inaugural addresses Jefferson made an urgent plea for preserving unity among the states.

Historian Alf J. Mapp, author of an acclaimed two-volume life of Jefferson, distinguishes a number of traits of character in his subject that seem to be found in the founder's devoted student also. In fact, they might have been used to describe Powell.

First, he has a large capacity for affection. Those who meet Powell, and especially those who know him well, consistently note how attentive he is and even how demonstrative he is in his affection. Women note that he is gentlemanly. Men notice that he is not afraid to embrace warmly. His son, Michael, tells a story inconsistent with the stereotype of a military general. The day was Michael's commissioning as an Army officer, following his graduation from William and Mary College. Following his public taking of the officer's oath administered by his father, the junior Powell saluted his father who returned the salute. Then the general kissed his son on the lips. Colleagues from the Weinberger era tell a story of Powell and best-friend Rich Armitage, then Assistant Secretary of Defense, seen wrestling playfully on the carpet in the office one day.

Like Jefferson, Powell is capable of strong masculine comradeship. Armitage is undoubtedly his closest friend; a day hardly goes by when they fail to start the morning with a phone call. Their discussion ranges the gamut—issues in Washington, the morning papers, and the news shows, family matters. It is a deeply bonded relationship that both guard. It is intimate and yet manly. There have been others along the way. In recent years his comrades have included superiors like Carlucci and subordinates like Bill Smullen. In childhood there was Gene Norman. His driver and Volvo hobby buddy Otis Pearson is another kind of male comrade. And one-time Soviet counterpart General Mikhail Moiseyev qualifies. In each case, these are devoted, caring relationships.

Especially in his youth Jefferson was known for hyperbole. In maturity his words were filled with pithy sayings, bits of wisdom, and only occasionally hyperbole that strikes like lightning. Powell guards his words. Apparently when he was younger, he was less measured. In recent years he has collected and coined a good number of expressions and rules to live and work by. A list of thirteen of "Colin Powell's Rules" was first published in *Parade* magazine in 1980 and has appeared often elsewhere. They include, "You can't make someone else's choices. You shouldn't let someone else make yours," and "Check small things." Recently he decided to add, "No kind deed goes unpunished," but it has not yet appeared on the cards he frequently gives to young people who visit him. His original list, neatly typed on three faded 3x5 inch cards, is kept under the glass on his desk. Among them is "Avoid conservatism." Gulf War press briefings were characterized by Powell's typically measured verbiage and characteristic self-control. He conveyed a cool determination to achieve the UN coalition's objectives, but his vivid soundbite describing the destiny of the Iraqi military—"First we're gonna cut it off, then we're gonna kill it"—will not be soon forgotten.

"In opposition to his habit of hyperbole was his passion for *precision*. Everything has to be measured," Mapp writes concerning Jefferson. Powell has been described as calculating. He weighs his probabilities. And he pays attention to small things. The matter at hand may be achieving a military objective such as the removal of Saddam Hussein's forces from Kuwait, or it may be cutting appropriations to the military budget in a way that keeps the fighting force capable of accomplishing its mission. An often-mentioned example of Powell's penchant for precision is the dispatch with which he conducts a meeting. He identifies the issue being discussed, lets each of the participants contribute his or her views, then summarizes the options and their strengths and weaknesses as he sees them. It is very clear, very precise.

He had on his staff as chairman one person, Bonnie

DiGiulio, whose primary duty was to review his outgoing personal correspondence. Powell saw every letter addressed to him as it came into the office and often directed staff members to prepare responses for his signature. Rarely, but on occasion, a letter drafted for him would make it past DiGiulio without her spotting some typo or a bit of bad grammar. Powell would almost certainly catch the mistake.

If he does not have Jefferson's developed aesthetic sense, found in an appreciation for nature and classical beauty in its many artistic forms including architecture, Powell nevertheless appreciates the second of the Greek transcendentals—truth, beauty, and goodness. Aided by his wife, Alma, Powell redecorated the Chairman's office with dignity and good taste, transforming it from a dingy space without light or color into a simple but dignified and sensually satisfying place. The view from the Chairman's office windows, like that of the defense secretary one floor above him, includes a parade field just outside the Pentagon's River Entrance. Beyond it is the water of the Border Channel, and still further lies the Washington of monuments. Upon arriving to serve Caspar Weinberger as military assistant, Powell noticed that the parade field where visiting dignitaries are met and official ceremonies are held was nothing but an ill-kept lawn. He took on its transformation as a pet project. Where there was once more clay than grass, today there is an inviting green. It is bordered with seasonal flowers. In springtime when tulips are in bloom and Washingtonians are eager to enjoy the warming midday sun, the formerly functional-at-best space is a haven for noontime lunch outings. More than one senior official has been seen briefly napping there at noon beside a stranger who slipped out with a sandwich.

Unlike Jefferson's college classmates who complained about his sober habits, Powell has always been fun-loving. His young adulthood had its moments of carousing. Jefferson did not smoke, drank wine only occasionally, and eschewed sexual innuendo in the presence of ladies. Apparently he never publicly cursed. With the possible exception

of impropriety among women, Powell is guilty of all the
other sins that Jefferson avoided. The recklessness of youth
never seems to have interfered with his ability to do his job,
however, and with age his occasional trespass has become
well-bridled. He quit smoking a number of years ago. He
watches his weight. Shortly after arriving in Washington to
take the top military post, his weight was a struggle for him.
There were too many banquets, dinners, and other social
functions to attend. But Powell simply decided to watch
what he eats, how much, and when. Likewise with alcohol.
Jamaican rum was a standard drink in his immigrant
household as a child, especially on special occasions and
during the holidays. To this day, Powell enjoys a rum-and-
Coke. From day to day he drinks Diet Coke. If Jefferson had
difficulty cracking a joke or telling a funny story, Powell
does not. There is no excessive sobriety in the disciplined
seriousness of Colin Powell.

Mapp points out that "it is good that [Jefferson] was
sober and industrious because his love of comfort was such
that he might easily have become a sybarite." Jefferson
loved luxury, and his personal financial problems were not
helped by his costly way of life. While the Powells do not
live in opulence, their taste for finer things has grown. And
yet they live simply, modestly, and without great comforts.
There are no lavish vacations. In fact, until recently there
were almost none. They enjoy getting away to the fashionable Hamptons, where they stay in a two-hundred-year-old
house known as "New Potato," owned by cosmetics
magnate Estée Lauder. Powell's favorite hobby, fixing
Volvos, involves piecing together old cars bought usually for
a few hundred dollars and sold for a modest profit. Until he
became Chairman, he had only bought one new car—a 1967
Chevy. He did so again in 1989 as a present for Alma who
had grown tired of the string of beat-up and often unreliable
station wagons the family had driven for so many years.
Due to the general's public acclaim, the Powells have
enjoyed Washington's most lavish gastronomical pleasures.
But ask Powell what his favorite food is, and he will say:

"Hamburgers." Is this a foil? By no means. Cooks in the Pentagon dining room that serves the Chairman and his staff agree that Powell has hamburgers as often as he can. When he does, the plate is left clean. At recent count he owned a half-dozen business suits, most of them several years old. He has a few jackets and pairs of shoes, besides his uniforms. He does not like to shop. He does, however, cherish the mementos he has collected through his career.

Powell and Jefferson share a tempered optimism. Like his mentor, Powell is not gloomy. Jefferson identified his own temperament as sanguine. He was probably a combination of sanguine and choleric. Jefferson: "How much pain have cost us the evils which have never happened." Powell: "Never take counsel of your fears or naysayers." Both men are forward-looking and have great hope. Powell refuses to despair over the conditions of society and the state of government in America today. One of his mottoes is, "It can be done." Both men believe in the strength of the human spirit, the great possibilities that lie ahead, and the enormous potential for America's future.

While Powell would not claim to be a latter-day Jefferson, certain elements of personal philosophy are uncanny in their similarities. Each passionately believes that knowledge, while not a panacea, offers great hope for solving a myriad of the world's ills. For both, education or knowledge is the key to making something of a person's life and essential to the future of the corporate life of America. For Jefferson, the practical epitome of knowledge was accomplished by the Enlightenment. Unlike Jefferson, Powell is not a serious student of Bacon. But he has insisted on the importance of learning in his own life and extends his personal experience to others as an example of what is possible for those who take it seriously. A college professor once wrote Powell a letter asking him the question, "What is an educated person?" His response is worth quoting at length:

"It seems to me that education is less a matter of knowing certain things than of knowing how to learn and of taking advantage of the opportunities to do so. The person who 'gets an education' and does not continue to learn has merely punched a ticket and makes a mockery of true wisdom and knowledge.

"Certainly, a degree of cultural literacy is a sign of being educated. It is hard to conceive of an educated American who does not know the basics of the Bible and has never looked at the Constitution, for example. But there are other social and cultural worlds beyond our own that need exploring. An educated person is interested in and acquires learning that crosses these new horizons. Such a person develops a probing mind that wrestles with life's most pressing issues—what is true, what is good, or beautiful, and what are their counterfeits.

"A certain kind of education is necessary for a career; this must be sought, whether its skills include aspects of Shakespearian criticism, or the way you change spark plugs and set an engine's timing. But it seems to me that job training is not what you have in mind when asking about the 'educated person.' Going to college to be employed in a white-collar environment, it seems, does not necessarily make such a person.

"An educated person need not hold academic degrees and honors, while school is surely most helpful. Rather, he or she is defined by being able to grapple with complex issues, ideas, and problems in a broad-ranging, 'strategic' way."

Powell and Jefferson both see the connection between knowledge and freedom. Jefferson's "I have sworn upon the altar of God eternal hostility against every form of tyranny over the mind of man" takes a variant, practical form in the final article of Powell's credo that he shared with prisoners: "I believe that God gave us life to use for a purpose." Both men know that the tyranny of ignorance and error, as well as oppressive domination, cannot be changed overnight, and both believe that it must be defeated. For Powell, there are distinct racial realities to be faced. That is why he so eagerly speaks to and challenges urban minority youth to pull themselves up by their bootstraps and make something of their lives. A demographically disproportionate number of prisoners, for example, are black. The undisputed key to breaking down racial, class, and ethnic barriers and leading an enlightened, purposeful life is education. He addressed the 1992 graduating class of Fisk University, the Harvard of traditionally black colleges and universities and his wife's alma mater: "You graduate as democracy and the rule of law are sweeping more and more of the world into their embrace. We graduated as Nelson Mandela stood trial for treason in South Africa. In 1964, he would be put in jail for what they thought was life. You graduate with Nelson Mandela a free man! And he and President de Klerk and other enlightened leaders are working together to destroy apartheid once and for all."

Like the working class immigrant's son he has helped inspire to achievement, the less modestly heeled Mr. Jefferson believed in hard work in pursuit of excellence. He advocated public schools without class restrictions that would award achievement. Mapp writes that Jefferson believed "to say that less than one's best was good enough was a sure way to provoke the wrath of this normally equable man. He believed that civilization was a constant struggle against the primordial pull of barbarism." Judy Kingman, in the *Inside Journal* article, asked Powell about his own commitment to achievement:

IJ: Many young people are prisoners today because of the lure of easy money through drugs as opposed to hard work. A big part of your message is the value of work.

Powell: Everywhere I have gone, I've tried to make that point. I don't know successful people who don't work hard. Success is hard work.

Many interviewers come and sit with me and say, "Gee, how did you do it?" Worked like a dog! That's how I did it. I work very, very hard. I always have. I worked hard when I was mopping floors . . . I've worked ever since I was fifteen years old. I was never without a job. Most of the time it was just pure manual labor while I was in college and high school. Got out of college and came in the Army, and I've worked very hard for thirty-four years.

Powell's commitment to excellence was tested with the end of the Cold War. The disappearance of the longstanding threat of Soviet forces' coming across the plain and into Western Europe in T-82 tanks, the dissolution of the Evil Empire, and the abrupt halt to the East-West arms race made it clear that there would be no further need for a massive American armed force on the ready. But deep troop cuts following World War II and Korea diminished both the size and the readiness of the nation's military. Powell opted to fight in Congress and public opinion for a smaller but ever-ready fighting force poised where needed, ready to defend American interests. It came to be called the Base Force. An indispensably essential element, Powell told the Senate Armed Services Committee in April 1990, is "quality people, superb training, a high state of readiness, and a pride in service to the nation."

Lastly, between Jefferson and Powell there is a keen understanding of society as a compact among past, present, and future generations. Part of the reason Powell is able to grasp this concept is because of his traditional family background and strong Jamaican clan roots. He is not an individualist. In this he differs from so many of his contemporaries. Powell has never felt a need to rebel or to assert his own desires and personal goals apart from others around him. Every choice he makes is taken with an awareness of those others made before him. Each is made with an interest in the effects it will have on others. And it is made with some thought given to the effects it will have in the days and years to come. There is almost a timeless, tribal wisdom imbedded in Colin Powell. It is not a common way of thinking prevalent in much of modern society and American government.

Powell reckons Jefferson as the chief architect of the nation. His most celebrated documents, along with the Constitution and its Bill of Rights, comprise the foundation of that edifice called America. Powell is loath to discuss his place in it, but he is aware that he has played, plays, and may go on to play an even greater role in that continuity called United States history. Whatever his future holds, Powell believes that both America's and the world's great hope is to be found in seeing things with the perfection of Jefferson's clear vision.

Jefferson was not immune from discrepancies between doctrine and practice, and the issue of black slavery is probably the most egregious case. Despite his programmatic assertion in the Declaration that "all men are created equal; that they are endowed by their Creator with certain inalienable rights; that among them are life, liberty, and the pursuit of happiness," Jefferson was a slaveholder. He did not believe it was possible for whites and blacks to live together in an integrated society. Rather, he thought that a plan to colonize freedmen and that even the establishment of a black colony on the frontier west of the Mississippi with the possibility of statehood, was the best idea. He refused to set his own slaves free because Virginia's laws exiled freed slaves. He held that they were better in his care. Certainly Monticello benefited from their presence. But he tried in earnest to include in the Declaration of Independence a passage condemning slavery. He argued that it was inconsistent to deny any human being the full range of God-given freedoms the Revolution sought to secure. In the end, the pragmatics of politics won the day. Slaveholders from the deep South and New England slave traders prevailed in maintaining the status quo. The United States was born of perfect ideals and imperfect flesh. Late in life he would foresee a breach in the Union growing out of conflicting economies in the North and South with differences magnified by ideological disagreements over states' rights and the emotional issue of slavery.

Abraham Lincoln inherited the still-unresolved issue of slavery and the world's model of democracy in its greatest

moment of crisis. It is often forgotten that the Civil War did
not begin specifically over keeping slaves. When the eleven
Confederate States seceded from the Union, it was over
interpreting the very principles of the Founding Fathers—
the true meanings of liberty and democracy. The South saw
the North in the role of the English monarchy. This time the
perceived oppressor was not King George III but King
Abraham I.

"The central idea pervading this struggle is the necessity that is upon us of proving that popular government is
not an absurdity," Lincoln said in 1861. "We must settle this
question now, whether in a free government the minority
have the right to break up the government whenever they
choose. If we fail, it will go far to prove the incapability of
the people to govern themselves." Lincoln recognized that
the issue of interpreting the founders' intent was not merely
a present one. It was as old as the nation's origins and was
"not altogether for today—it is for the vast future also."
And it "embraces more than the fate of these United States.
It presents to the whole family of man, the question whether
a constitutional republic, or a democracy, conceived in
Liberty, and dedicated to the proposition that all men are
created equal can long endure" as he would put it at the
graveyard on Gettysburg Battlefield.

But Lincoln was a man of his times no less than any
other. It is absurd to hope that he might have anticipated the
civil-rights movement or the demonstration of blacks' capabilities as equal to that of whites. True, anti-black sentiment
in his home state of Illinois was strong. Lincoln's political
instincts surely told him that to make strong pro-black
assertions would have signaled political suicide. And it
seems he believed, as he asserted, that blacks are not equal
to whites in every way. While he did not believe in the
modern notion of social and political equality, he still
insisted that blacks are included in the Declaration's guarantee of equality. Persons are not equal in all respects, he
would hold, but *in natural rights* as defined by Jefferson—
life, liberty, and the pursuit of happiness. Lincoln insisted

that the Founding Fathers hoped slavery would die out. But
like Jefferson, Lincoln refused to condemn Southerners for
the institution of slavery.

When the Dred Scott decision declared Negroes ineligi-
ble for citizenship, Lincoln spoke out. In a speech delivered
on June 26, 1857, Lincoln addressed the subject of the
Supreme Court's decision and the turn of events since the
nation's founding: "The Chief Justice does not directly
assert but plainly assumes, as a fact, that the public estimate
of the black man is more favorable *now* than it was in the
days of the Revolution. The assumption is a mistake. In
some trifling particulars, the condition of that race has been
ameliorated; but as a whole, in this country, the change
between then and now is decidedly the other way; and their
ultimate destiny has never appeared so hopeless as in the
last three or four years."

In two states, New Jersey and North Carolina, free
blacks had been given the right to vote, but this was
reversed. In New York the right was abridged. Lincoln
noted that state legislatures held the power to abolish
slavery but that it was becoming fashionable to make the
right to hold slaves a part of state constitutions themselves.
This was just the beginning of a decay, he asserted. In days
past, said Lincoln, "our Declaration of Independence was
held sacred by all and thought to include all; but now, to aid
in making the bondage of the Negro universal and eternal, it
is assailed, and sneered at, and construed, and hawked at,
and torn, till, if its framers could rise from their graves, they
could not recognize it at all."

The United States was torn. By the summer of 1858
Lincoln would use biblical language to issue a prophetic
warning: "A house divided cannot stand." By the time he
became President in 1861, the nation was shaken to the very
bedrock. Democracy was at stake. Could there remain a
Union of states? A civil war would ensue on home soil. It
was the bloodiest war ever fought by Americans. Lincoln
issued an Emancipation Proclamation. Slaves were to be free
men and women. The significance of the moment in

American history was noted by Lincoln in the conclusion to his 1862 Annual Message to Congress: "The fiery trial through which we pass, will light us down, in honor or dishonor, to the latest generation. We say we are for the Union. The world will not forget that we say this. We know how to save the Union. The world knows we do know how to save it. We—even *we here*—hold the power, and bear the responsibility. In giving freedom to the slave, we assure freedom to the free—honorably alike in what we give, and what we preserve. We shall nobly save, or meanly lose, the last best, hope of earth."

Colin Powell admires Abraham Lincoln as second only to Jefferson. The reasons are simple. First, the sixteenth President did not waver concerning the intent of the Declaration on fundamental issues of human rights and individual liberties. Second, he insisted upon the full implementation of the Declaration and Constitution in the matter of slaves. Third, he refused to allow differences of interpretation between North and South to permanently rend the seamless garment of one democratic United States. And lastly, the strength of character Lincoln demonstrated in his single-mindedness of purpose is enormously inspiring to Powell. There are other, less philosophical reasons for Powell's respect for Lincoln. Perhaps the most compelling of these is his support for the idea of creating black military units and allowing 186,000 African Americans to fight in the Civil War.

On November 19, 1992, a cold and misty morning, General Powell spoke to a crowd gathered on the Pennsylvania battlefield to commemorate Lincoln's Gettysburg Address on its 129th anniversary. He was the first African American to be invited to do so in the fifty-year-old tradition. While paying tribute to Lincoln, his words sound the call of a global Jeffersonian. "Abraham Lincoln would come to this place where we now gather and bring meaning to the enormous sacrifice and pain of Gettysburg. Lincoln came simply to dedicate the soldiers' cemetery. With coffins still stacked nearby and spent shells still littering the fields, Lincoln did much, much more than that.

"He spoke to thousands of people who had gathered for the dedication ceremony. He also spoke to every future generation of Americans. He spoke of what Gettysburg meant in the great sweep of world history: that America, humanity's greatest experiment in democracy, should have a new birth of freedom and that government of the *people*, by the *people*, for the *people* should not perish from the earth.

"Lincoln knew that if the great American experiment failed, then freedom failed. If the Union lost, the great progress of the world was set back a century or more; perhaps forever. At Gettysburg, the world's future was in the balance. And at Gettysburg, the world won.

"That great victory, and the ultimate victory that would follow at Appomattox Courthouse, set the stage for a revolutionary change in the world, just as Lincoln knew it would. The preservation of the American Union and the struggle for basic human dignity that became its primary motivation, established the foundation for America's growth.

"Politically and economically we became the world's leading power. Our example proved to people everywhere what liberty in harness could do, what powerful values could create, what a union of free men and women was capable of accomplishing.

"Lincoln had told the Congress in December 1862, seven months before Gettysburg, that 'In giving freedom to the slave, we assure freedom to the free—honorable alike in what we give and what we preserve.' Father Abraham would be very proud today, for today our example has shown the way to liberty and independence to so many around the world: to Poles, to Hungarians, to Czechs, Slovaks, Lithuanians, Latvians, Estonians, Bulgarians, Romanians, Ukranians, and a host of others. Yes, it is true that many of these newly freed people are confronting wrenching and difficult situations—just as we did in 1863.

But how hopeful it is that they wrestle with their liberties instead of with their chains."

———————

Martin Luther King, Jr., completes Powell's trio of great inspirations. The text that moves him is not one of the civil-rights leader's compelling speeches, nor his famed letters from jail in Birmingham and Selma, but his life itself. It is an icon that speaks more loudly and profoundly than any utterance.

While serving at FORSCOM, Powell had his staff hang a framed picture of Dr. King on the wall in a small conference room adjacent to his office. It was a gift from Coretta Scott King, who inscribed it to Powell. When he entered the room, Powell discovered that his staff had hung the picture directly across from Powell's chair. Whenever he conducted a meeting, the portrait, along with the words printed at its bottom, confronted him: "Freedom has always been an expensive thing."

Powell sees King as bringing the work charted by Jefferson and consummated by Lincoln toward its proper end. "Lincoln freed the slaves, but Martin Luther King set the rest of the nation free," he often says. While Powell was fighting one war in Vietnam, another war was being fought in the streets across America. For King's part it was a wholesale conflict of nonviolence aimed at disarming the violence of racial hostility. In 1989 Powell wrote in an op-ed piece published in *The Washington Times*, "Martin would see that institutional racism is still part of our society. He knew that character and ability are formed in the home and in the school. If he were alive today, he would be working hard to strengthen the black family. He would not be satisfied with educational systems that still do not prepare our young people to take advantage of the opportunities available to them. I am sure he would have as a major goal a quality education for all Americans. He would also be determined to provide a good job for every American as a solution to the underlying causes of second-class citizenship."

Powell spoke on Martin Luther King Day in 1992 to an audience gathered at the D.C. Public Library in a Southeast Washington neighborhood, a world away from the marble and monuments. He told the group of blacks and whites and Asians and Hispanics that "many people think that Martin was a black leader, but he was really an American leader. . . . It was his example and his sacrifice that forced America to look deep into its heart and see the continuing reality of racism and intolerance and violence that threatened to destroy us as a people. It threatened to destroy us as a nation. And that was the purpose of his work, to make sure that it did not happen to our Nation. He didn't finish that work with us, but he brought us a long way along the road."

North and South, democrat and republican, conservative and liberal, black and white. In the seeming irreconcilability of such differences Colin Powell, like Jefferson, Lincoln, and King before him, tries to bridge divisions with hard work, reason, faith in God and in man's ability to side with the better angels. He spoke at Fisk University shortly after the bloody beating of Rodney King by four police officers that set off in Los Angeles the worst urban violence since those five scorching hot days in August 1965 when Watts was ravaged. The match that set the emotional tinderbox aflame more than two-and-a-half decades earlier was a similar incident involving a motorist and alleged police brutality. Powell was speaking particularly about divisions between the races, but he might have been referring to any of the destructive, exclusivist criteria that persons and groups use to define "us" and "them." Almost preaching, he said, "Divided, fighting amongst ourselves, walking separate lines of diversity, we are as weak as newborn babies. Together, intertwining our many differences and diversities into a mosaic of strength, we will prevail over the darkness. . . . I want you to love one another. I want you to respect one another, see the best in each other, share each other's pain and joy."

chapter ten

A COMPLETE SOLDIER

O R D I N A R I L Y the full honor ceremony would mark the beginning of a chairmanship. But the first official day of General Colin Powell's term of service as Chairman of the Joint Chiefs of Staff, October 1, 1989, was a Sunday. He spent the day quietly at home and retired that night expecting to get into the Pentagon early on the morning of the second. The ceremony, traditionally held on the green outside the Pentagon's River Entrance, was scheduled for 3:00 P.M., Tuesday, October 3. By the time he got there, he had put in more than a full two days as Chairman.

Powell's new job began when the phone rang in the wee hours of Monday morning. It was Lieutenant General Tom Kelly, the Joint Staff's Director of Operations, the J-3. There were indications that a coup was imminent in Panama. Powell called Defense Secretary Dick Cheney and General Maxwell Thurman in Panama. Just a couple of hours later, as drizzle fell on its River Entrance steps, Powell slipped into the Pentagon virtually unnoticed. There were several hours of impromptu briefings and discussions in the Pentagon. By nine o'clock, Cheney, Powell, Kelly, and intelligence officer Rear Admiral Ted Sheafer were at the

White House to brief the President. George Bush made a comment about the new Chairman's jumping right into things. The Bush administration wanted to see the despotic, drug-dealing, dictator-president of Panama—Manuel Noriega—out of power. Powell observed, though, that neither the coup leaders nor their plan was reliable. They wanted U.S. help. Powell's recommendation: Stand back and see what happens. The U.S. should not get involved despite wanting to see Noriega removed. George Bush agreed. The coup to depose General Manuel Noriega did not happen that day. But when it did, on Tuesday, it failed. American hands were clean.

It was a balmy, breezy, Indian summer afternoon on the lawn between the five-sided building and the Boundary Channel. Powell had been sworn in privately in Cheney's office with just family and friends present. This was the public ceremony. Every seat was filled, and others were standing well before the ceremony began. The Powell family sat in the front row. Colin's sister, Marilyn, and her husband, Norm Berns, had come for the occasion.

Powell and Cheney reviewed the ceremonial Old Guard troops. Cheney spoke in glowing language about the new Chairman. Then Powell rose to the podium. He described an enormous painting that hangs in the wide, open staircase that connects the Bradley Corridor on the Pentagon's second floor with the Eisenhower Corridor on the third floor. It is a picture of the inside of the Strategic Air Command chapel, painted in the early 1960s by Woodi Ishmael. Bright sunlight streams through a beautiful, modern, stained-glass window. There is a single family kneeling at an altar rail in what otherwise is an empty church. There is a mother and father, a daughter beside her mother, and a son beside his father. The father is in uniform. There is a sense that the family is praying together one last time before the father must go off to war, or to an assignment alone without his family.

"Everytime I pass that painting, a silent prayer comes to mind for all who serve this nation in times of danger.

Beneath the painting there is an inscription from the prophet Isaiah. The words read: 'And the Lord God asked: "Whom shall I send? Who will go for us?" And the reply came back: 'Here am I, send me.'"

Each day as Powell entered the doors of the Pentagon en route to his office he passed in front of this testament to what he once described as "the essence of what we are supposed to be doing in this building—that's serving. . . . That's the ultimate statement of selfless service: 'Send me.'"

It was such service, over more than thirty years, that led Colin Powell to the top post in America's armed forces. George Bush remembers that Powell was the hands-down choice. "Dick Cheney felt very strongly about it, and I was most interested in his view," Bush notes.

Powell was chosen from among fifteen four-star officers. At age fifty-two he would become the youngest Chairman ever and the first black. "I do remember some advisors suggesting to me that 'he doesn't quite have the experience and he might not be able to get the confidence of the other chiefs if he jumps over a lot of other potential candidates.' He had just assumed a four-star command," Bush recalls. "That was an argument not made in rancor, or in a way to tear him down, but the argument was that maybe he needs a little more seasoning so that when he does become Chairman—which inevitably he would—he would have the unquestioned support, right from the first day, of the other military. I decided, and I give Dick Cheney great credit for his counsel on this, that because of Colin and because of this *character* that he is possessed of, and the way he works with people, he would have the confidence of the others from Day One. And I think that history will show that he certainly did."

Apparently Frank Carlucci played a role in the process, too. Just after Cheney was nominated by George Bush to be his defense secretary, Carlucci and Cheney saw each other. Carlucci made a point of mentioning that Cheney would get to nominate a Chairman to serve for most of the four-year presidential term. "There's only one person it should be:

Colin Powell," Carlucci said. Cheney agreed. The choice was made.

It was common knowledge by the time Powell was National Security Advisor that he was expected to at least become Chief of Staff of the Army. Like Bush, many claim to have known that some day Powell would be the nation's top troop. General Jack Wickham was Chief of Staff of the Army when Powell was a two-star. "Colin earned the ranks he received. Up to major general—brigadier general and major general—were done by boards of his seniors. Therefore, selection was based upon merit. I selected him for three stars because of merit and because I saw in him a contender for four stars." Wickham put Powell in the command of V Corps. "When the fourth star rolled around he went down to command Forces Command. He held commands at every level. He just missed [commanding] a division," Wickham observes.

"When he worked for Weinberger, Colin had very high visibility. Even then Jack Marsh [then Secretary of the Army] and I talked about Colin's becoming Chairman," says Wickham.

Many misunderstand the Chairman's role. He is not a commander of troops. Troops are under the jurisdiction of what are called unified and specified commanders. The Chairman has a personal staff of only sixty. But he is the highest ranking officer in all the armed forces, and his responsibilities are singularly great. He serves as the principal military advisor to the President, the National Security Council, and the Secretary of Defense. He is the head of the Joint Chiefs of Staff, made up of the Vice Chairman and the top officers in each of the four services. The Chairman, while not in the official chain-of-command between the President, defense secretary, and the commanders, functions within it as a conduit communicating between the civilian leaders and the top uniformed commanders. The Joint Staff, a diverse group of sixteen hundred military and civilians, develops the military's strategic plans under the Chairman's direction.

The chairmanship of the Joint Chiefs has not always been the uniquely powerful position it has become. America's top military leaders started meeting early in World War II as a de facto group in sessions with senior British officers to map out a broad strategy for the war. This group of so-called Combined Chiefs of Staff consisted of the British Chiefs of Staff and their "United States opposite numbers." The functions and duties of the Joint Chiefs of Staff were not formally defined during the war, but they reported directly to the President regarding Allied war plans. When the Joint Chiefs of Staff were formally established by the National Security Act of 1947, its members were corporately designated principal military advisors to the President. A 1949 amendment to the legislation created the Office of Chairman who was first among equals. World War II hero General Omar Bradley became the first officer and the only five-star general to become Chairman of the Joint Chiefs. Although there was a chairman, the Chiefs of Staff of the Army and Air Force and the Chief of Naval Operations (to be joined in 1952 by the Commandant of the Marine Corps) gathered collegially. Over the years the Chairman's responsibilities broadened. However, it was not until they were focused and redefined by the Goldwater-Nichols Defense Reorganization Act of 1986 that the Chairman's role became singularly important.

The Goldwater-Nichols Act had been in place for three years when Colin Powell became Chairman. His predecessor, Admiral William Crowe, had begun his four years in the office before the new legislation was enacted. Crowe relied upon consensus building and was the epitome of what had formerly been an important quality in a chairman working between services with their almost legendary rivalries. Although he assumed his duties as the President's principal military advisor, he made a point of gathering the service chiefs around the table to shape recommendations for the civilian leadership. Crowe was just naturally inclined to work in committee.

Powell, however, had spent the years since Goldwater-

Nichols at NSC and briefly as Commander-in-Chief of FORSCOM. His day-to-day experience with the Joint Chiefs was his contact with the Chairman. Besides, he had studied what the new role was supposed to be. Further, he realized that the best recommendation to any commander, and especially the Commander-in-Chief, is not usually a committee compromise but a bold, unvarnished plan. Or, it might amount to laying out all the options with their anticipated consequences. By the nature of the military art these might be disputed among colleagues. Powell decided that he would assume the full reign of responsibilities as the President's advisor. Indeed, it would be valuable to hear from the top officers at each of the services, but the mind of the military would have to be not a partisan one nor a compromise among parochial ones but, rather, a truly "joint" one. Powell was the youngest Chairman ever who first assumed the position's full role and, following the Gulf War, started to clearly express what it means for the different services to fight together jointly.

The Chairman does not hold an Army job. As the top GI he is a man for all services, and his staff includes members of all four services. Those who work for the Chairman and the Chairman himself talk about being "purple suited," presumably a combination of Army green, Air Force blue, and the darker blue of the Navy. They are not one color or another but all colors at once without prejudice or rivalry. They must work together and appreciate and respect one another because in the end their interests are the same—to win, to successfully accomplish their assigned mission. Powell knows that just as in society where cooperation makes for social cohesion and stability, the services all need to work with one another if they are to be certain of victory in war.

It did not take Colin Powell long to settle into the Chairman's office. Many long days would be spent there in what would be his last and longest assignment. While his duties expanded over the years, the Chairman's office itself remained essentially the same. The space for staff is cramped. The chairman's own office, while refurbished under Alma Powell's supervision, is still modest. The room that is used both ceremonially and for day-to-day work is smaller than many other senior officers'.

Surrounded by mementos, awards, and gifts he received throughout his career but especially during his chairmanship, Powell moved between a large executive desk and a high, standing desk where he sat on a stool looking out the mylar-covered, one-way, bulletproof glass. Outside, only feet away, Pentagon employees could be seen waiting for shuttle buses, limousines dropped off distinguished visitors, and traffic came and went past the River Entrance steps. In the distance are the grassy square that serves as a parade ground and the Boundary Channel with its sailboats. Powell could watch the boats with binoculars that sat atop the desk, just beside the brass reading lamp with its green glass shade, and a pen set. This is where Powell chose to pore over the morning newspapers, often listening to tapes of Carly Simon, Benny Goodman, Strauss waltzes, Louie Armstrong, the Statler Brothers, Mozart, Paul Simon, and Count Basie from a portable radio-stereo on the wall shelf to the right and behind the larger office desk and its leather executive chair. Beside the tape machine, family photographs. The shelves were lined with books, mostly on military and historical subjects. There were mugs bearing military unit crests, gifts from the soldiers. A brass model of a 1927 Volvo, received at Christmas 1992. A bronze bust of Thomas Jefferson. A shotgun, the gift of Mikhail Gorbachev at one of the U.S.-Soviet summits. Sabers from commencements at the Merchant Marine and Coast Guard academies; two Desert Storm GI statues—one of a male, the other of a female soldier. Powell had squeezed the balloon stress-ball with a caricature of the face of Saddam Hussein on it to the point of bursting. The sand that was formerly inside had mostly poured out and onto the shelf. There was a sizable chunk of the Berlin Wall and a piece of a Scud missile. A bottle of beer from Panama and a door knob from his alma mater, Morris High. Next to a Desert Storm baseball card bearing a likeness of Colin Powell was one fifty years older, sealed between plexiglass. On it, the face of World War II ace Colin P. Kelly and a plane dropping bombs in the background on one side. On the verso, a bio and the words: "Gum, Inc. Phila., Pa. Buy US Savings Bonds." A set of green hardback books, the official history of the U.S. Army in World War II. On the credenza below, Powell laid out part of his collection of military awards from around the world. Every country he had visited since becoming Chairman had given him its highest military honor.

On the wall-length cabinet behind the desk were two banks of phones with "drop lines," direct hook-ups to cabinet members and key government officials and push-buttons connecting him with all of the major commanders. From here he could talk "secure" on a scrambled signal to anyone with a similar phone. On the wall space between the bookcase and the cabinets hung a simply framed quotation from President Abraham Lincoln. It reads, "I can make a brigadier general in five minutes, but it is not easy to replace 110 horses. A. Lincoln." It was a promotion gift from a protocol officer and colleague in the Office of Defense Secretary Harold Brown in the Carter administration. On the back is an inscription: "Presented to BG Colin Powell by Lt. Col. Stu Perviance, civilian USA, on 23 June '79 with a prediction, not to be opened until 23 June 89." Attached is an envelope containing the prediction that Powell would become the first black Chief of Staff of the Army, made three weeks after he was promoted to one-star general.

A third phone with buttons to ring each member of his personal staff sat on Powell's desk with one in-box, one out-box, each cleared out daily. Under the desktop glass the general had positioned 3x5 cards and various notes, as well as a cartoon from the New Yorker showing older men dressed in uniforms riding swings in a park. The caption: "The Joint Chiefs of Staff taking advantage of a lull in world affairs." One of the notes was a quote from ancient Greek historian and general Thucydides famous for his sharp analysis of causes and effects: "Of all the manifestations of power, restraint impresses men most." Another is a line from the movie *The Hustler*, "Fast Eddie, let's shoot some pool." The thirteen aphorisms in the official list of Colin Powell's Rules were first published in *Parade* magazine and have been reprinted often since. But the longer, original list, typed out on three index cards during the Weinberger era, was still ever in Powell's sight as Chairman. In order, they are: Have a vision. It ain't as hard as you think. Be demanding. Don't take counsel of your fears or naysayers. Perpetual optimism is a force multiplier. Act at $P = .70$, not P_s equals .99 or .2, l'audace. Avoid conservatism. Remain calm. Be kind. It will look better in the A.M. Share credit. Check small things. Get mad, then get over it. Humor. Don't let adverse facts stand in the way of a good decision. Be careful what you choose, you may get it. You can't make someone else's choices and you shouldn't let someone else make yours. Decisions should be timely, neither early nor late. Avoid having your ego so close to your position that when your position falls your ego goes with it. It can be done.

The strange-sounding pseudo-equation (*Act at $P = .70$* . . .) is actually a shorthand for how to make decisions. Powell insists that they must be both timely and have probability of bringing success. The "P" means both probability and perfection; the "s" has to do with success. Powell asserts that decisions are to be made with sufficient information that will yield seventy percent probability of success, rather than when there is virtual certitude (his 99 percent) or when doing so would be foolishly precipitous (20 percent). Such timing takes a stroke of boldness (*l'audace* is the French word often translated as "audacity" or "boldness") to achieve the optimum true success. In a speech given to new generals, Powell told them, "Don't seek perfection and don't come up short. Make timely decisions."

Powell is most certainly the first Chairman to have proudly displayed a picture of a dishonorably discharged soldier on his office wall. On the side of the room opposite his desk was a sitting area with a couch and two chairs around a coffee table. Above the couch was a Stivers print of Lieutenant Henry Flipper among other cavalry officers mounted on horseback, his arm extended, his finger pointing the way forward. In 1881, Flipper, the first black graduate of West Point, was brought up on trumped-up charges associated with missing commissary funds. He was acquitted. The real problem seems to have been his friendship with a white woman. When the court martial failed, Flipper was dishonorably discharged for conduct unbecoming an officer. He went on to become a prominent land surveyor. On another wall there is an image of another African-American, a Buffalo Soldier. This image, *Scouts Out*, by Lee Brubaker, inspired the Buffalo Soldiers Monument at Fort Leavenworth, Kansas. During his chairmanship Powell was present for both the ground breaking and its dedication and was instrumental in seeing the project through.

Powell was always keenly aware that he had "climbed on the backs" of other black men and women who had gone before him both in American society and in the military. He makes frequent reference to the Buffalo Soldiers, the 54th Massachusetts Regiment made famous in the movie *Glory*, and officers such as Brigadier General Benjamin O. Davis, the first black general in the U.S. Army, and Air Force General Daniel "Chappie" James, the first black to reach four-star rank.

Powell was proud to have chosen as his aide-de-camp a young man who followed in the footsteps of Captain Roscoe Brown, a black and the first American pilot to shoot down a German jet in World War II. Speaking at a 1991 reunion of the all-black World War II-era Tuskegee Airmen, Powell surprised Major Rod Von Lipsey by introducing him. Powell boasted of Von Lipsey's forty fighter missions in the Gulf War for which he was highly decorated. Powell took particular pride in being able to further the military career of the outstanding Marine by bringing him into the inner circle of the Chairman of the Joint Chiefs. In May 1993, Von Lipsey was selected to be a White House Fellow.

In the last months of his chairmanship, prominently displayed near the door where guests enter and leave the office, was a tiny picture taken of Powell as a brigadier general, with the autograph of General Omar Bradley, the nation's first Chairman of the Joint Chiefs and the last of the five-star generals. Under the photo is Bradley's honor guard. A Reagan-Powell grips-and-grins shot is signed: "Dear Colin, If you say so I know it's all right. All the very best wishes and warm regards, Ronald Reagan." A photo taken at a White House meeting was signed by then Vice-President George Bush, "Dear Colin, Now here's the way I see it." On another wall was the Certificate of Appointment making Powell Chairman. It is displayed behind glass with the pen George Bush used to sign it and a note that the pen "has ink left for further action. Good luck, George Bush."

Two other pictures were hung side-by-side in the spring of 1993, fewer than six months before his retirement. One of them was taken at Bush's full-honors military farewell ceremony presided over by Powell. It is inscribed: "Colin, this was the nicest thing in my whole presidency. Bar and I will never forget. Thanks, my noble friend. George Bush." The second, a black-and-white taken in the Oval Office after a winter-weekend meeting, shows Powell and Aspin wearing sweaters and President Clinton dressed in a business suit. The three men are smiling and talking. It reads: "Colin, on a rare day I am more dressed up than you. With thanks on your birthday for your service to America. Bill."

On a table was a foot-high Boehm porcelain bald eagle, one of only three, with a delicate porcelain American flag clutched in its beak. It was a gift on receiving the Horatio Alger Award. One of the first presents he received upon assuming the chairmanship was from the Kuwaitis. It is a small wooden ship. He refused to let it out of his sight. A replica of the tattered 1st Infantry Regiment colors given to him by the Chicago Mercantile Exchange, was mounted in a frame and displayed between the ceremonial American and Chairman's flags.

Powell used a small, round mahogany table between the sitting area and his desks for most meetings. Instead of going into the formal Joint Chiefs of Staff meeting room known as the Tank, Powell often invited the service heads into his office. It was his turf and informal. Assistants and aides were left outside. He also met guests and reporters at this table. It completed the room. It was a workspace, a meeting room, a ceremonial hall, a study, and a home away from home—there is a small private bathroom as well— through the long hours in crises such as the Gulf War.

What neither Powell nor anyone else might have imagined when he returned to the Pentagon was the range of crises he would face. Not only was there an October coup attempt in Panama, but an American military action there two months later. In November 1989 a Special Forces detachment was held hostage in El Salvador. Also in December the U.S. helped put down a coup in the Philippines with U.S. Air Force fighter jets intimidating rebels. American forces were involved in actions on and around the African continent—including Liberia, Somalia, Sierra Leone, Kenya, Zaire and Angola—that received little attention in the press. Troops returned to Somalia for the kind of humanitarian mission that became so commonplace between 1989 and 1993 that it could probably be called the Powell Doctrine. The first of these, Operation Provide Comfort, was to assist the Iraqi Kurds following the Gulf War, beginning in March, 1991. While soldiers remained behind in northern Iraq, forces helped the people of Bangladesh when a devastating typhoon swept through that country in May. Some of the local people called the Marines who were dispatched "angels of the sea" and so the operation was named Sea Angel. A month later American GIs kept a Fiery Vigil as the Philippine volcano Mt. Pinatubo erupted and Subic Bay was evacuated. In what started out as an attempt to save Haitians who were fleeing their homeland in rickety boats, taking them to the American base at Guantanamo Bay on the island of Cuba became a controversial operation. In the winter of 1992 United States forces airlifted medical supplies and foodstuffs to the former Soviet Union. Other airlifts brought goods to the desperate people of Sarajevo and other parts of Bosnia. GIs were deployed at home after a hurricane ravaged Florida and served beside California National Guardsmen in Los Angeles when rioting, looting and violence overtook parts of that city after the police beating of motorist Rodney King.

In all, it was a time of great turmoil in the world and notable triumphs for both democracy and United States foreign policy. It is worth recounting the events. Barely a month after Powell became Chairman the Berlin Wall that separated East and West came down; Germans mingled freely once again. Before the year was out tyrannical President Ceausescu of Romania was overthrown and executed, and the first Bush-Gorbachev summit was held off the coast of Malta.

In January 1990 President George Bush proposed cuts in the numbers of U.S. and Soviet troops stationed in Europe. South African leader Nelson Mandela was freed in February. A month later Colin Powell would begin publicly talking about the Base Force concept describing a deliberate reduction of the Armed Forces. In the summer months, the East-West thaw would change forever the relationship of cold hostility that had dominated the world stage since the end of World War II. Following a winter and spring of reforms throughout the Eastern bloc, in June George Bush and his Soviet counterpart Mikhail Gorbachev met in Washington for a second summit. The same month the Russian Federation declared its sovereignty. In July Gorbachev agreed to a reunified Germany with membership in NATO. NATO declared that the Cold War had ended, and continuous twenty-four-hours-a-day, seven-days-a-week "Looking Glass" flights by Air Force command post aircraft were ended. On August 2, Saddam Hussein's forces invaded Kuwait; the build-up of forces for Operation Desert Shield began. In September Bush and Gorbachev met in

Helsinki for their third summit to discuss the Persian Gulf crisis; the U.S. announced its unilateral reduction of forces in Europe. In October General Powell welcomed the Soviet equivalent of the Chairman of the Joint Chiefs of Staff to the United States on the second of three such exchange visits. It was the first of Powell's chairmanship. A month later agreements were signed to cut forces and ballistic missiles in Europe and the Warsaw pact announced the dissolution of its military arm.

In January 1991 Operation Desert Shield became Desert Storm as the coalition of forces led by the United States began the air war that would wear down the Iraqis. At the same time Powell addressed congressional committees on the emerging and enduring realities of a new world order. New strategic concepts, the kinds of military forces needed to face the changing world, and the Base Force were discussed. In February the Gulf War turned from an air war to ground operations and in four days the U.S. evicted Iraq from Kuwait and reduced Saddam's military from the most powerful one in the region to a battered, mostly disarmed force. In April Georgia followed the example of Russia and became the second republic to declare its independence from the U.S.S.R., and the Warsaw Pact military arm was dissolved. Intermediate nuclear missiles were eliminated by the United States and the Soviet Union in May. A month later Boris Yeltsin became the first popularly elected leader of Russia, apartheid was repealed in South Africa and a unified Yugoslavia collapsed and civil war commenced.

In their fourth summit, held in Moscow in July, Bush and Gorbachev signed a treaty to reduce strategic nuclear weapons. During the same month Powell visited Moiseyev in the Soviet Union and in a further attempt to cut U.S. military costs and the size of the force, base closures were announced. A coup attempt by Soviet officials failed in August. Marshall Akhromeyev, a stalwart communist and World War II hero, with whom Powell had a friendly working relationship, committed suicide. Powell's counterpart and good friend, General Moiseyev, was exiled. Also during August eight more republics declared their independence and both the United States and the European Economic Community recognized the sovereignty of the three Baltic states of Latvia, Lithuania, and Estonia. A month later their independence would be recognized by the new Soviet State Council. France and Britain followed the lead of President Bush in announcing cuts in theater nuclear weapons in September and in October President Gorbachev announced his own nuclear reduction initiative and suspended nuclear weapons testing. By December the effects of the collapse of communism were driving events elsewhere. South Korea announced the withdrawal of American nuclear weapons from their soil. North Korea and South Korea signed a non-aggression pact and agreed to ban all nuclear weapons in Korea. In early December the Ukraine chose to withdraw from the Soviet Union. Before month's end Ukraine, Belarus, and Kazakhstan agreed to put all former Soviet nukes under Russian control, the Soviet Union was dissolved and replaced by a Commonwealth of Independent States (CIS) comprised of eleven republics, and Mikhail Gorbachev retired.

The dynamic, quickly-changing world warranted the publication in January 1992 of Powell's new National Military Strategy. At the same time a second Bush nuclear initiative was announced, cutting strategic nuclear forces. Bush and Yeltsin met at Camp David in February and a seventeen-day airlift took food and medicine to the CIS. By March, Slovenia, Croatia, Bosnia, and Herzegovena declared independence from Yugoslavia. In South Africa, whites voted to continue negotiations on ending white rule. Russia and other formerly Soviet republics joined the International Monetary Fund and the World Bank in April, a new Yugoslavia was formed by Serbia and Montenegro, and heavily armed Serbs attacked Bosnia in a raging civil war.

By June the United Nations voted sanctions against Yugoslavia, and a second Bush-Yeltsin summit was held in Washington yielding a number of new security agreements. In one of many rounds of sparring with the world, Saddam

Hussein still resisted United Nations attempts to inspect its military facilities but backed down after hassling inspectors in July. By October the U.N. established a no-fly zone over Bosnia but declined to enforce it. Conditions there worsened through the devastating winter and only began to see hope of relief by spring. In Russia, the winter meant long lines for meager foodstuffs, the rise of neo-Communist sentiment, and by spring Mr. Yeltsin faced his strongest opposition from the Soviet hold-over Congress of People's Deputies.

Colin Powell not only lived through some of the most exciting of modern times but participated in their shaping. Much of what happened, especially between East and West, Powell foresaw. Immediately upon assuming the job of Chairman he articulated a distinct philosophy to the members of his staff and also seems to have expected, at least in broad strokes, the major events on the horizon.

Air Force Colonel Dave Patterson, who served on Powell's staff, recalls Powell's visiting the NATO Defense College while he was a student. "With one exception every speaker of any merit, and these were often European Chiefs of Defense, said the following words in their first or second paragraphs: 'First, we live in interesting times. Second, who would have guessed two years ago that we would see the collapse of the Soviet Union and the disarray of Eastern bloc nations? And three, I don't have a crystal ball on the future.' General Powell said three things when he spoke to us, too. He said, 'You will hear people say we live in fascinating times. You will hear them say that life is moving so quickly that there is no way to predict the future. And you will hear them say, 'Who would have predicted the present circumstances?'" And his next words were, 'Let me tell you, I would have predicted this. I would have told you that the changing times are going to bring about such turbulence in Eastern bloc nations as to make them unsustainable. I would have told you that we are going to live in a time now that the complexion of the American forces are going to be drastically different from how you have seen it in the past or even hoped to have seen it in the past.' He also said, 'I will tell you that in 1995 we will see a military force that is far, far smaller than you see it today, perhaps as much as one-third less.' He was making the point that there were signals around if you were willing and astute enough to see them. The students from all these NATO nations agreed that Powell was the most persuasive and impressive. And this parallels very closely his position amongst the other CHODs [the top military officers in each of the NATO countries]."

Within the first two weeks as Chairman, in October 1989, Powell gathered his staff to lay out his worldview. Among his key points were that a future lay ahead in which the military could be diminished by one-third, that they could expect to see a requirement to have possibly as few as two divisions in Europe, that forces would be drastically reduced in Korea because there would be little or no requirement for us to be there, that American nuclear capability would be essentially removed from Europe, and that the focus of U.S. efforts in the world would become very, very regional with well-tailored packages of forces.

As elsewhere in his career, Powell garnered great support from those assigned to him. Staff members report having been made to feel that whatever they were doing was important to the general, even tasks as mundane as typing letters of regret in response to the thousands of invitations Powell declined. Once again, Colonel Patterson: "He made it matter that you personally were doing that certain job." But Powell is not effusive with praise. Verbal affirmation came in small phrases, usually reserved for big occasions such as ceremonies, or through short notes with "Yes!" or "Good!" written on them. No one, however, despite what was a busy time and an enormous workload seems to have been disgruntled, disillusioned, or disappointed with the boss's usually silent appreciation.

John Primm tells a story of Powell's understated affirmation involving this book's author. Upon joining Powell's small team, I recognized that something had to be done about the number of invitations he received to visit schools and speak to young people. He was a natural role model but had to decline all but a very few of the opportunities. My proposal was to produce a role-model video called "General Powell Talks to Young People." Its message would be simple: Stay in school, don't take drugs, work hard, have a vision for life and stick to it.

Since there was nothing in the defense budget for a production of this sort, I begged permission to use pieces of video that others had taken of Powell, including two speeches he gave at high schools, his own alma mater in the Bronx and Dunbar Vocational High School in Chicago. The finished product was seen by tens of thousands of teenagers. Primm recalls, "We put together the video. We promised [special assistant] Bill Smullen that we would be finished but were making changes up to the very last moment. Bill said, 'Guys don't embarrass me'—he had not seen the final cut on the video. It was 6:00 P.M., and we went into the general's office. We put the tape in his machine. He just sat there with his hand on his chin staring at the screen, not moving, not saying a word. Bill stood there looking for hints of reaction. Somewhere about two or three minutes into it, Powell quietly went, 'Uh, huh. That's really funny.' And then I got the feeling he really, sort-of, liked the vid. He moved from really intense concentration to just a wisp of a smile. He never really smiled. When he got through the whole thing he shifted in his chair and smiled. I was beginning to stop sweating at that point, thinking that we might have done okay. Then Powell said to the two of us without too much excitement, 'Damned fine job. You guys did a good job, a really fine job. I guess I can get the President off my back now.' We thanked him and left."

This was the first project either Primm or I did for Powell. Little did we understand that Powell was particularly proud of his "Kidvid" as he called it. The next day Smullen let me know that some of Powell's closest aides, while never feeling unappreciated, have never once as much as overheard a three-fold declaration of approval. Powell left the office that afternoon for the White House and gave President Bush the tape. Apparently Bush had been encouraging Powell to do something more to reach kids, and particularly minorities and the poor in the inner cities, with a message of hope.

He had visited schools more often when he was at the White House. It was shortly after his nomination to succeed Carlucci at the NSC that he also became involved in the work of a private homeless shelter in southeast Washington, an area where drugs and tourists never dare venture. Powell was invited to speak to the ladies' auxiliary of the oldest black American Legion Post in the nation's capital. Its president was the Reverend Imagene B. Stewart, herself once an uneducated young woman living on the streets. But Stewart, determined to make something of her life, got menial jobs, worked hard, and eventually went to college. She never forgot where she came from and decided to found the shelter known as the House of Imagene. Powell braved a record-breaking Veteran's Day 1987 snow storm and Washington traffic to deliver an emotional luncheon speech. Once there, Stewart nabbed him. Powell has been a friend of Stewart and a supporter of her shelter ever since.

The House of Imagene is an intentionally modest project that seeks no government money. It is the only shelter in Washington that takes families in and keeps them together; others segregate men from their women and children. "I get them out looking for work," Stewart stresses, remembering the way she escaped from a life on the streets. Powell understates the support he has given the shelter over the years. In 1992 he raised money to buy turkeys for the Thanksgiving Open House that feeds hundreds in the neighborhood. He has been delivering his own care packages from the trunk of his car quietly for years. One day Chairman Powell sent a memo to those on the Joint Staff at the Pentagon. He was conducting a clothing drive for Imagene. The memo conveyed the specific wishes of the Reverend Stewart: "Don't send me down here no worn work clothes for these folks. I want suits for them to go to work in," Powell recalls being told. Staff members dug into their closets, and Powell delivered business suits, nice dresses, trousers, and coats and ties to the shelter. At a Martin Luther King Day celebration in Washington, Powell spoke, and Stewart was honored. Powell leaned over to Stewart and whispered in her ear: "Imagene, just keep on keepin' on. God loves you, and so do I."

As in the past, Powell liked to lie low despite his highly visible position. He is essentially a very private man and although being Chairman meant a life in the limelight around Washington, frequent social occasions both as a host and as a guest, press briefings and interviews—all essential parts of the job—his inclination was to keep whatever privacy he could. For the more than three years when Dick Cheney was defense secretary, except in times of great crisis, Powell kept to the Carlucci tradition of not coming into the office on weekends. This worked until Clinton's man Les Aspin, who does not know the meaning of the word *weekend*, made it more difficult. Even then, whenever work absolutely needed to be done and could be carried home in a briefcase, it went home to Quarters 6. He and Alma enjoyed the designated Chairman's house on Fort Myer's Grant Avenue, perched atop a hill with a spectacular view of Washington's monuments. The first floor was largely for entertaining. The upper floors made for a roomy, comfortable private home. Each Friday afternoon, Otis Pearson, the general's driver made sure there were two movies on videotape for the Powells to watch over the weekend. As long as there were not too many interruptions, Powell had a good weekend routine worked out.

He and Otis Pearson looked forward to Saturday mornings because they worked on cars together. The two of them go back to the days of Powell's assignment as V Corps commander in Germany. Pearson, who is an Army sergeant first class trained to be an artilleryman, began driving in 1979. His first such job was as the driver to the highest ranking enlisted man at Fort Benning, the post command sergeant major. Ten years later he was driving for the top GI in the country and was a friend, even like a second son, to him.

On Saturdays Pearson arrived at Quarters 6 well before nine o'clock. Often Powell would already be out in the garage behind the house working on one of his old Volvos. Powell became Chairman and bought his wife a new Mazda. For more than twenty years the Powells had driven used cars. In Atlanta it was a source of startled amusement when, in April 1989, the Forces Command's new four-star general drove the four blocks to work each morning in a beat-up, old 1973 Chrysler station wagon that showed every one of its 150,000 miles. It was the family car, and Powell kept it running. But Powell's real affection was for Volvos. His first Volvo, named Vince, a white 1977 240 model, got him hooked. It became the car that each of the Powell children would use while attending William and Mary College. Its odometer has been stuck at 77,000 miles ever since Powell bought it, but Annemarie Powell still drives it today. Pearson estimates it has been driven more than 200,000 miles.

What started out as taking care of one Volvo turned into something more like a combination hobby and used car business. Over four years in Washington Powell and Pearson bought more than twenty-five and resold more than fourteen Volvos, often salvaging parts from one to fix another. At one point in late 1992, the two men were working on 1953, 1956, 1966, 1967, 1977, and 1979 model year cars. What sounds like an expensive hobby has actually been a modest one. "We look for things, we scrounge," Pearson admits. Most of the cars they have worked on cost little or nothing. "My family says I am a cheapskate," Powell confesses. With so many cars, and a collection of used parts, it was necessary to find places for all the Volvos. Otis would regularly move the cars around from one parking spot to another on Fort Myer. "The general is not gonna rent space," Pearson says quite matter-of-factly.

Recently people who have heard that Powell fixes up Volvos have called and written to offer him their cars. But even before owners sought him out because of his renown, he and Otis would leave notes on the windshields of cars seen on the side of the road, a practice Pearson continues today. The two men are well known at local Volvo dealerships and at used parts stores. Before the Gulf War brought him so much attention Powell himself used to walk in regularly, grease up to his elbows, asking if they could help him find a particular part.

Powell's personal favorite and the car he takes the most pride in is a black 1953 Volvo 444. He received a letter from a family in South Carolina offering him the car so Otis called to find out more. The next day, a Saturday, while Powell was out of Washington on business, Pearson drove from Washington to see the forty year-old car. Its friendly owners lived in a beautiful wooded spot and invited Otis to go fishing. He declined but had lunch and saw the car which, while beautiful, could not be driven. When Powell returned to Washington he asked Otis about the car. "It's nice," Otis told him. "How much do they want?" Powell inquired. "Three thousand dollars," said Pearson. "Whew!" Powell responded. But its owners liked Otis and wanted Powell to have the car, so they wrote him a letter. Pearson and Powell decided they needed to figure out how to move it. Otis took his truck, borrowed a car trailer, drove to South Carolina where he spent the night, loaded the Volvo onto the trailer and drove back to Fort Myer. The owners took one thousand dollars for the car. Powell and Pearson have restored it. Unlike many of their cars that were sold to friends or listed on the Pentagon message board, Powell intends to keep this one.

One of the cars they sold was not a Volvo but a Honda that had been owned and driven by Michael Powell. Since his near-death jeep accident in Germany, Mike found riding in a compact car less than comfortable. At a social occasion one evening Colin Powell was talking with Judge William Webster, former FBI director, and the subject of Powell's weekend avocation came up. Webster had been driving a Chrysler New Yorker but had nothing but problems with it. Powell invited him to bring it by for a look-over. Webster and his wife dropped the car off at Quarters 6 one Saturday, but while Powell was looking it over the couple went scouting new cars and decided to buy one. On returning to Fort Myer they told Powell that if he wanted it, he could keep the New Yorker. He bought it, then gave the comfortable luxury car to his son and sold the little Honda.

On a typical Saturday at Fort Myer, Powell and Pearson spent the morning in the garage, with the radio playing one of Washington's light rock or easy listening stations. On occasion Powell, who gave up smoking cigarettes years ago, would puff on a cigar. They would work until it was time to take a break for lunchtime. Most often Alma would call them into the kitchen for a quick cold-cut sandwich, some soup and a Diet Coke. Both men preferred to get cheeseburgers. Otis would run over to the PX or, even better, to Burger King. After lunch Powell's routine took him to the barber shop for a weekly trim, and Pearson would find his way home and to the racquetball court. Before the afternoon ended, Pearson usually stopped by the garage where the general was typically working once again on one of the cars. Many Sundays were spent back in the garage.

Without qualification each of the Powells acknowledges that Otis, who has no immediate relatives at home in what he calls "L.A.," short for "lower Alabama," has become a part of their family. Alma Powell says simply and proudly, "He's family." When Pearson was released from the hospital following surgery for a racquetball injury the Powells would not let him go home to rest in bed and hobble around alone. They put him in their spare bedroom at Quarters 6, and Alma and Anne waited on him. The thirty-five year-old bachelor says, "Yeah, they took me in. I feel I'm very lucky. I know I am." Pearson is a humble, self-effacing man who does not presume upon the relationship. The family draws him in, but he confesses, "Sometimes I just try to get out of the way." Are he and "the general" or "the boss," as he refers to Powell, business partners? "I just like playing with cars, but he takes care of me." Pearson echoes another member of Powell's personal staff told on the first day he came to work never to as much as buy a stamp for the general without getting the money from him first. "He won't let me spend a dime or waste a penny on something that he's been doing. I'm there to help," says Otis Pearson. Pearson wouldn't think of leaving Powell to work in the garage alone at his singular form of relaxation. Besides, Otis adds, "I like to see him happy."

Washington has become home for the Powell family. With the exception of Linda who is pursuing a career in acting in New York the whole family has chosen to stay in the nation's capital. The youngest of the Powell children attributes the family's strength to their naturally simply liking one another and choosing the company of family first and foremost. When she finished college in 1992, Annemarie moved back with her parents and got a job at the CNN bureau in Washington where she works for the news-discussion program, *Larry King Live*. Following his accident in Germany, Michael Powell came home to continue recuperating in his parents' house. When he and Jane Knott were married, they moved to nearby Alexandria, Virginia, close enough for son Jeffrey to grow up with his grandparents. "We couldn't move away from here. Jeffrey's grandparents would never allow him to be far away from them," Mike Powell insists.

There was some concern when Linda Powell decided that she wanted to leave the nest. She had decided that her secret junior-high school desire was something she would act on—she wanted to be an actress. On the occasion of a Powell family visit to Norm and Marilyn Berns' home in California, Linda and her father were alone, sitting in the living room when Powell raised the subject of what she might want to do when she got out of college. "My heart started racing because I knew that this was the chance to say it. And I said, 'No, I don't know what I want to do yet.'" Linda got up to get a Coke in the kitchen, her heart still racing. Ten minutes later she returned to the living room and told him the truth. He said, "Oh, [pause] I don't know how you do that. How do you go about that?" And I said, "I don't really know, either," Linda recalls. She continued, "I think I am going to need some training."

Powell replied, "I saw a cousin of yours yesterday who is an engineer. I asked her how she liked it. She didn't seem to be at all excited about being an engineer. I think you should do what's going to make you happy."

Alma Powell observes, "I felt she had the right to go and do whatever she wanted to do. It was not exactly what I wanted for her. I would rather she had selected something safe, something that you could be proud of and say, 'Oh, my daughter the anesthesiologist, my daughter the program planner, or whatever.' But a long time ago Linda played a record for me and it said, 'Your children are not your children, you only have them for a little while, don't expect them to duplicate what it is you have the idea of, they're individuals.' And so, I always try to keep that in mind. She certainly had every right in the world to go do it and deserved the chance to try becoming an actress. I admired her for her independence in striking out to do it. Her dad was not happy about it. No, you know him, a very realistic person, if that's the word for it. But he's come to terms with it."

There was not a great deal of discussion about Linda's decision. Alma Powell reflects, "We don't sit down and have long talks. We don't do that. Somehow you get the message across in a few sentences. What she said to him when she finished college was, 'You would send me to graduate school. Will you send me to acting school? That's what I want.' And he said, 'Yes.' Even though that was not what he wanted."

Family members observe that Linda is temperamentally most like her father, while Anne is the epitome of her mother. "We're both focused. We both like to be alone," Linda says. Mike Powell asserts that Linda's leaving home resembles their father's striking out from New York as a young man to do something that his parents could never have imagined—to become a soldier.

Linda confesses that Army life was not easy. "When

someone is as dedicated to his work as my father is, the family is bound to sacrifice. He worked very long hours and there were times when we were without him either because he was away or because he was so focused on other things. And our lives revolved around his career," she says. "I adored him. I still do. But I missed knowing him. I missed having him for a friend. That's starting to change—since I've gotten older and less in awe of him. Since Jeffrey was born. And I think since there is a sense now of change coming, of a cycle of our life coming to a close as we leave the Army. Because that's really what it is. It's not just him retiring. It's all of us retiring from his commitment to the Army."

She will miss the rituals she grew up with. "The fun parts are the ceremonies and waking up and hearing the guys doing their chants as they run past your house in the morning. There is the bad part of the ceremonies: meeting and greeting and having to shake everyone's hands. Everywhere you go you represent your father. In Army families everybody is in the Army. Your father gives his life to his country and so everybody in the family is sort of serving the country. It makes you very patriotic. I think I am very patriotic."

Like their parents, the Powell children seem to have mastered diplomacy. They have learned how to fit in in many different social settings and can readily switch cultural codes when necessary. "We learned how to relate to our Jamaican relatives and also our black relatives in Birmingham. Then when we got back to wherever we were living we were usually the only black family. As we moved up in the ranks we started to interact with a lot of different classes of people. We would go to the house of people who were really rich, which was not us, but they treated us as though we were the same," Linda says. But she likes living in New York because there are all types of people, and there she lives outside her father's shadow and can make a life for herself. Nonetheless, she chooses to return home to visit her parents and siblings at least once or twice a month.

In the aftermath of the Gulf War General Powell decided that there was a need for a military manual that talked in very simple terms about how the services should and could fight wars. The result was not your run-of-the-mill, everyday government publication with its annexes and appendices and charts. Instead Joint Publication #1, which was distributed more widely than any other manual ever bore a distinctive Powell touch. Its language was that of teamwork, its principles are moral ones and its model seems to be the family. "It isn't anything more than common sense," Powell says. Powell says it was written for those who dismiss the moral attributes of warfighting, that it is an attempt to capture the lessons of America's experience in Panama and the Gulf. The bedrock of warfare, he says, is "trusting people, working as a team, being a family." On the inside cover is a quote from General Dwight D. Eisenhower. It begins, "War is taking any problem exactly as you take a problem of your own life, stripping it down to its essentials, determining for yourself what is important and what you can emphasize to the advantage of your side." This leads to making a plan and then giving your all and fighting not to be distracted. Often in the past, services have fought amongst themselves. But, Eisenhower continues, "we have got to be of one family, and it is more important today than it ever has been."

The slim book focuses on values: integrity, competence, physical and moral courage that includes taking risks and tenacity, and teamwork built on trust and mutual confidence, delegation, cooperation, and cohesion. The book has illustrations, is full of stories, and there are pictures. Powell played a role in choosing the photos. His favorite was taken in the spring of 1944 and portrays Ike, along with the British general Sir Bernard Montgomery, inspecting troops in the field. On Eisenhower's face is the visible burden of command and yet his eyes are focused with personal concern for the troops under his command.

Whether it is his own children, now grown, the youth of America, or the troops in America's armed forces,

Powell's convictions about life remain. Powell put his signature to a message inside Joint Pub #1 that betrays his personal philosophy:

> When a team takes to the field, individual specialists come together to achieve a team win. All players try to do their very best because every other player, the team, and the home town are counting on them to win. So it is when the Armed Forces of the United States go to war. We must win every time. Every soldier must take the battlefield believing his or her unit is the best in the world. Every pilot must take off believing there is no one better in the sky. Every sailor standing watch must believe there is no better ship at sea. Every Marine must hit the beach believing that there are no better infantrymen in the world. But they must also believe that they are part of a team, a joint team, that fights together to win. This is our history, this is our tradition, this is our future.

This is the conviction of the man whom George Bush called the "complete soldier" when he chose Colin Powell to be Chairman of the Joint Chiefs of Staff. And it was a guiding factor in how the greatest crisis of Powell's chairmanship was conducted—the Gulf War.

chapter eleven

DESERT SHIELD,
DESERT STORM

CERTAIN MOMENTS in history are pivotal, or have the potential to be so. The Cold War was over. In a warming world climate of cooperation, the Gulf War established a new role for the international community of nations in the U.N. Both leading up to it and in its execution, the Persian Gulf War showcased the military strength that America had developed through the Reagan and Bush years.

The guiding strength was found in the people, civilian and military, who planned and conducted the war. In what is almost certain to be the legacy of his career in uniform, the Gulf War persuasively demonstrated Colin Powell's diverse talents.

Desert Storm was one of the greatest military victories of all time *and* it was a military campaign waged with an eye on political outcomes. Powell's focus on the application of political and military power to achieve national goals stems from a deep and sincere patriotism harnessed to an intellect excited by historical complexity and nuance, especially in the military sphere. In the end, to use Richard Armitage's words, "Powell fixes things."

Historian and journalist Austin Bay describes Colin

Powell as "a military man who understands the political context of war as well as the intricate operational details of modern combat. During Desert Shield and Desert Storm, Powell was the perfect politically savvy warrior. As Chairman of the JCS, he understood his role was to provide General Schwarzkopf and the field forces the opportunity to achieve a decisive, overwhelming military victory within the exacting political circumstances of the coalition, within the framework of the various United Nations resolutions, and within the context of American democratic institutions."

In January 1993, a young future officer at the Naval Academy in Annapolis asked Powell about his role in the Gulf War as a "go-between between the politicians and General Schwarzkopf."

"Without fear of being a little immodest, I was slightly more than a go-between," Powell responded; then he laughed in his distinctive, wheezy way. His audience joined him in laughter. "But your characterization is not bad," he added.

A clarity of purpose and focused objectives are vital to conducting successful military operations. Powell brings a broad scope of vision to what led up to the Persian Gulf War and what led Saddam Hussein to attack Kuwait. Powell came to the chairman's responsibilities with the uncommon experience of years of direct experience in the geopolitics of our age. As both deputy and as national security advisor in the Reagan White House he was involved not only with world issues but also the processes used to address them. Powell did not merely look upon the unfolding circumstances with an eye to war and how to conduct it; he brought to discussions in the Bush White House a keen sense of the larger picture and how to effectively work within the framework of national security decision-making.

Explaining the unfolding events and his role in them, Powell told the Chicago Council on Foreign Relations in November 1992, "My responsibility [as Chairman] is to lay out to my political leaders the full range of military options, to let them know what we can do, to let them know how we can solve a political problem, to let them know where I do not believe military force will solve a political problem, and to make them understand all of the consequences of the use of military force.

"The President of the United States, the Commander-in-Chief, has no more important responsibility than the commitment of the lives of young men and women to combat and possible death. My responsibility is to lay it all out—the good, the bad—so that the President can make an informed choice. . . .

"At the end of the day, when the President had all of the options laid out to him and asked, when it was time to make a choice [about conducting war against Iraq], we said, 'Yes, Mr. President, let us know what you want to do. You have got all the information you need to make a decision.' He then made his decision, having put the right amount of force in place. And we did it in a way that was decisive, that was perfectly matched to the political objectives, and that was absolutely successful in accomplishing the objectives laid out for us."

From a perspective more than two years removed, it is now cachet in certain circles to "blame the war" on George Bush. This kind of instant revisionism is regrettable and bodes ill for building better international structures for peace-making and peace-creating. If anything, the Persian Gulf War established a historic precedent for combined political, economic, and military international cooperation. Colin Powell, as a member of the Bush Administration and senior military officer of the most powerful member of the coalition, played a central role in establishing that precedent.

American participation in what became Iraq's fateful exploitation of its southern neighbor began with the muddling comments of U.S. Ambassador to Iraq, April Glaspie, just prior to Saddam's invasion. It seems she told the Iraqi president that in the American view we "can never excuse settlement of disputes by any but peaceful means." The State Department acknowledges that she told Saddam that the U.S. has "no opinion on the Arab-Arab conflicts, like your border disagreement with Kuwait," as if political and economic issues in the region are mere parochialism.

Glaspie's was actually a no-win situation. Bellicose language from her would have been played by Saddam as interventionist threats from the Bush Administration. Saddam could have attacked and said he was doing so because he was provoked by threats from the United States. A chorus of liberal members of the press in the West would have touted such tough talk by a Bush administration official as American warmongering.

Any unprejudiced analysis of the last few weeks before the invasion must acknowledge that Saddam Hussein is one of the twentieth century's grandest miscalculators. He thought he could invade Iran and take its oil province of Khuzistan. The unprovoked invasion brought his nation bitter suffering. He thought he could build a nuclear reactor (Osirak I) for purposes of making a nuclear weapon and that Israel would not react. They bombed. Saddam did not look or listen before he leaped.

Colin Powell suggests looking at the crisis through a much larger lens than the month of July 1990, and the last-minute discussions between a dictator with an army massing on a weak neighbor's border and an American ambassador's attempting to strike some mediating chord. One has to consider Iraq's long-term objectives in the Persian Gulf and the self-created predicament Saddam Hussein found himself in after the end of the Iran-Iraq War. That war left Iraq with the world's fourth-largest army, a well-equipped and experienced armed force rivaled in the region only by Israel and Turkey. It also left Iraq with huge monetary debts, much of the amount being owed to Arab states in the Gulf littoral.

In early 1990 the Cold War was also ending, with the Soviet Union rapidly pulling away from regional conflicts. James Dunnigan and Austin Bay, in *From Shield to Storm*, note that: "From a strategic perspective, Saddam saw Russia declining, thus the growing 'preponderance' of Israeli power as linked to the increasing U.S. power to intervene in the Gulf. If Iraq stagnated, if an Arab power did not fill the vacuum created by Soviet political and military retreat, then a great opportunity would be lost. Yet in 1990, both Israel's and Turkey's regional 'freedom of action,' Saddam believed, were limited by domestic and international politics."

Saddam had as much given away the game in his now famous speech of February 24, 1990, in Amman, Jordan, and his equally noted interview with *The Wall Street Journal* on June 28, 1990, where he threatened "to burn half of Israel." In the most crucial line in Saddam's February 1990 speech, the Iraqi dictator told the audience, which included Egypt's Hosni Mubarak as well as Jordan's King Hussein, that "The big does not become big nor does the great earn such a description unless he is in the arena of comparison or fighting with someone else on a different level." Dunnigan and Bay translate this as meaning "If a minor-leaguer wants to move up, he has to take on the majors."

In the summer of 1990 Iraq faced extraordinary economic, and political pressures. In 1961 Iraq, well before Saddam Hussein came to power, threatened to invade Kuwait. For years Iraq's claims to Kuwait as a nineteenth province, though spurious history, were trumpeted to the Iraqi people. There were long-term preparations on the part of Iraq. They established bunker systems in the south and forward supply depots. These weren't hidden. Given the scale of military operation undertaken, based on the size of the forces and the commitment of the Republican Guard, it is fair to estimate that the invasion of Kuwait was at least a year in the making.

Powell argues that it is always a soldier's duty to prepare for war. Scipio Africanus, the Roman general who defeated Hannibal, said: "If you want peace, prepare for war." Our own wargaming and analysis of the situation had prepared us for just such an attack. Schwarzkopf and Central Command played out a contingency game in July. Other preparations were also made. The U.S. had the ready reaction forces of Schwarzkopf's U.S. Central Command (CENTCOM), and forward-deployed naval elements as well as pre-positioned supply ships at the U.S. Navy base on the British Trust Territory of Diego Garcia in the Indian Ocean. U.S., British, and occasionally French naval forces were always present in the Persian Gulf. There were also continuing exercises with friendly nations in the region. The so-called "tanker war," where the U.S. intervened to convoy Kuwaiti oil tankers which were then under attack by Iran, stood as a precedent for U.S.-Kuwaiti cooperation.

Yet when the Iraqi forces actually launched their attack on 2 August 1990 the world seemed transfixed. But the glue that would bind the allied coalition and see it from despair to triumph was already beginning to harden. In retrospect the great achievement of the Bush Administration, in those first three or four days, was getting the Saudis and the Security Council to admit that a consensus existed. What was lost in the alarm of August 2, 1990, and what Saddam himself failed to see, was the extent of common interest on a planet increasingly linked by communications and economic interests. Between August 2 and August 5, this emerged as a fact solid enough to form what in the past would have been thought an impossible coalition. But deep mutual, economic, and military interests sealed the coalition. Increased Russian cooperation with Western Europe and the United States laid the groundwork for dialogue and decision in the U.N. Security Council.

The initial build-up phase of Operation Desert Shield was one of the most delicate politically and most dangerous militarily. From the U.S. the 82nd Airborne Division and several Special Forces units were dispatched, linking up with Marine Expeditionary Units in or near the Persian Gulf. An initial concern was firepower on the road from Kuwait City to Dhahran. How could a possible Iraqi armored thrust down the coast be stopped?

The weight of military action fell on CENTCOM and its commander, General H. Norman Schwarzkopf. A feisty bear of a man and an intellectual, Schwarzkopf epitomized the rugged field commander, somewhat in contrast to Powell's demeanor of efficiency, smoothness, and cool-headedness. The combination of personalities and personal skills gave the Goldwater-Nichols Defense Reorganization Act of 1986 its perfect test. It was a success. Powell described at length how it worked when he spoke at the Naval Academy: "The beauty of the system was that, as principal military advisor to the President, Vice-President, Secretary of State and Secretary of Defense, the Chairman provides advice in his own right. I consult widely with the [individual Service] Chiefs and I always know what the Chiefs are thinking. But in the final analysis, I provide advice in my own right. So we don't vote on anything. Voting went away after the Goldwater-Nichols law was passed. But I always know what the Chiefs are thinking.

"And so there was a single point of contact out of the Pentagon, and it was the Chairman to the Secretary to the President. And so whenever recommendations were presented to the President and to the Secretary they were coming from one person, the Chairman, representing the interests of all the services and General Schwarzkopf. General Schwarzkopf took no instructions or guidance from anyone else. And everybody in theater worked for General Schwarzkopf. We didn't care what [service's] suit you were wearing. Once you crossed that line you belonged to Norm and you did what Norm said to do. And if you've got a problem with that then go to Powell. But otherwise you do what Norm says. We had very few problems. I mean, who wants to screw with Norm?"

Powell provides his own analysis of its success. "It worked! It worked exceptionally well."

Powell explains how it worked. "The system we had for managing the war was one where the President would assemble his advisors and the Chairman was always included. On occasion, Chiefs went. And on some occasions individual Chiefs went to see the President because the President wanted to know about particular issues. But we were always there. And we—the Chairman representing 'we'—were included at the very earliest stages, so that our military advice was shaping political judgments from the very beginning. And as we went through it, we were able to constantly bring the political decisions back to what we could do militarily. And if there's one story that is going to be written out of Desert Storm and Just Cause and everything else we've done, it's how political objectives must be carefully matched to military objectives and military means and what is achievable."

Some observers suggested that Powell was sometimes on the outside of a civilian-led, political force that drove the Gulf War. But Powell describes a pyramid-shaped chain-of-command with the President at the top and how it operated with success in the Gulf War. "In terms of President Bush and Secretary Cheney, I think it was absolutely perfect. The President never took exception to anything I said. I was free to say anything I wanted. I was never constrained. I was never seen as the spoiler or somebody who was going in a different direction. President Bush wanted to hear all views and our job in the military was to make sure he heard all views, and we examined every option, he looked at every alternative. . . .

"The President was so good about this, in terms of following the chain of command, giving us guidance, knowing what we were going to do, and then letting us do it, he was so good about it that he never would call General Schwarzkopf, for example, except to say, "Well done," or a Christmas greeting of some kind. But otherwise he would not call General Schwarzkopf. Mr. Cheney only called General Schwarzkopf from the Pentagon once or twice, and only after we had talked about it and he let me know he was going to do it, for one particular reason or another. The chain of command was always preserved. If they wanted something from Schwarzkopf, I would get it."

Powell tells a story to illustrate his point. "One morning at about five o'clock I was in my office. It was that kind of period. And my hotline rang. There were a bunch of hotlines and there's one button on my bunch of hotlines that rings differently from all other buttons. And it rang. It almost never rings. And so I looked around and saw that it was the President's button. So I picked it up, 'Good morning, Mr. President.' And he said, 'Colin, I [pause] got up early.' This was during the war. He said, 'I' and he was a little hesitant in his comments. He was sort of searching for what to say. And he said, 'I really want to get an update on what is going on and I haven't heard from the Sit[uation] Room yet. And could you tell me what's going on?' And then he said, 'I know I'm supposed to talk to Dick Cheney first, but Dick isn't in yet. And I really want to know.' I said, 'Mr. President, you can call me anytime you want. I'll tell you anything you want to know because I know where you are in the pyramid.' But the point is that the President, having put this system in place, was religious in protecting that system, to include the White House and himself, so that he would talk to Secretary Cheney, and I would only talk to the President when we were all together in a meeting."

A similar modus operandi was used when American forces went into Panama. Powell recalls that "the night of that operation we were all in the Command Center, myself, [Lieutenant General] Tom Kelly . . . and Secretary Cheney was there with us, beginning at about eleven o'clock at night. And we stayed all night long. And Secretary Cheney knew where every single squad was going. He knew everything about the plan. But he sat there all night long and never asked me about anything or offered a suggestion about something or wanted to talk to General Thurman down in Panama. And once every hour he would go into another room and he would call the President and tell him what was going on, and then come back. But I never talked to the President. The President never talked to me. The President never talked to Panama. It was that system that, I think, helped make the operation in Desert Storm so successful." Powell says he tells these stories to illustrate what a "great, great military Commander-in-Chief President George Bush was, and what a superb Secretary of Defense in wartime we've had in Dick Cheney."

As in Operation Just Cause in Panama, Powell's advice and strategy throughout the Desert Shield build-up phase was clear and relatively uncomplicated: if we choose an offensive option we must have decisive force or risk terrible consequences. This stance on Powell's part greatly influenced what became a group decision. It occurred sometime in mid to late October of 1990: the decision to place in the combat theater overwhelming military forces.

Powell himself has said very simply, "There wasn't a single decision, but a gradual increase in forces based on the expanding presence of Iraqi troops." In the end, a half-million troops were deployed. They included the equivalent of more than six armored divisions and a variety of other "lighter" forces.

Such overwhelming force not only put military capability in the combat theater—it also made a political statement that Powell hoped might even convince Saddam to pull back. November through January, however, in military terms, was a difficult interregnum. Many U.S. heavy mechanized and armored units had to be shifted from the continental U.S. and Europe. This would not have been possible without the end of the Cold War.

In Colin Powell's mind this period calls into question future conflicts. Will there even be sufficient forces for future contingencies? This was the fundamental rationale behind his Base Force concept and his protestations before Congress that the world remains an unstable place where contingencies must be met and the U.S. as its sole superpower is faced with enormous global responsibilities. Cut forces? Yes. Emasculate them? Not on my watch.

Making it from October to January was a grind. Howard Means and Bob Woodward both make much of the personal disputations between Powell and Schwarzkopf. Yet Powell continues to refer to Schwarzkopf as "my friend Norm." Mere forgive and forget? A smokescreen perhaps? Not quite. It seems that, in search of controversy or sensationalism, Means and Woodward fail to appreciate the professional level of Powell's and Schwarzkopf's relationship and their commitment to achieving victory. An army is a rough place for anyone who wears his feelings on his sleeve. Long hours and crises take their toll. Soldiers learn to anticipate personal friction as part of warfare. You pick up and move on. For the press it's fodder for sensationalism, for the soldier it's an obstacle that's usually a lot less deadly than a minefield.

Although Powell is not usually too bothered by the media, it is also true that he is not completely happy with Schwarzkopf. His displeasure has very little to do with his fellow general's colorful style. And it is not a matter of envy. Rather, those closest to Powell say that Stormin' Norman's book, *It Doesn't Take a Hero*, portrays certain events in the Gulf War inaccurately. Powell feels betrayed by factual untruths and what he feels are unfair characterizations of him by his fellow soldier. When asked to identify specific instances, Powell graciously declines to discuss the matter. One problem seems to be the way in which Schwarzkopf pays Powell a compliment and then criticizes him as either weak or political or a puppet of the civilian leadership. For example: "Officially, as a Commander-in-Chief I reported to Secretary Cheney, but Colin Powell was virtually my sole point of contact with the Administration.

"It's my job to keep the President and the White House and the Secretary of Defense informed,' Powell would say. 'You worry about your theater and let me worry about Washington.' This arrangement was efficient: I'd tell Powell we needed something done in Washington, and he'd make sure it happened. And there is no doubt in my mind that General Powell was the best man for the job during this crisis. Not since General George Marshall during World War II had a military officer enjoyed such direct access to White House inner circles—not to mention the confidence of the President. Powell could get decisions in hours that would have taken another man days or weeks. But I also found the arrangement unnerving at times, because it kept me in the dark. Often, after White House meetings, Powell would call with questions that made me wonder whether our civilian superiors had grasped military realities." Schwarzkopf implies that Powell was giving in to administration officials' expectations that Schwarzkopf develop a ground-offensive plan without having enough troops and weapons to be successful.

Schwarzkopf recounts a story in which he took out his frustration on the Army's Chief of Staff, General Carl Vuono. "Dammit, Carl, you guys on the Joint Chiefs are supposed to be the President's principal advisors on warfare. Why am I being required to send back an offensive plan I don't believe in? These are our Army troops we're talking about! You, the Chief of Staff of the Army, ought to be telling the President we're in no position to go on the offense unless we have more forces." Powell, as Chairman and the principal military advisor to the President, sees such an appeal to Vuono as Schwarzkopf's failure to trust his own dedication to the troops committed to the Gulf.

On another occasion Schwarzkopf suggests that Powell had to come around to the view that there would be more than a halfhearted commitment to war effort. Concerning events on October 22, 1990, he writes, "Though Powell had focused on supplying additional forces, he hadn't said what I most wanted to hear: that we could scrap the high-risk, go-with-what-you've-got offensive plan. That meant he hadn't yet crossed it off the list of possibilities, and I wasn't surprised the following morning when he asked to be briefed again on that option." Schwarzkopf recalls dismissing members of his staff from the room and appealing to Powell for more forces. Powell reportedly said that a mandate from the Congress and the American people was needed to bring more troops to the Gulf. Schwarzkopf continues: "Nobody wanted another Vietnam, and I understood Powell's determination to avoid political as well as military mistakes. Unless we were confident of public support, it would be better not to launch an offensive at all. In the course of that conversation, he made up his mind. 'If we go to war,' he promised, 'we will not do it halfway. The United States military will give you whatever you need to do it right.' He'd finally crossed the bridge, and as he left Riyadh with our troop request, I felt as though he'd lifted a great load from my shoulders." And yet a week later, the next entry in the book, Schwarzkopf writes, "My sense of well-being didn't last long. That Saturday Powell got back to Washington and called with a bombshell." In what amounted to much ado about nothing Schwarzkopf once again casts doubt on Powell. Upon reading the characterization, Powell was not amused. His job included managing the political side of things in Washington and from all indications he did so well. He was never willing to gamble with the lives of America's young men and women in uniform and certainly was not shaken to his senses by the pleadings of Norm Schwarzkopf.

On another occasion Schwarzkopf contradicts himself on the agreed starting date for the ground war but implicates Powell. When Defense Secretary Dick Cheney and Chairman Powell visited Schwarzkopf in the desert on February 8, Cheney asked the CINC if he was ready to launch the ground offensive. "I think we should begin the ground attack now. We'll never be more ready," Schwarzkopf answered. Cheney asked him what date he wanted to go. "The twenty-first," Schwarzkopf said, adding that he might need three or four days of latitude to be certain the weather was good.

On returning to Washington, Powell called Schwarzkopf to let him know that the President approved. Schwarzkopf decided to plan on going on the twenty-fourth. Schwarzkopf suggests, however, in an account dated February 20, that he was under pressure to "launch the ground war early." The weather forecast for the twenty-fourth and twenty-fifth was not good, so Schwarzkopf wanted a delay. But Powell insisted that it was expected that they would attack. Schwarzkopf accused Powell of dashing his "military judgment for political expediency" when, in fact, both the forces were ready and the agreement (which Schwarzkopf himself notes) was to begin the ground assault on the twenty-first, or within three or four days. But the weather cleared and troops moved on the twenty-fourth.

Schwarzkopf did an excellent job of managing his own

political responsibilities with coalition partners in Saudi
Arabia and on the battlefield. Where should the Kuwaitis
and Saudis go? Working with General Khalid, there were
never any problems. Schwarzkopf had extensive cultural
experience in the region and was sensitive to host-nation
issues. He determined where the multi-national forces
went. He dealt with various sensitivities, such as working
with the Syrians. Likewise, there was the age-old American
inter-service politics. Here, Goldwater-Nichols once more
proved its value, as Schwarzkopf tailored combat missions
based on weapons and unit capabilities rather than on the
competing turf claims of the various services.

Powell was essential to the Bush Administration's
conduct of the political confrontations at home. His personal
prestige in Congress forced wavering Democrats to take
note. Future Secretary of Defense and then-Congressman
Les Aspin also emerged as an important figure in solidifying
political support for the campaign in the Gulf. Aspin's
House Armed Services Committee hearings featured the
testimony of Colonel Trevor Dupuy whose estimates of
combat costs were important. But Congress also became a
forum for dozens of dire predictions. From the Senate floor
Senator Paul Wellstone (D-Minn.) said "We stand on the
brink of catastrophe." In the House, Representative Lee
Hamilton (D-Ind.) said solemnly "War will split the coalition, estrange us from our closest allies, make us the object
of Arab hostility, endanger friendly governments in the
region, and not be easy to end, once started." One of the
predictions heard in the halls of Congress, which Powell
found particularly noxious, was that it would be a war of
"blacks and browns dying for oil for whites." There were
battles in the House and Senate and a movement of certain
members of the Congress from gloom and doom to an
understanding of the historical significance of the gathered
international coalition and the cost to be borne for its failure.
Senate Armed Services Committee Chairman Sam Nunn
could not be convinced to support the war. However, on
January 12, 1991, Congress passed a joint resolution giving

President Bush the authorization to "use U.S. Armed Forces pursuant to U.N. Security Council Resolution 678 (1990)." War was virtually inevitable. What began as a protective shield in the desert would become a furious storm with devastating effects.

The night of 16–17 January 1991, was a long one for a soldier with the field experience of Colin Powell. He knew that the first twenty-four hours of combat could be decisive in how the war evolved. New weapons and equipment, such as cruise missiles, were being counted upon to attack critical targets. Stealth fighter-bombers were getting their first real test against sophisticated radar systems.

The raids went well. From the first attacks, launched by U.S. Army Ah-64 Apache helicopters against radar sites in southern Iraq, it became clear that the months of planning, the years of training troops, and the years of developing and procuring robust, high-tech weapons were paying off. In what amounted to the largest helicopter offensive in history, the attacks "opened an electronic hole" in Iraqi defenses for the air offensive. Testifying before the House Appropriations Committee just after the war, Powell noted that "our decade-long investment in training, readiness, equipment and, above all, people, has paid off. There has been some heavy criticism in recent years of the weapons we purchase for our troops, and accusations that many of the weapons are too technologically sophisticated to perform well in actual combat. Before this conflict began, armchair strategists informed the public that many of our systems would not stand up under operational conditions. Yet every American who has watched television in the past several weeks knows that these pundits were wrong.

"Other critics," Powell noted, "suggested that our weapons, designed at the 'high end' of the technological spectrum to counter the Soviet threat, were not suitable for the 'low end' regional threats we would more likely face in the future. The experience of DESERT STORM has proven them wrong here as well. The 'high end' of technology clearly excelled in the Gulf War."

No doubt the problem of bomb damage assessment and determining just how badly the Iraqi Army had been damaged plagued both Schwarzkopf in the field and the staff at JCS. American and coalition forces were scrupulous about their selection of targets. On March 5, 1991, Powell reported to Congress that "Throughout its execution, our campaign was also designed to minimize civilian casualties and damage. The guidance that our pilots operated under was to attack only military targets. They went to considerable lengths to avoid striking civilian targets, as well as religious and archaeological sites." He continued, "Last week we provided photographic evidence to the Iraqi people and the world that, despite allegations by Iraqi authorities, the holy shrines at Najaf and Karbala are intact and undamaged. There could be no more credible testimony to the success of our targeting policy than the fact that Iraqi soldiers were seeking shelter in civilian surroundings because they knew we were avoiding such targets." Coalition casualties were always a consideration as they always are for any warrior who cares about his troops. But their numbers stayed remarkably few. There would be no American air-to-air combat losses and a total of only seventy-five (63 U.S., 12 allied) aircraft downed, including both combat and non-combat losses, out of 116,000 missions flown.

The air campaign prepared the battlefield for the decisive ground war. CUT IT OFF AND KILL IT. This was the coalition military strategy for dealing with the Iraqi Army expressed in simple words, without obfuscation.

In retrospect, several military aspects of the war have come under criticism. The U.S. anti-aircraft missile, the Patriot, seemed like a sure thing on CNN, intercepting incoming Iraqi Scud missiles fired at Israel and Saudi Arabia. But it was neither originally intended to intercept other missiles nor 100 percent accurate. Almost immediately the Israelis began questioning their effectiveness. But Powell is a realist and pragmatic when it comes to weapons systems. "The Patriot missile, first developed in the mid-1960s as a weapon to defeat aircraft, was upgraded in recent years, at an additional cost of about $200 million above the $12 billion total system cost, to attack tactical ballistic missiles," Powell told members of Congress after the war. "The antimissile version uses the same launchers, missiles, and infrastructure as the earlier one, but adds a significant new capability, as anyone living in Riyadh, Haifa, or Tel Aviv will tell you. Extending the mission or effectiveness of proven weapons systems through low-cost improvements is another way we ensure that American taxpayers are getting their money's worth."

Ground operations began on February 24, 1991 at 4:00 A.M. Saudi time. President Bush told the nation that "the liberation of Kuwait has entered its final phase." As Saddam Hussein urged his troops to kill "with all your might," they were being trampled so badly that by the end of the first day field commander Schwarzkopf would declare the coalition's accomplishments a "dramatic success." Two Marine Divisions and Arab forces attacked toward Kuwait City. The XVIII Airborne Corps and VII Corps conducted a wide-sweeping left-flanking movement into Iraq to cut off Iraq's forces before decimating them. More than 5,500 Iraqi troops were captured. On February 25, Saddam issued a call by radio for all Iraqi forces to withdraw from Kuwait to the positions they held on 1 August 1990. The Iraqi president hailed the accomplishments of his troops and boasted of taking a victorious stand against the evil Americans. A stray Scud missile hit a U.S. barracks in Al Khobar, Saudi Arabia, where Army National Guard troops were based. Twenty-eight died; ninety were wounded. It was the last of seventy-eight Scuds that Saddam fired. The Soviets presented a new peace plan. On February 26 it was rejected. CENTCOM spokesman Marine Brigadier General Richard Neal announced that the Saudi ground forces were in "full retreat" as coalition forces pursued them. VII Corps attacked Republican Guard divisions along the western Kuwaiti border as XVIII Airborne Corps troops completed the encirclement of Iraqi forces by reaching the Euphrates River. Saddam announced a complete withdrawal as Kuwaiti resistance groups celebrated an end to occupation. On February 27 Kuwaiti troops raised their national flag upon entering Kuwait City. Republican Guard units were decimated in a large tank battle with VII Corps and 24th Mechanized Infantry units. President Bush again went on television. "Kuwait is liberated. . . . Iraq's army is defeated. . . . Our military objectives are met." A suspension of offensive military operations was announced. The war was ended.

The war was quick. Force was overwhelming. After nearly 100,000 numbing air sorties a decisive ground attack paralyzed the largest military force in the region. But it was a key maneuver that amputated the most fearsome parts of Saddam's military Goliath. It was the sweep of forces, referred to by General Schwarzkopf as the Hail-Mary play, that was decisive. The name is really a misnomer. It is an allusion to the football play where the quarterback draws back and fires the ball into the air far downfield in the hopes that it will be caught. It is often a pass of desperation when a touchdown is needed and there is little hope of moving the ball slowly but surely downfield. This was a calculated move, not a long shot. What's more, although Schwarzkopf takes credit for coming up with the plan, it was actually Colin Powell whose idea it was to "cut it off and kill it." In Schwarzkopf's memoir, *It Doesn't Take A Hero*, the impression is left that the plan originated with Schwarzkopf. Actually, planners on the Joint Staff under Powell's direction were already working on such an idea at the time, some developments were concurrent, and the actual operation was a combination of elements put together by the Joint Staff and the CENTCOM planners.

The ground war and "Schwarzkopf's Hail Mary," that deep left hook around Kuwait by coalition forces, ranks as one of the greatest tactical and operational achievements in military history. One hundred hours were all that was needed. But was the war stopped too soon?

American high-tech JSTARS planes that can see through clouds were tracking the Iraqi Hammurabi Republican Guards Armored Division as it escaped across a bridge over a marsh lake, the Hwar al Hammar in the Shatt-al-Arab region of the Tigris and Euphrates Rivers. Later, these surviving Iraqi forces would attack defenseless Shiite farmers in southern Iraq.

So why didn't the coalition go on to Baghdad? Powell repeatedly reminded those who were disappointed that toppling Saddam was not part of the assigned mission. Talking with editors at the *San Diego Union* in September 1991, he said, "the objectives that the President, our friends in the region, and the United Nations agreed on was to get the Iraqi army out of Kuwait and restore the legitimate government in Kuwait and provide for regional security." To the objection that the Iraqis live under a despot, Powell adds, "It was never one of our objectives to change the form of government of the Iraqi people. So our political objectives were clearly stated.

"And when after forty-three days [of military operations], which included a four-day ground war we reached the point where those objectives had been accomplished, the President ordered us to stop offensive operations. At that point we had pretty much smashed up the Iraqi army, and it remains smashed up. We had not destroyed the entire Iraqi army because we knew that a very significant percentage of the Iraqi army was never in the Kuwait theater of operations to begin with. So we didn't go in there and invade Iraq and go to Baghdad chasing Saddam Hussein and destroy the rest of the forces."

No doubt the people of Iraq would be better off with someone other than Saddam Hussein in charge. But Powell warned members of the American Stock Exchange on Election Day 1992 that simply doing away with Saddam would not guarantee that Iraq would become what the community of nations might like it to be. "I think his people will be better off with a different leader. But there's this sort of romantic notion that if Saddam Hussein got hit by a bus tomorrow some Jeffersonian Democrat is waiting in the wings to hold popular elections. And you're going to get— guess what?—probably another Saddam Hussein. It would take a little while for them to paint the pictures on all of the walls. But there should be no illusions about the nature of that country or its fight. And the American people—all the people who second-guessed us now—would have been outraged if we had American soldiers in Baghdad, patrolling the streets two years later, still looking for Jefferson."

Powell's conclusion: "We did it right. We accomplished the mission we were assigned by a powerful international coalition. I have not had any second thoughts about it, or regrets about it. I think we did it correctly."

Powell did not want to get bogged down in Iraq and Kuwait. His thinking is not atypical for his generation who studied the early nineteenth century military strategist Clausewitz at the National War College. For Clausewitz war is an instrument of policy, a means to be used toward a specified end. In conducting the Gulf War there was a political end to be achieved, and it should be achieved decisively. Powell was also influenced by his Weinberger-era colleague Fred Iklé's short book, *Every War Must End*. Powell excerpted, photocopied, and sent copies to key generals during the build-up of Desert Shield. Iklé makes the point that because fighting a war is an undertaking of great magnitude, governments often lose sight of its proper end. He asserts that in conducting a succession of military campaigns military men can "remain curiously blind in failing to perceive that it is the outcome of the war, not the outcomes of the campaigns within it, that determines how well their plans serve the nation's interests." Iklé asks, "If generals act like constables and senior statesmen act like adjutants, who will be left to guard the nation's interests?"

Several historians have amplified this point. Writing in the *Houston Chronicle* on January 12, 1992, a year after Desert Storm began, Austin Bay argued that "Enforcing the string of U.N. resolutions passed between August 2, 1990 and March 1991 (Resolution 678 as a particular example) represents the first time in human history that so absolute a majority of the globe acted to resolve a military conflict with cooperative political, economic, and military means. . . . If

U.S. forces had gone 'on to Baghdad,' much of the world would have seen the coalition as nothing but a cover for U.S. imperial policy and Saudi vengeance. By living up to the Security Council's 'grand bargain,' the U.S. proved to be an honest leader and political broker. The result: We now have the first genuine opportunity to resolve a host of Middle Eastern troubles . . . Desert Storm gave the world a view of twenty-first century high-tech war; its aftermath gives us a view of what could be the path to twenty-first century peace.. . . . The Desert Storm coalition provides the model for such cooperation."

Saddam's power was greatly diminished by the Gulf War and its aftermath. He remains in the surprisingly strong grip of U.N. sanctions and poses no immediate threat to the peace of the world.

Desert Storm is a testament to clear and exacting military goals. General Colin Powell played a central role by precisely matching the coalition's achievable political ends with specifically military means—to defeat the Iraqi army in Kuwait, to do so swiftly and decisively with a minimum of allied casualties, and to do so within the constraints of the U.N. resolutions—no more and no less.

chapter twelve

THE WARRIOR'S
RELUCTANCE

P O W E L L W A S N O T pleased when more than three million copies of the May 13, 1991, issue of *Newsweek* hit the street. The cover story was titled "The Reluctant Warrior." The art showed a serious Chairman of the Joint Chiefs. *Newsweek* had secured the magazine rights to the Bob Woodward book, *The Commanders*. In addition to the excerpts was a story about the book. Its lead: "The scene will undoubtedly be used in campaign videos when George Bush runs for re-election in 1992. 'This will not stand,' the President sternly vowed only a few days after Iraq invaded Kuwait. 'This will not stand.' Resolute words from a strong leader, sure to move voters and make them relive a famous victory. But at the time, the reaction of the President's chief military advisor, Chairman of the Joint Chiefs of Staff General Colin Powell, was less enthusiastic."

Had the Woodward book appeared without the magazine article, perhaps there would have been less fanfare.

But the *Newsweek* article keyed in on Powell's supposed response upon hearing George Bush's words that afternoon of August 5 as he returned to the White House from Camp David. Powell was reportedly "stunned" at not being consulted. There had been no National Security Council meeting. Bush was clearly too gung ho. *Newsweek* asserted that "General Powell, it turns out, actually favored a strategy of containing Saddam Hussein with economic sanctions." In short, Powell was a reluctant warrior.

Such a description would not have carried so much weight had another assertion also been made. "Without question, Woodward's main source was Powell, who spent hundreds of hours with *The Washington Post's* top investigative reporter." The suggestion was made that "The fact that Powell privately supported sanctions over force—just like many Democrats on Capitol Hill—led political insiders to joke that by leaking to Woodward, Powell was launching his bid for the Democratic Presidential nomination in 1992."

Powell is the hero-figure in Woodward's fascinating book. He is its centerpiece, a measured, sensitive, principled, and compelling national leader. There is nothing of the impulsive or self-contradictory pall that touches the other main Washington characters. If this is so, does it mean that Powell was able to prevail over the savvy, even cagey, author Woodward to be portrayed in such a light? Does moving Powell to center stage with both footlights and a strong spotlight make him the key interpreter and communicator of the drama? Is Powell so self-seeking, or was he at that moment, that he would risk ruining his relationship with George Bush and tarnishing an otherwise pristine image by cavorting with a journalist? Did he, in fact, talk with Bob Woodward ad infinitum or, at least, ad nauseam? And if he did not, where did Woodward get so much inside information, whether accurate or inaccurate?

If Powell was Woodward's main source, the book would have been a much smaller tome. No slouch on research, Woodward and his assistants conducted interviews with four hundred people over twenty-seven months. Many key participants in the events from November 8, 1988 through January 16, 1991, the start of the Gulf War, were interviewed repeatedly. Several were interviewed two or three dozen times. "I interviewed one important source forty times, sometimes in a rushed four-minute phone call during a crisis, at other times in free-wheeling one-hour conversations," Woodward writes. Some allowed him to tape the discussions, others did not. Some sources provided "access to documents, memos, contemporaneous handwritten notes, schedules, and chronologies."

Powell publicly acknowledges that he spoke with Woodward. Furthermore, Powell has called Woodward a "friend." There is no secret about their relationship, which began when Powell was on Caspar Weinberger's staff and reporter Woodward was roaming the hallways in the Pentagon.

Woodward's initial purpose was simply to write a book about how the Defense Department works. Events took over. Instead it became an account of how military decisions were made during the time that included the U.S. incursion into Panama and American response to Saddam's invasion of Kuwait. In January 1989, Woodward enlisted the help of F. William Smullen III, Powell's confidant and special assistant for public affairs. But it was before Powell was chosen to be Chairman that Smullen, then with Powell's predecessor Admiral William Crowe, recommended that Crowe meet and cooperate with Woodward. He did so numerous times, allowed Woodward to accompany him on a three-day trip to Oklahoma, and all was well. Access to and success with Crowe served as a set of credentials to open other doors. The research continued.

Powell became Chairman on October 1, 1989, just as events in Panama began to heat up with a failed attempt to overthrow the despotic dictator Manuel Noriega. Operation Just Cause followed in December and Noriega was caught and extradited. Powell met with Woodward in his office on July 30, 1990, three days before Iraq invaded Kuwait and shortly after the Russian federation declared its sovereignty and NATO declared the Cold War over. They discussed the operation in Panama and Powell's views of the role of the Chairman. Again on January 7, 1991, they met face-to-face. Subsequently Woodward called Powell at home. Smullen, also a longtime friend of Woodward, advised Powell that such calls were not in Powell's best interest, and Powell agreed. There were several brief phone conversations. In the spring and summer Woodward was writing. Then Iraq invaded Kuwait on August 2. Woodward decided to include in his book the U.S. deliberations on military possibilities that led to the Gulf War and to shift the focus altogether. The general was under one of his Volvos, grease to his elbows one weekend when Woodward called Powell at home. From the garage he told Woodward that he simply could not discuss operational matters. Powell did not talk with him again until the book was finished.

So who was Woodward's "main source?" Perhaps there was none. He never asserts that the person he interviewed forty times was his *main* source. Powell was not the source. Following the *Newsweek* allegations, those closest to the Chairman were eager to find out who really provided accounts of supposedly confidential White House and NSC meetings. The Bush White House was a tightly sealed ship by any administration's standards. Leaks, so routine in previous presidencies, occurred very rarely. Clearly many of those involved in the unfolding events talked with Woodward. Cheney publicly acknowledged that he did so repeatedly. Is he the supposed main source? Whether by one source or by many, Woodward got his hands on insider information.

Those closest to Powell came to believe that the primary source helping Woodward was not a principal player in the events at all but a well-placed person at the NSC identified by name. Woodward acquired some very detailed information that comes only from official meeting notes and minutes. Such documents would have given Woodward just what he needed to establish his own credibility as someone "in the know." Powell's associates believed they had identified the leak. But after probing, it seems that Powell was misinformed. It is true that ordinarily only those at the NSC would have had copies of the all-important papers. Exactly who compromised the information is today and may ever remain unclear. The single, named source who was suspected and reported to Powell is almost certainly not the culprit. The general himself has never uttered a bad word about the accused or even defended himself. He knows that such things just feed those in Washington whose appetites for controversy and sides-choosing are insatiable. Further, Powell does not see his job as that of enforcing moral standards inside the Beltway or pontificating from the lofty heights of integrity. Besides, he has no proof that the allegations are true; Washington is full of scuttlebutt. Even if he could expose Woodward's supposed source, defending himself is simply not his way of doing business.

Senator Sam Nunn, chairman of the Senate Armed Services Committee (SASC), would not let Powell off the hook. As Washington buzzed with rumors about the Woodward book, some who came down on the wrong side of the issue as events unfolded saw in Colin Powell a very popular potential ally who may have been on their side after all. If Powell had really been reluctant and had truly hoped that sanctions had been given more time, Nunn and others would be in the best of company. Perhaps Powell saluted smartly when the Commander-in-Chief gave his order to go but had, in fact, personally resisted using American GIs. Perhaps Powell, through Woodward, had broken the silence of a soldier who actually opposed military intervention. This was a chance to save face for those who had *gone on record* as reluctant.

Senate approval for a second two-year term for Powell was supposed to be simply pro-forma. In July, the Chairman's staff and the Senate Armed Service Committee staff began scheduling a reconfirmation hearing. But as the end of Powell's term approached, a date for the hearing before Nunn's committee was never fixed. Months before, Powell had planned an Asian trip for the last week in September 1991, the final week of his first term. Finally, around the first of September a mid-month date was set, then postponed. At first, no new date was set. Then it was decided that the hearing should be held on the last Friday of the month. Powell's Asian trip was cancelled.

A week before Powell's term would expire, Colonel Paul Kelly, Powell's special assistant for legislative affairs, received a call from the SASC's staff director, Arnold Punaro. He had some questions for Powell to answer in writing, not an uncommon request. Kelly went to Capitol Hill to pick up the questions. They were labeled TOP SECRET. In the car Kelly opened the envelope and discovered pages and pages of very specific queries related to the Woodward book. Kelly arrived at the Pentagon's River Entrance, passed through security, and immediately turned right into Powell's office. The general was sitting on the stool at his high-window desk. "General, I've got the questions for the hearing," Kelly said. "You've finally got them? Let me see them," Powell responded. He gazed down at the first page, flipped it, then glanced at the next page, flipped it. He glanced and flipped, page after page. He stopped. "Unh-uh," he grunted, "we're not getting into this. I have no statement to make. You go back and tell those guys I'm not answering those questions." The two men discussed the repercussions of not answering the committee's questions and how far they might try to force the issue.

Kelly returned and reported Powell's response to Punaro and Pat Tucker, staff director for the Republican minority. "We're going to have to send this up to Senators Nunn and Warner," they told Kelly. They did. The committee leaders said that they wanted each and every question addressed. Kelly reported back to Powell.

The Chairman had consulted with Cheney. It was decided that there would be one, general written response. It was delivered on Thursday, September 26. Kelly returned to Punaro's office and watched as he read Powell's statement. Punaro was not satisfied. "That's his answer?" Punaro asked.

"That's his answer," Kelly replied.

"Well, as far as we're concerned, it is not satisfactory

but I don't know if Nunn and Warner will accept it. Wait here," Punaro told Kelly. Punaro went to find the senators and Kelly waited about forty-five minutes until Punaro returned. "The committee will not accept this answer." Kelly returned to the Pentagon and reported in to the Chairman.

"Well, they can find somebody else," Powell exclaimed in frustration. He was visibly upset and vented his frustration on Kelly. In a moment he regained his composure. "It's nothing personal," Powell apologetically told his assistant, "you're just delivering the mail." But Powell continued, "I shouldn't have to take this. I've done nothing wrong. *The Commanders* book is a lot of hearsay and innuendo." The senators immediately sent Powell a second letter, which he answered bluntly.

The hearing was scheduled for the next day, Friday, September 27. Usually before testifying Powell went into Punaro's office, sat down, had a cup of coffee, chatted and waited for the committee members to show up before entering the hearing room to testify. This day Powell was all business. He went directly to Room 222 in the Russell Senate Office Building where the hearing would be held. "General, why don't you come into my office until the members get here?" Punaro suggested. "No, I'm fine right here," Powell answered. He was ready for a showdown.

The senators arrived. Among them was Senator Bob Byrd, representing the Democratic leadership. Byrd was an ex-officio member who rarely if ever attended SASC hearings. There was significant Democratic interest, however. Byrd wanted to weigh in. Clearly Chairman Nunn was not the force behind the confrontation with Powell. Nunn opened the hearing and was cordial but not back-slapping. The subject of Woodward's book never came up. The committee adjourned until the afternoon of Monday, September 30, when they wanted to talk with Powell again. Powell worked in his garage over the weekend. In a closed session at 1:00 P.M. on the last day of his first term Powell quickly put the subject of Woodward's book to rest by appealing to the privileged nature of his conversations with the President. At 2:00 P.M. the public hearing continued and he was reconfirmed by the full Senate in time for there to be no break in terms.

Powell has been around the nation's capital too long to hold a grudge. Politics is politics, and he knows it. Besides, Powell sincerely respects Nunn as a professional. The senator studies the issues, conducts business fairly, and is an ally of the military. Shortly after the September hearing, the general hosted Nunn for breakfast. The reconfirmation process? It was nothing personal.

If Powell was not Woodward's key informant, how is it that he became the book's hero? The fact is that among the principal players—Bush, Scowcroft, Cheney, Baker, Gates, Quayle, Sununu, and Powell: the so-called Big Eight—none is as compelling or well-placed a character as Powell. Mediator between civilian leadership and field commander Schwarzkopf, the principal military advisor to the President and the Commander-in-Chief's key communicator to the military, a former national security advisor himself, a non-partisan, and a national hero with the highest public approval rating since World War II, Powell is more than a tempting choice as the central figure in a book that is about "the commanders." Powell did not need to prevail over Woodward, who knows how to weave a good yarn. Woodward knew that Powell is the most attractive subject in his book, whether he was talkative or not. He made him its central figure.

For a man who plays his cards close to his chest and who is as media smart as anyone in Washington, Powell would have had to be convinced that providing Woodward the information he is reputed to have given was more than worthwhile. He would have had to be convinced that his otherwise good relationship with George Bush was worth putting in jeopardy. Those who speculated that Powell might have been interested in challenging the President in the 1992 campaign know nothing about the conditions under which Powell might consider elective politics or how he works with journalists. Powell admits to being "a political general" and does not see that as an epithet. But political acumen is different from being a politician. Powell's view of duty to the President, however, is a distinctly military one. For Powell the fundamental "duty, honor, country" issue looms so large that it is not only at the fore of his mind but something deep in his constitution. Such words are not mere precepts to be observed or even principles to be applied. Helping Woodward while compromising the President's confidence simply does not make sense to Powell. His personal and professional integrity would be thoroughly compromised. Is Colin Powell a friend of Woodward and the media? Yes. A turncoat? Inconceivable. A fool? Not by anyone's estimation.

Following the publication of *The Commanders*, George Bush was reported to have been depressed and saddened by what was undoubtedly betrayal from within. If so, did he blame Powell? Was the thesis put forward by *Newsweek* accepted by the President? Less than two weeks after the magazine appeared and just after the book appeared in stores, George Bush chose to make a media event of his announcement that he intended to reappoint Powell for another two years as Chairman. On May 23, in a 9:00 A.M. ceremony in the White House rose garden, Bush said, "He has done a fantastic job, and I'm taking this step now to demonstrate my great confidence in his ability and the tremendous respect that I have for him. . . . I've seen it firsthand and it has not diminished in any way."

Following statements by Bush and Powell, Brit Hume of ABC News asked the first question: Would Powell like to comment on the recent account that he had serious misgivings about using force in the Gulf, "at least at one point?" No, he responded, he would not comment on accounts or books on the subject. The President knows the advice that he gave him. "We all worked together." Reports of distance between those involved "are incorrect." Bush jumped in: "Let me add something, Brit. We had several meetings. And General Powell leveled with me, and Admiral Jeremiah leveled with us, and Norm Schwarzkopf leveled with us. And to the degree they were not on—rushing to commit our young men and women to battle—that's exactly the way they should have been. And I wasn't rushing to commit our young men and women to battle. And he gave me sound advice. He gave me straightforward advice. I never had any concern about where he stood. I expect the Secretary of Defense feels exactly the same way.

"And I just want to be on the record as saying that he spoke his mind; he did it openly. And then when we had to get together in meetings and figure the next steps, he was a constructive force all the way along the line. And it was Colin Powell, more than anyone else, who I think deserves the credit for the time we had to—after all options, in my view, were exhausted—draw the line in the sand. It was he who suggested to me, sitting right up here in that office.

"And so I feel that he did what any general officer should do. He told me the risks; he told me what was at stake in human life; he told me what his view is to how it would go, which was always very positive, if we had to commit forces. And I am unhappy about revisionistic views of things." No further questions on the subject were raised.

When interviewed for this book, Bush was asked if he thought General Powell was a prime Woodward source. He responded, "I couldn't tell. But I put my faith in people. And I say, 'This guy would never do anything to hurt me or anything to blow himself up, to be a peacock. It's out of character.' I put my bet on a human being, and with Colin I never have any doubts of any kind. I know the book caused concern in certain quarters, but it never did with me because I had total confidence in the man's character. For me it was a question of integrity and honor. There's no one that has those more finely honed than Colin Powell." Did they discuss the book? Bush does not remember.

Bush claims that in reading *The Commanders* so many things attributed to him were untrue that he simply could not believe the veracity of those attributed to Powell. Others claim that the book is accurate in what it reports but that much of the story was left out. Perhaps Woodward did not have all the relevant notes and minutes.

But the question remains: Was Powell in fact a reluctant warrior? Did he resist taking military action in the Gulf? The answers are not so simple as yes or no. Woodward is careful to nuance his presentation of events. Nowhere is Powell portrayed as opposing military action. Neither does he ever recommend, as the President's principal military advisor, abandoning sanctions for war. All true. The key to understanding where Powell stood on the issue is found in how he conducts business and especially how he operates in a meeting such as those crucial ones at the White House and Camp David before the Gulf War.

Unlike colleagues who approach the table with their positions fixed, their arguments ready, and their goals in view, Colin Powell's approach is to offer "if-then" analyses of options as best as he can. He is respected as the master of volumes of information boiled down to laymen's terms. He rarely says, "I believe we must do such-and-such." He prefers to get the options on the table and look at them.

In the case of the Gulf War there was never a time that Powell specifically recommended taking military action. Nor, apparently, did he ever resist. An equivocal position? Not really. The variables were numerous, and all needed to be weighed. They included assessing the probability of Saddam's caving in under the pressure of sanctions or being overthrown by his own people, the likelihood of holding the U.N. coalition together, and the fact that the Muslim holy month of Ramadan when Arab partners could not be counted on to participate in any action that was approaching, and more narrowly military operational interests such as the likely weather should an offensive be mounted.

"That's just the way that he operates," Colonel Bill Smullen observes. "He watches. His approach is to offer both sides of an issue so that no one is surprised when something goes wrong. It's his approach to decision making."

Powell insists that he supported the President's decision to take military action. But it was the President's decision to make, not his own. Perhaps the fullest statement Powell has made about it was at an editorial board for the *San Diego Union* newspaper in September 1991. He was asked about published accounts suggesting that, in the period of November, December, and early January, he had favored "a strategy of waiting and containment versus an early attack on Kuwait and Iraq." His response: "There was no disagreement. . . . We hoped sanctions would work. As we watched the weeks and months go by, it wasn't clear sanctions would work. My responsibility in this whole matter was to make sure that we knew what the military component was for whatever policy choice he made. And so it was my responsibility, which I discharged to the very best of my ability, to let the President know what military strategy and force structure associated with the continuing sanctions would be and what military strategy and force structure associated with going on the offensive would be. And we talked about it. We talked about the pros and cons. And we talked about at what point we should shift the strategy. And the President made the decision that he had to preserve all of his options. And that is what he did when he built up the force [on the ground] to the required 100 percent we told him it would take if he decided to attack.

"It was clear to me by late December that the sanctions were not working, that Saddam Hussein was quite prepared to suffer a great deal, more important, to have his people and army suffer a great deal before he was going to get out of Kuwait. Meanwhile, Kuwait was being systematically destroyed."

Powell continued, referring to testimony he gave to the armed services committees of the House and Senate in December 1990, prior to making a commitment of military action: "What I said was: How long sanctions should be allowed to go is essentially a political question, whether it be six, twelve, eighteen, twenty-four months. It's a policy and political judgment, but there is a cost to waiting. My responsibility is to let you know the force structure. If you want to wait that long, I'll tell you what it'll take to win.

"When the President made the policy choice and political judgment, based on a large number of factors, that the situation couldn't continue, he went to the U.N. and he went to the American people in the form of the Congress to get permission to undertake offensive operations. I was fully, 100 percent, unreluctantly behind that strategy. And I am very proud of the manner in which the armed forces of the United States executed that strategy. But I will also point out that we would now have sanctions in place for a year and he's still there, and I doubt if he would have left Kuwait if we hadn't kicked him out. So that's as forthcoming as I can be."

When asked about Powell's participation in the meetings and decision-making process that led up to taking military action in the Persian Gulf, George Bush responded this way: "I never had the feeling as the Commander-in-Chief that Powell was doing anything other than giving me his best judgment and, when the decision was made, carrying out that decision. I don't remember his 'hanging back' or his unwillingness to do something. I think he wanted to do it right." In Powell's mind "doing it right" meant having overwhelming force at the ready to be assured of a swift victory.

Dropping by at a small Pentagon luncheon for Lutheran bishops, Powell was asked about being characterized as a "reluctant warrior." It set off forty minutes of preaching on a broad range of subjects. Was he a reluctant warrior? All good warriors are reluctant to jump into a fight, he told them. War is a tool of last resort. Those young men and women in uniform are "my kids." If war is necessary, let's do it decisively and quickly. But one thing is certain, America does not troll for war. War is always a tool of last resort.

chapter thirteen

POWELL, POLITICS, AND THE PRESIDENCY

D O E S C O L I N P O W E L L want to be President? As the 1992 campaign unfolded, there was more than a little speculation that the black general might emerge as the Great White Hope in what seemed, at least initially, to be a season of voter malaise and weak candidates.

In the minds of some, Powell would be the vice-presidential candidate that George Bush needed to push him clearly ahead of any contender. Others imagined him the Democrat in disguise who might lift a traditionally defeated party from its Executive Branch desperation, whether pursuing the Oval Office or as its heir apparent in the number-two role.

From the start of the campaign to its end, Powell would have nothing to do with it. His stock answer to the most often asked interview question during the '92 election season was, "I have no political fire in my belly." Or, "I know who I am. I am a soldier."

Powell had no intention of running for either place on either party's 1992 ticket. He's too smart to be co-opted by either party's political machinery. His basic good judgment and military reluctance to enter a fight he cannot clearly win was aided by an authentic absence of personal aspiration. Powell would rather fix Volvos in the privacy of his own backyard than fight the political, social, and economic battles of the presidency.

Interest in Powell's political possibilities began in 1987 when he was Deputy National Security Advisor. And in the November 16, 1987, issue of *TIME* magazine, in a story about his succeeding Frank Carlucci, a former colleague is quoted saying, "Colin would make a great President of the United States." Republican colleagues in the Reagan White House played with the idea of drawing him out of the military and into the political arena. Although an Army officer, he wore a business suit to work each day. Powell was black and by virtue of his West-Wing job associated with the GOP de facto. It was a sign of admiration, but it was also a nice political move for the GOP to support this up-and-coming black kid into a political cauldron." Powell asserts that "nobody has ever come to me with a plan" for his entering politics. However, he adds, "A few friends have said to me that '[a political bid for office] could be in the future, and you need to preserve your options'. . . . There have been people who talked with me about it, claiming to be emissaries of one person or the other. My answer has always been the same: 'I'm on active duty. This is fun to listen to but you're not going to get a reaction.'"

This does not mean, however, that he has closed the door on a future role in leading the United States of America. Speaking of his response to the unnamed "agents and surrogates" who have approached him about seeking public office, Powell says he has told them, "I'm flattered, I'm glad you think that I may be able to do that. I don't want to foreclose anything I might want to do in the future but I'm on active duty; I don't want to discuss politics."

In 1992, before Bill Clinton was a serious contender, the governor of New York, Mario Cuomo, was the clear Democratic favorite in the early polls. On November 24, 1991, he suggested on ABC's *This Week with David Brinkley* that he and Colin Powell shared the same views concerning

United States' and coalition's use of sanctions leading up to the Gulf War. Powell balked. First Powell's special assistant, Bill Smullen, faxed a letter to Ann Crowley, the governor's press secretary, about the matter. When Cuomo mentioned Powell again in a December 3 *Washington Post* op-ed piece, the general himself wrote to Cuomo. His point was clear: Stop trying to identify yourself with me, do not read your position into the facts, and if you are trying to lure me into the ring as your tag-team partner you overestimate your attractiveness.

Mario Cuomo chose not to run. Whether Powell's rebuff played a role in Cuomo's decision may never be known. But he was not the only one to make his interest in Powell known. Office of Management and Budget Director Dick Darman was more explicit. Upon the appearance of an article by Joe Klein in *New York* magazine titled "Candidate Colin?", Darman penned a short note to Powell, enclosing just the headline and photo of Powell riding atop a limousine, waving to the crowd gathered for the Gulf War Victory Parade in Manhattan. The text read something like this: "Dear Colin, As you know, we don't do politics here at your local OMB. But to my way of thinking Candidate Eisenhower sounds a whole lot better than Candidate Stevenson. Regards, Dick." The implication was clear. The World War II hero Dwight Eisenhower ran for President as a Republican and won. If Powell had any political aspirations, he would find great support and even victory in the party whose administrations he had served for the better part of three continuous terms. Darman was the sort who liked the sound of "President" Powell.

In the summer of 1992 Bill Clinton trailed in the polls behind Bush and the renegade billionaire Ross Perot. The choice of a running mate seemed essential if Clinton was going to move ahead and take the lead. A June 23 report by Bruce Morton on the weekend *CBS News with Bob Schieffer* suggested that Powell was the right man for Clinton, but as *TIME* magazine's article on running mates in the July 6 issue pointed out, "There are no signs that the Chairman of the

Joint Chiefs of Staff wants to be the first black candidate on anyone's national ticket." Powell never spoke with Clinton, about the campaign or any other subject, despite a close mutual friendship with Vernon Jordan.

Throughout the campaign many thought George Bush should sack Vice-President Dan Quayle. Columns and editorials across the land suggested that the President needed a heavy hitter, someone the public would perceive to be more potentially presidential than the former junior senator from Indiana. In a July 30 piece, Mary McGrory asserted that former Republican Senate colleagues were praying that Quayle would step down so that Powell could "lift Bush out of the mire, lock up the black vote, reclaim the South, galvanize the cities, inspire the nation and reelect the Republicans." *Houston Chronicle* commentator Austin Bay sketched out a "Program for Continued Prosperity" that Bush should articulate if he hoped to be reelected. It included initiatives in economics, education, tax accountability, deficit reduction, crime, and civil rights. His final paragraph takes a different turn: "But what if the Republicans want to win and win big? Forget all of this advice and get Colin Powell, Chairman of the Joint Chiefs of Staff, to agree to run for Vice-President. Bush will get 65 percent of the popular vote. Quayle? Dan Quayle? Isn't he a character in *Doonesbury?*"

From the start, the attention embarrassed Powell. As early as March 1991 he called the Vice-President to say that he was chagrined by speculation that Bush might choose Powell as his partner in a second-term race. Quayle assured Powell that he did not see such reports and recommendations as a problem between them.

What did Bush think about asking Powell to be on the ticket? He denies ever telling anyone that he might want to approach Powell. "I never wavered in my belief that [Dan Quayle] should remain there," he told me. "We got a number of suggestions from others about [approaching Powell], however. A lot, and from very good people, good close friends of mine, people whose political judgment I respect. But in my view I had a Vice-President, the country had a Vice-President—I think still that he got a bum rap—and so I never felt that I would dump him."

Apparently, however, 1992 was not the first time Powell's name came up in the Bush camp. *Vanity Fair* reported that on the eve of the 1988 Republican convention Prime Minister of Great Britain Margaret Thatcher had recommended to George Bush that he select Powell as his running mate. But it would have been unthinkable for Bush to raise questions about politically sensitive issues with his friend Colin Powell whose own integrity as a soldier in uniform prohibited it. Speaking after his retirement Bush told me, "Maybe it's old-fashioned, but the way I dealt with the military, it never would have occurred to me to engage him in any conversation that would relate to domestic politics. I went out of my way to make sure he and the other Chiefs knew that I wasn't going to get them involved in one way or another and that would certainly include discussing his views." Insiders agree that for all the Powell hoopla, the President was not to be enticed. For him it was a matter of personal honor.

Privately, those who are closest to the general say that while he was comfortable with both Bush and Reagan in most military and foreign affairs matters, the Republican Party was not a political home for him. The emergence of a strong, vocal right wing was repulsive to Powell and even frightening in its lack of trust in the will of the people and the democratic system. Polarizing, venomous verbiage at the Republican National Convention led by Pat Buchanan and the sociologically exclusivist appearance of mostly clean-cut, all-American, predominantly white delegates, signaled something unsettling to Powell.

Mike Powell, traditionally a conservative like his dad in matters of foreign affairs, tells how he and his sister reacted to the convention. At one point he called her to ask if she was watching it on television. She said yes. Then what did she think? It looked like a 1990s American Nazi Youth rally, she thought. Hmm, that is what he thought, too. He could not imagine his dad involved in what the Republican Party had become. When asked if his friend Colin Powell might emerge as a Republican, Rich Armitage echoed Mike Powell's doubts given the party's current state.

If Powell is not entirely at home in GOP circles and stands at ideological odds with much of the domestic side of the Reagan-Bush legacy, is he any more at home among traditional Democrats? It seems not. Young Lieutenant Powell's support for the socially conscious presidency of Lyndon Baines Johnson, whose stand on civil rights was decisive in changing the way of life for blacks, does not translate into an abiding party allegiance. Mike Powell puts it this way: "A twenty-two-year-old black in 1964 rooting for LBJ doesn't necessarily make a Democrat at all. Back then almost all blacks were Democrats out of necessity. . . . But as times have gotten better, the freedom produces different affiliations."

So where does that leave Colin Powell? His son continues: "He's really a moderate in his thinking, and he's not really an ideologue on any end of the spectrum. He probably tends to be driven away by polarities on each side. He has a quiet disdain for the way the political game is played and what politics produces. I think he thinks that many people sell their principles in the name of party."

"I wouldn't be surprised—and I don't know—to find out that my dad has never had a party affiliation," the younger Powell adds.

He is a man without a party. Yet there is a widespread belief that Powell will one day appear on the ballot. No one was taken aback during the second debate among 1992 presidential candidates when Ross Perot predicted that either as a Republican or a Democrat in 1996 the name Colin Powell would appear on the ballot. "I have a fearless forecast. A message just won't do it. Colin Powell will be on somebody's ticket four years from now—right? Right?" Neither Clinton nor Bush disagreed. In fact a close listening to the tape of the debate reveals two distinctly different "uh-huh" and "mm-hmm" responses of affirmation. Are these men dreaming, do they know something Powell himself refuses to face, or is Powell simply playing hard to get? The answer may be probably "none of the above."

Certainly Powell is attractive in a way that any would-be king-maker would find hard to resist. He is not a racially polarizing black. He is Jamaican but through marriage and association identifies himself with African Americans. He is not a WASP, but he functions perfectly naturally among them. He is not Jewish, but is comfortable with the culture, religion, and language. He lived in a neighborhood and went to school with Hispanics as a kid and has lived for thirty-five years in the racially and ethnically integrated military. Thus he transcends traditional racial and ethnic boundaries. He is not poor, but he is not rich in the same way that America's elite families are. He has worked for everything he has but worked side-by-side with the privileged elite in Washington for half of his adult life. He dines as comfortably at Burger King as in the palaces of royalty. He is at ease either greased to his elbows while working on an old car or riding in the back of a limousine. Lastly, both he and his family are attractive—they all look good (but not too glamorous), they behave themselves socially (but are not boring), they convey all the things that inspire admiration and confidence and yet they are ordinary, real people.

There are other, more substantive reasons why he might be an attractive candidate for the land's highest office. There is probably no one on the current political scene who has Powell's broad experience in international affairs. Certainly no one's track record is as strong. His successes began with the reorganization of the National Security Council under Reagan following the Iran-Contra affair and include the preparation of the key Reagan-Gorbachev summit meetings. His military experience runs the gamut from being the high-level commander who makes decisions for his subordinates, to the staff officer who figures things out to serve those others who make decisions. He has shown both consummate restraint and overwhelming determination in the use of military force. He knows how to lead and

how to conciliate. When the rumors began to fly that Powell
was being considered by Bill Clinton for the position of
Secretary of State, the foreign and especially the European
press waited with hopeful anticipation. Little was it known
that at the first-ever meeting between Clinton and Powell,
the President-elect implied that not only would he like
Powell to be a player on the new team but that Powell could
choose his position if he had any interest in trading in his
Army green uniform for a civilian one. As word traveled,
heads of state and foreign ministers privately expressed
hopes that the State deal would be sealed. When asked why
they welcomed a Powell appointment, their answers were
similar: "He's a known quantity." "We know and trust
him." "He's an honest dealer." "He understands the
issues." "You can work with him."

In fact, Powell was never directly offered the position.
And despite strong hopes on the part of many including
best-friend Rich Armitage, Powell never made an overture
toward the President-elect. Clinton was impressive, Powell
thought, but still an unproven and unknown quantity in
Washington. Besides, there was as yet unfinished business
in the Pentagon—the Base Force reductions, and Roles and
Missions of the services, for example.

Powell has the additional advantage of having worked
successfully with Congress. He has dealt with the powerful
Senate Armed Services Committee, the Budget Committee,
the House Armed Services Committee,and the Appropriations Committee. He is a savvy broker who knows the key
players in Congressional leadership. He is respected on
Capitol Hill. Until the arrival of the Clinton administration
he was unique in having virtually no enemies in Washington. Despite the inevitability of facing ideological adversaries, virtually no one would speak a bad word about him. He
was the teflon general.

Powell has taken an active interest in certain domestic
issues that do not conflict with his military duties. These
largely fall under headings the Army calls health, welfare,
and morale. They have to do with troop readiness in the

services. In the wider population these are domestic issues. They include education, about which he has spoken most publicly. In fact, at the time the video "General Powell Talks to Young People" was released, certain members of the press asked whether General Powell wanted to be known as the "Education Chairman."

Regarding fiscal policy, it was no congressional committee that convinced Powell that the defense budget needed to be cut following the collapse of the Berlin Wall and the dismemberment of the Warsaw Pact and Soviet Union. Powell himself took an active part in bringing about fiscal responsibility. And it is worth remembering that he spent a year working as a White House Fellow in the Office of Management and Budget and a short while in the Department of Energy.

Lastly, Powell is as media-smart as they come. He knows how to present himself and communicate in front of the cameras. He also knows who's who and what's what in the business. Every day he reads closely the *Washington Post* television insider's column often simply referred to by the last name of its author, John Carmody.

No one denies Powell's appeal as a candidate. The key question is whether Powell is interested and if so under what conditions. Any equation must take into consideration certain personal matters. By Washington standards Powell is a poor man. He needs to earn enough income beyond his military retirement to live comfortably in Washington. He has promised his wife that after more than thirty-five years in military service he would no longer ask her to live just above the subsistence level. In addition, despite his high celebrity status, the whole Powell family enjoys a degree of privacy uncommon among prominent public figures. The prospect of losing their privacy is unappealing. Alma, in particular, admits that she looks forward to a less tumultuous life. Just two-and-a-half weeks after the 1992 election, at a luncheon of the Joint Armed Forces Officers Wives in Washington, attended by his wife, Powell was asked a question by the wife of a GI working on the Joint Staff in the

Pentagon. The woman also works for a small newspaper, the *Voice*, in suburban Virginia. Her question was simple and direct: "Will you consider throwing your hat in the ring in the future for a Senate seat or the presidency?"

His response: "Alma and I are in our last ten months of service. We really do not know what our future holds for us. I don't rule anything out, but we would have to think long and hard about a political life. And Alma has said to me often, with a very unpleasant look on her face, 'Don't you even think about it.' Tell your editor you asked the question and he was very noncommittal."

Only in his mid-fifties, Colin Powell has a lot of life left in him. He decided not to return to his native New York upon retirement. And he did not withdraw to a quiet, out-of-the-way place to take up fishing, or hunting, or skiing. Washington has been his home for half of his career and the Powells' circle of friends is tightly knit in the nation's capital. As an info-maniac he finds there no more exciting place to be. He may give some speeches, write, do some consulting, and serve on a few corporate boards. And he has stated without being more specific, that he intends to continue to serve the nation in one form or another.

So what might the conditions be that could thrust the only black American ever to be received approvingly across virtually all racial, ethnic, and class boundaries, into that single spotlight reserved for the President of the United States? His friends and closest associates generally agree upon the following terms.

Powell has no intention of taking on Bill Clinton in the 1996 election if the nation shows significant signs of recovery. If, however, Clinton's proposed economic reforms fail in Congress, if he himself continues to waver, if he seems incapable of delivering a strong economy, reducing the budget deficit while stimulating economic growth, if confidence in government erodes further and a Democratic hold on both the White House and Congress fails to break the gridlock that characterizes Washington, then Powell might take a look at politics. If American leadership around the world seems to flag, foreign policy stagnates and morale declines in the defense department, he could be tempted. But even this is not enough to set him running. For Powell the real issue is simple. He is a Jeffersonian democrat who believes in taking his cues from the people. Although he has spent thirty-five years serving commanders above him and especially the Commander-in-Chief, he does so because this is serving the American people through their representative. He is not likely to set out on a political career, but he could be lured into serving his country once again.

His longtime best friend and closest confidant, Rich Armitage, explains it this way. "The only way it would happen would be to be drafted because he wouldn't be involved in the primary process," Powell could possibly emerge in a time of national crisis, and Armitage can foresee such a crisis. But a forgetful public and a 1993 retirement could dim Powell's magnitude by 1996. "He would have to have a way of staying somewhat in the public eye. If you ask him what he's going to do, I'll tell you what he says to me. He says, 'We're gonna go out and run something.' That's what we do, we run things. That's what I do. I solve problems. That's what he does. And I say, 'What are we going to run? What's big enough for the two of us?' And he says, 'I don't know, Jake.' (I'm Jake, he's Elwood.) And we figured out we'll get the band together and we'll run something. But it never gets much past that. But we both have a desire to fix something. How do you maintain yourself for three years out of the limelight? It's possible, but it's a tough sell. I don't know how you maintain yourself sufficiently in the public arena to be the charismatic figure who's called upon in time of crisis."

Armitage continues, "We were talking about presidential politics, and I said to him that there are certain people who could wrestle back to the Republican Party. After all it was the party of Abraham Lincoln and of Thomas Jefferson. There are several architects of American policy, foreign and domestic, a lot of master builders. Woodrow Wilson is one, Franklin Roosevelt is another and I think this brings us to the point that it is less the party [that matters to Colin] than the idea [of building democracy] that he would like."

After losing the 1992 election, George Bush asserted that his own political life was over; he intends to have nothing to do with the 1996 campaign but, concerning the possibility of a Republican approach toward Powell he says, "I don't know his politics. I've never talked politics with him. I don't have the vaguest idea how he feels about domestic issues, and he's too much of a professional [soldier] to show those cards. I don't know how comfortable he'd be with certain economic policies that we pride ourselves on, but if he wanted to be in politics it seems to me he would have an all-star future with unlimited potential. That's based on character and what I hope he feels, and I know I feel, is a certain friendship. . . . I think a lot depends on what happens between now and [1996]. . . . In terms of character and in terms of stature you could easily make such a prediction [that he might run]."

Speechwriter Larry Wilkerson echoes Armitage: "The need would have to be clear, the mandate would have to be overwhelming, and the call would have to come in a way that the call came to him from President Reagan [following Iran-Contra] for him to be National Security Advisor or to be Deputy [NSA] when he was V Corps commander. . . . It would have to be a clear crisis. Some would say we're in a clear crisis right now, myself included. . . .

"The issue is really tied to Jefferson and what really is the essence of this country. If the mandate for him, if the call were clear and loud enough, I could foresee its happening. But it would almost have to be like the mandate that existed in a lesser sense—because I really do believe the crisis then was a lesser crisis—for Franklin Roosevelt when he came to his first term. Most of my economist friends laugh when I say that. They say I'm crazy. But I tell them that the combination of the economic and the cultural crisis we're in right now is much worse."

Mike Powell confirms that his father could emerge as a white knight should the nation face a time of serious need for leadership. But by nature he is not inclined to go seeking a political future, especially elective office. While he may seem a natural, his own experience is one of waiting for orders to assign him here or there. He simply does not go looking for jobs. They have always come to him. He salutes smartly and does whatever is required.

Powell is a patriot. He is politically savvy but not a politician. For him the real issue is not merely fixing an economy but rather making a democracy, a home, an example to others! He has the vision to rally forces and hold them together for a mission. For him this is family. Family pulls together. If the nation needs a contemporary father to help refound it, he could rise to the occasion. But he is not about to insinuate himself for personal gain or the satisfaction of his ego. He is comfortable taking orders having done so for most of his life. While he can also give them, he is neither tempted nor possessed with a need to make himself a demigod under the guise of serving democracy.

Powell knows that politics is the art of the practical and true democracy often requires compromise. Nevertheless, contrary to the primarily pragmatic rhetoric of many professional politicians, Powell really talks in the language of Jefferson—and he believes it. And Powell is not naïve. He knows that Jefferson was onto something when he asserted that "no man will ever carry out of the Presidency the reputation that carried him into it." If, in the course of events, however, the nation finds itself at a point where the American people cry out for a leader of proven confidence and whose integrity is uncontested, Colin Powell could be made to come forward to move the nation toward a restored health, a new security, and greater domestic and international cooperation.

For Powell there are timeless principles at stake. He would be hard pressed to shrink from the Declaration and charter that Jefferson and the Fathers signed. Like them, Powell's deep conviction is that certain truths are self-evident, and that the American experiment is the best hope among those that mortals have tried. This conviction leads him to share their categorical pledge—of life, of fortune, and of sacred honor.

chapter fourteen
SACRED HONOR

GENERAL COLIN POWELL looked on the wintry morning of January 20, 1993, Inauguration Day, as William Jefferson Clinton was sworn in to be America's forty-second President. It was a bitter morning in Washington perhaps sweetened by ceremony, a changing of the guard. One generation of leaders left the White House to be replaced by a younger one. Between the two administrations and two generations stood Colin Powell.

Dignitaries sat in the reviewing stand waiting for the arrival of the new First Family. Among them, the Chairman of the Joint Chiefs of Staff sat with his wife beside him, looking ahead with a solemn gaze. On such a day, whether due to weather or the changing political climate in the nation's capital, the faces of all those bundled to temper the cold may have seemed strained, fixed.

Two months earlier, on Tuesday, November 3, 1992, Bill Clinton defeated George Bush, signaling an end to twelve years of Republican presidency. Two days later the phone rang in Quarters 6, and Colin Powell answered it. It was Barbara Bush calling. "Hi, Colin, how are you?" she asked. The general called to Alma to get on the phone. They chatted, and Barbara asked them to join the Bushes for the weekend at Camp David. The President could be heard in the background yelling, "Tell them to bring the kids."

Jane was asleep when Mike Powell came home late and slipped into bed. "Your mom called, and she wants us to go to Camp David with the Bushes tomorrow," Jane groggily mumbled. "What!?" Mike responded with astonishment. The next day Alma called the White House just to be certain the invitation stood.

It was a two-hour drive to Camp David from Washington for Alma and the family. The general had been out of town and flew in by helicopter. The Powells arrived and parked, their timing perfect, for Colin's helicopter had just landed. As the Powell family convoy rode golf carts, they turned a corner, and before them stood Barbara Bush. She wore a comfortable winter parka, and her two dogs were beside her. They chatted briefly and Mrs. Bush invited everyone to the President's private cabin.

They sat around the fire, talking. There was a search for blocks and other toys kept on hand for the Bush grandchildren, to occupy Jeffrey. The phone rang, and Mrs. Bush picked it up. It was the President. "The Powells are here," she said. "Get on up here." A few minutes later Bush arrived. The smiling host greeted everyone. "Who's up for a walk?" he asked.

The Powells stopped at the three lavishly appointed cabins where they would spend the night. Bicycles were parked out front for each guest's use. Every detail was thought of. In front of the cabin assigned to Mike, Jane, and Jeffrey Powell were a big man's bike with a crossbar, a medium-size woman's bike with a low bar, and a tiny two-wheel bike with training wheels just right for a four-year-old.

After dropping their bags, everyone donned parkas and set out for the woods. There was snow on the ground but the trails were clear. The President and the Chairman walked out front, with George Bush setting a brisk pace. Barbara, Alma, Mike, Jane, Anne, and Jeffrey, with the dogs, followed behind. The walk lasted an hour and a half. There was chit-chat about everything imaginable. After another stop by the cabins to freshen up, everyone gathered in the main lodge where the President has his office and where official meetings are held.

The Bushes and the Powells gathered cozily around a single round table in the dining room. It felt like family. The kitchen staff had prepared Texas steak. The President bobbed up and down, full of energy, as the phone rang incessantly—first Baker, then Scowcroft, then Baker.

Bush seemed to have enormous energy. He talked about the election without animus. The world had changed, he reflected, and there were issues of social change that Clinton had brought out during the campaign that Bush did not share such strong feelings about. George and Barbara seemed convinced that they had grown too old-fashioned for America. "It seems the country is ready to make this generational shift," Bush noted.

There was talk about the Bush children and grandchildren. Bush mentioned possibly seeing a movie and complained about how movies had become so violent in recent years. As Bush jumped up from his seat to move on to the next activity, four-year-old Jeffrey exclaimed, "I'm not done yet." "Oh, Jeffrey's not done," the President confirmed. He sat down again, so everyone sat back down, and Jeffrey finished his ice cream. With the exception of some parental embarrassment, it was remarkably like being at home.

After dinner the Powells and the Bushes watched a movie, *Enchanted April*. Mike, Anne, and Jeffrey went to the bowling alley.

The next morning everyone gathered once again for breakfast. The President's brother and family from New York dropped by. As the day unfolded, Barbara was on the phone, trying to line up meetings with real estate agents in Houston. President Bush loaded Jeffrey down with mementos (presidential yo-yos, flashlights, pens) and showed him some of his own collection of keepsakes—ships and planes—and before the day was over, the President was trying to line up a wallyball game. The Powells decided to beat the snow that was forecast and drove south for Virginia just before sundown.

Colin Powell and George Bush had become friends over many years of working together. Bush had confidence in Powell because of his character, integrity, patriotism, and reliable performance of duty. Powell's respect for Bush grew over the years and was sealed with the President's handling of the Gulf War.

That respect for Bush caused Powell to go out of his way to honor him in the last days of his presidency. At a military salute just a week before Bush stepped down, General Powell began his remarks, "Mr. President, there comes a time every so often in a soldier's life when he has to say good-bye to an especially honored, respected, and revered leader. It is always a profoundly emotional moment." Using distinctly military language, Powell continued, "A loyalty grows in the unit—the loyalty of family—and the heart and soul of each member of that family is touched when the time comes for the leader to depart." Bush had not only been Commander-in-Chief but was an aviator in World War II. It was Bush's distinct oneness of heart and mind with the service that Powell could not overlook. "You have been unstinting in your faith in us, your pride in us, your respect for what we do for the nation. You have lived by the code we set for ourselves as warriors: dedication to one's troops, moral integrity, judgment, tenacity, courage . . . or to put it in military terms: duty, honor, country."

Powell went on, in true military fashion, to recognize Barbara Bush. In the Army it is customary to recognize the wives, now spouses, who "stand behind" those in uniform. In what is an especially affectionate description, however, Powell took note of the First Lady's role. "American troops in some of the most desolate corners of the world have warmed to the sight of Mrs. Bush—Barbara, as she has so often ordered me to call her—bundled up in a field jacket, shaking hands, hugging soldiers, her face full of the life and sparkle that have made a nation fall in love with her. For all of us in uniform, she has been a symbol of dignity, wit, love, and grace under pressure."

Admittedly Powell is a sentimentalist. His favorite film is the Humphrey Bogart-Ingrid Bergman World War II-era classic *Casablanca*. Powell's fond remarks concerning George and Barbara Bush could seem to be nostalgic hyperbole, but they are deeply sincere. The affection seems to be mutual. When Barbara Bush was asked about Colin and Alma Powell, she could not hold back her effusive praise. "He is my precious friend. I love him, and I adore Alma. We are devoted to them."

Mrs. Bush continued, "George's great respect and admiration for him rubbed off on me. George trusted him so enormously, and still does, as do I. We feel a great friendship with him. We wanted to be with warm friends [at Camp David]—this is right after the election—and Colin Powell is the man George chose. It was a good choice. . . .

"A lot of people from humble beginnings forget them, but Colin doesn't do that. I think you have got to put him down as the great Renaissance man. He's an extraordinary man. The cabinet wives love Alma. She's funny, warm, very bright. . . .

"Look at the leadership and the strength. George wouldn't have trusted Colin so enormously if he hadn't really had those things. Look at how he spoke to the American people. He really did give people confidence. He is a great leader. You had the feeling he had no personal agendas. I think that's why he led well. He really thinks of his troops and he really thinks of the men and women who serve under him, and I think they feel it enormously.

"It has everything to do with this great warmth. . . . He is a sensitive, warm, very emotional man. Put me down for every superlative you can think of when it comes to Colin Powell and his whole family. He's a good friend, relaxing to be with. And there's a good twinkle in his eye."

Powell had never met Bill Clinton before the Arkansas governor was elected. They met when the President-elect visited Washington and stayed at the Hay-Adams Hotel. On leaving the first meeting, Powell was impressed. He described the President-elect as smart. While intelligence and charm make for good impressions, they do not guarantee a President success in a town where power bases are more diffuse than they are in the capitals of most Southern states.

The natural inclination for Bill Clinton was to serve as President in the fashion of the governor of Arkansas. Accustomed to working with a weak state legislature, Clinton's temptation was to play part-populist and part-monarch. No one doubted his conviction on the issue when Clinton promised to allow homosexuals to openly serve in the military. However, some believed that, like so much campaign rhetoric, it was merely a means of garnering votes. Others knew that Clinton intended to see the exclusion of gays changed, but virtually no one thought he would spend his first week in office trapped in a self-woven web of Washington naïveté.

Senator Sam Nunn, powerful chairman of the Senate Armed Services Committee and a Democrat who supported Clinton, made it known on national television that the President had not consulted him about the matter and that he would oppose the President. The first signal sent to the new President from Capitol Hill was: "We were here before you got here and will no doubt be here when you leave; you had better remember the legislative branch of government and learn the ways of Washington."

A few days later in a meeting with the Joint Chiefs of Staff, President Clinton sat on one side of the table with his staff and advisors. Powell sat directly across the table from him, flanked by the service chiefs. The affable, smiling Chairman was seen comfortably leaning forward for the mandatory photo-op, looking like the man in charge, while Clinton looked apprehensive.

The gays issue was one that Powell cared enormously about. As the President's principal military advisor it was his job to tell Bill Clinton news that he did not necessarily want to hear. Yes, the "old chestnut," to apply a term Dick

Cheney had used, of homosexuals as security risks was a bogus reason to keep them out. But the fact remained that the military is a closed society with a distinct culture and a cohesion all its own.

The prospect of maintaining "good order and discipline" was integral to the military's being able to accomplish its mission, Powell held. Unlike skin-color, which is a benign, non-behavioral characteristic, sexual orientation is perhaps the most profound of all human behavioral characteristics, Powell argued in a letter to Congresswoman Pat Schroeder in May 1992. "Comparison of the two is a convenient but invalid argument," he wrote. Unlike a job in the society at large, military service is a twenty-four-hours-a-day life, especially in combat situations. "I believe the privacy rights of all Americans in uniform have to be considered, especially since those rights are often infringed upon by the conditions of military service." He closed, "I believe the policy we have adopted is consistent with the necessary standards of good order and discipline required in the armed forces."

To support his assertions he turned to the work of sociologist Charles Moskos. "Sex between service members does undermine order, discipline, and morale. So does invasion of sexual privacy. That's why the military separates the living quarters of men and women." If the military were like civilian life, Moskos asserted, there would be no problem. Gays could clearly acquire the same technical skills that heterosexuals could and, in fact, many gay veterans had proved that point. But military life is not civilian life. "It is an institution that requires enforced intimacy and lack of privacy," according to Moskos. Just because there are bad reasons for excluding homosexuals from military service does not mean that good reasons are either invalid or should be ignored. Powell was not a gay-bashing homophobe. His concern was for keeping and maximizing the capability of the force. That is why he advised the President against changing the policy.

Powell's staff had been working on the issue ever since

the election through the Democratic leadership on the Hill. Following a process that had become ritual, Powell's legislative assistant Marine Corps Colonel Paul Kelly had been in touch with principal staffers to work out a reasonable compromise. Certain terms seemed to be coming together for what looked like an appropriate revision of the categorical policy against gays in the military. A thorough study of the issues would be conducted. In the meanwhile a four-part plan would include no longer seeking out gays who are already in uniform to kick them out.

Clinton moved unilaterally. An interim directive required the services to no longer ask if new recruits are homosexuals. In a memorandum of January 29, Clinton directed that the issue was to be studied by the Defense Department and by July 15 the Secretary of Defense was to draft an executive order revising the policy. But by late March, the Defense Department was in gridlock with a lack of civilian leadership. No study of the issue had yet begun. The President had a Secretary of Defense. But from among the nearly forty politically-appointed high-level Defense Department posts, Les Aspin and his one deputy were the only two to be nominated and approved by the Senate.

On March 23, in his first formal press conference as President, Clinton seemed somewhat embarrassed by a question concerning the as yet non-existent study and attributed Department of Defense sluggishness in part to Aspin's recent heart problems. (Aspin was hospitalized with a congenital heart ailment a month earlier and had just received a pacemaker.) Clinton said he did expect the report, however, and hinted that if homosexuals were allowed to serve openly in the military there might be certain restrictions on what duties they could perform, in the interest of good order and discipline. Powell had argued that having homosexuals on the front lines and on ships might cause the same problems as might women at the forward edge of the battle area. Clinton's concession implied one of two things: Either Powell's argument was worthy of serious consideration and probably correct, or at least that

Powell and Nunn represented a constituency that should not be dismissed lightly.

Powell did not hold Clinton's lack of military service against him. He knew other men who opposed the Vietnam War, and he is not the sort of man to hold a grudge. But the fact remained that Clinton had no experience with soldiers, sailors, airmen, Marines, or coastguardsmen. That lack of experience was a definite handicap for the Commander-in-Chief. If anything, Clinton was blessed to have a non-partisan like Colin Powell as his principal military advisor. Powell could not solve the administration's problems with the lack of politically-appointed civilian leadership within the Pentagon. That was outside his portfolio. But Powell's character and professional devotion to the Commander-in-Chief was something he would not compromise at the end of his career. He had served all sorts of men in the past, experienced and inexperienced, ones he personally agreed with and ones he disagreed with, some he especially liked and others he merely tolerated. For a matter of months he could salute smartly and carry on his duties.

Unfortunately, problems were building. Powell's three-star assistant was rebuffed when he went to a White House meeting in the first days of the new administration. Lieutenant General Barry McCaffrey, who commanded the 24th Mechanized Infantry Division as it led the coalition storm into Iraq during the Gulf War, was told by a young woman on the Clinton staff, "Listen, I'm not interested in talking to the military." And Powell himself was repeatedly cut off by young turks at a National Security Council meeting even though Powell was the most experienced person in the room and, indeed, the only person with significant experience in national security matters.

From the first day of the new administration, stories began floating throughout Washington that the Clinton White House was simply not comfortable with the military and all its accoutrements. They were part truth and part fiction. Some said that Chelsea Clinton, the thirteen-year-old daughter of Bill and Hillary Clinton, had asked her military escort not to wear a uniform to the inauguration. Uniformed ceremonial guards were removed from outside the offices of the Secretary and Deputy Secretary of Defense. The President showed up for a Marine honor ceremony, but did not know how to salute.

Powell's greatest concern was not ceremony. He was not the sort of general who inspected his wife and children at attention in the morning on his way out the door, or who insisted that everything in life was a military "dress right, dress!" He, too, had worn a business suit to work at the White House and came home to change into casual clothes at night. The important issue at stake was the readiness and morale of the troops. Forces must not be cut to such low levels that a hollow force was left. Like a caring father, he would not have them on the battlefield unready, under-equipped, or too few to face any bully on any block. Not that they should continue as they had during the Cold War. But the world was still a scary place with lots of threats, some known and some unknown. It took much effort to get the military up to par after Vietnam. Just because the Soviet Union came apart and the Warsaw Pact was extinct did not mean that the United States could demilitarize. The advent of "smart" bombs and stealth aircraft did not reduce the need for a strong, cohesive force. The world needed American military might more than ever. It just didn't need as much of it.

The new Secretary of Defense, Les Aspin, was an old colleague and sometime adversary on Capitol Hill. As chairman of the House Armed Services Committee, he differed with Powell on the issue of how large the military needed to be. Aspin proposed a counter to the Powell-Cheney-Bush Base Force plan that saw the collapse of the Soviet Union as a justification for severe cuts in the number of troops. Powell encouraged caution at counting the so-called peace dividend too soon in what remained a volatile world. There were hot-spots around the globe. Three former Soviet states still had massive nuclear stockpiles. Russia was not yet a stable democracy. The world was littered with petty despots. No doubt forces needed to be cut, but so did other aspects of the military budget. And because the military is a hierarchical society with many specializations, sane personnel cuts would have to be gradual.

Powell warned of "breaking the force." A reduction of twenty-five percent of those in the military seemed a good plan for the time being, but of course the Base Force plan could be reassessed at some point down the road. Aspin was smart about the armed services and especially about military policy, but he was insensitive to intangibles that make a force into true warriors, the "moral factors" that Clausewitz identified as the ultimate determinants in war. No systems analyst can validate or assign the full value to these moral factors.

Aspin was a key Democratic leader in the House who garnered support for authorizing military action in the Persian Gulf. But philosophically he and Chairman Powell were light-years apart. In October 1992 Aspin castigated Powell for what he wrongly characterized as the general's "all-or-nothing" approach toward the use of force. Powell actually holds that decisive or "overwhelming" force is important to assure that military victory is achieved. Like Clausewitz, he would not have the military caught in murky quagmires. Rather, he believes that military force is an arm of political policy and that clearly spelled-out political objectives are required before generals can know how to fight. The question to be asked is: "What are we trying to achieve politically?" When answered, professional men of arms can work out a plan for achieving that end.

While acknowledging that not every situation is crystal clear, Powell wrote in the October 8 *New York Times* that what makes generals nervous is when *objectives* are not clear and the military does not know what it's getting into. Besides, not every problem in the world can be solved by using big guns from the world's only remaining super-power. "If force is used imprecisely or out of frustration rather than clear analysis, the situation can be made worse," Powell wrote. "Decisive means and results are always to be preferred, even if they are not always possible. So you bet I get nervous when so-called experts suggest all we need is a little surgical bombing or a limited attack. When the desired result isn't obtained, a new set of experts then comes forward with talk of a little escalation. History has not been kind to this approach," Powell concludes in a clear allusion to Vietnam. That protracted conflict ended in defeat and an enormous waste of lives and livelihood for the people of both America and Southeast Asia. Powell did not want U.S forces caught in another Bay of Pigs, failed desert raids, or Beirut bombings either.

Aspin, whose support for funding the best in high-tech weapons in the 1980s was an important boost to the Pentagon, disagrees with Powell. He prefers using the military as a precision tool to achieve so-called limited objectives.

When rumblings of U.S. military action in Bosnia began, however, Powell made it very clear that he was not convinced there was sufficient clarity of purpose to commit American forces to provide "limited" assistance. Before the election he wrote, "The crisis in Bosnia is especially complex. Our policy and the policy of the international community have been to assist in providing humanitarian relief to the victims of that terrible conflict, one with deep ethnic and religious roots that go back a thousand years. The solution must ultimately be a political one. Deeper military involvement beyond humanitarian purposes requires great care and a full examination of possible outcomes." Powell wanted to make sure that he was not dismissing Bosnia, should there be a clear, well-defined mission. "Whatever is decided on this or the other challenges that come along, Americans can be sure that their armed forces will be ready, willing, and able to accomplish the mission," he wrote.

The State Department and members of the NSC were the driving forces for the use the American military in Bosnia. Aspin was acquiescent and seemed simply to want to please the President. When NSC meetings started going the way of "let's try this now and see what happens,"

Powell discouraged them strongly. Admittedly, the suffering was great, and the atrocities against civilians were revolting to any civilized person. Television news brought the horrors of Bosnian ethnic cleansing, its shrapnel-hit children, the raped women, and displaced elderly, the freezing and hungry and amputated, into every American living room at the dinner hour.

Authentic pathos moved Colin Powell. And it is not as though he was opposed to specifically humanitarian missions. Quite the contrary. He was the prime mover behind American assistance to the Kurds, following the Gulf War, to the people of Bangladesh when a typhoon hit there in May 1991, to Somalian refugees in Kenya, and even to Sarajevo in July 1992. But recent American military successes around the world did not mean military airdrops of food and medical supplies should launch an incremental commitment of American forces to Bosnia. Further, unlike the Gulf War, which was prosecuted with a global mandate, American unilateral jumping into Bosnia simply seemed foolish. The issue was a matter of concern for the whole community of nations.

Between gays and Bosnia, some Washington observers noted that Powell did not seem to be getting along with Clinton in the same way he had with Bush. The real issue was not policy but something more fundamental. Powell had worked with Bush since 1987 when Bush was Vice-President. All relationships take time to grow and develop. Powell served Bush closely through many crises over a long-time period. It was only natural that the degree of warmth and camaraderie between Powell and the new President would be less.

Clinton himself was new enough at military and foreign policy that the differences between Powell and Aspin did not mean that the President dismissed Powell out-of-hand. In fact, Clinton quickly realized that Powell was not a hold-over from the previous administration but a professional soldier of the highest caliber. He could be trusted to serve Clinton faithfully, honestly, and without a personal, political agenda. Powell was an enigma in a highly manipulative, partisan town. Within a few weeks of taking office, Clinton got into the habit of calling Powell directly. They discussed a wide range of issues. Bush was not nearly so frequently in touch with his principal military advisor.

When Powell-Clinton differences were reported in the press, a story soon appeared in the *New York Times* that Powell would resign. Just hours after the presses stopped rolling, Powell was on every television network's morning programs, denying the story. The fact is that before the end of the Bush presidency, Powell spoke to his boss Dick Cheney about retiring from the Army a few months before his full second two-year term would run out on September 30, 1993. He let the new administration know of the possibility of his leaving by summer rather than fall. After more than thirty-five years in uniform, Powell was beginning to think about life after the Army. It had been a long, full career and a life he would miss, but his wife and family were ready for him to retire. Summer seemed like a natural time to make the change. No, he had not made a decision to leave then, but he wanted it known that he was thinking about the possibility. His decision would not be an attempt to bail out of the Clinton boat. But when he does retire, what he might do in retirement is not certain.

Colin Powell is inspired by certain lofty principles, and he thrives on putting them into practice and generating them in others. Deep inside is the heart of a patriot. But his convictions go deeper than that. Life is a matter of duty, of honor, of country, and also of things even more quotidian: dedication, moral integrity, courage, good judgment, justice, honesty, responsibility, faithfulness, industriousness, fairness, forgiveness, devotion, love. This sort of character is meant to reach deeply into the life of home and family but so inclusively as to include all of humankind.

In our time, Powell himself has said it, there is no escaping the fact that such words sound corny. But for an uncommon man like Colin Powell it is not only possible to believe in but also possible to live—and if necessary, to die—for one's sacred honor.

INDEX